Grant MacEwan's

ILLUSTRATED HISTORY OF WESTERN CANADIAN AGRICULTURE

Grant MacEwan's

ILLUSTRATED HISTORY OF WESTERN CANADIAN AGRICULTURE

Western Producer Prairie Books
Saskatoon, Saskatchewan

Printed and bound in Canada by
Modern Press
Saskatoon, Saskatchewan

Jacket & book design by Mac Thorpe.

Western Producer Prairie Books publications are produced
and manufactured in the middle of Western Canada by a
unique publishing venture owned by a group of prairie
farmers who are members of Saskatchewan Wheat Pool. Our
first book in 1954 was a reprint of a serial originally
carried in *The Western Producer*, a weekly newspaper
serving western Canadian farmers since 1923. We continue
the tradition of providing enjoyable and informative
reading for all Canadians.

CANADIAN CATALOGUING IN PUBLICATION DATA

MacEwan, John W. Grant, 1902-
    Grant MacEwan's illustrated history of
western Canadian agriculture

    Includes index.
    ISBN 0-88833-059-6 bd.
    ISBN 0-88833-068-5 pa.

    1. Agriculture - Prairie Provinces - History.
I. Title.
HD1783.M23   338.1'09712   C80-091064-8

TABLE OF CONTENTS

FOREWORD

Agricultural history offers a new frontier in the study areas of both agriculture and history. We were slow in discovering it. For understandable reasons, the pursuit of agricultural history suffered the same misfortunes that plagued Canadian history in its broader aspects, namely, neglect for many years. Boys and girls at school in the pioneer period studied English history until they were sick of it, and were left with the impression that Canada had no history or its history was of no importance.

If the Centennial Anniversary of Confederation in 1967 did no more, it proved useful in making Canadians more conscious of their past and more eager to know about the struggles and triumphs of the formative years. Then, having discovered interest and fascination in the history of their country, some scholars and others came to realize that agricultural history, fully as much as any branch of history, possessed charm springing from its own character. They found it possessing more than charm; it held practical value for the lessons it was capable of teaching, lessons about pioneer human fiber and resourcefulness, about the penalties which have always followed abuse of soil, about the applications of weather history in farm planning, about the waywardness of markets, and so on.

It had been overlooked for too long that the messages of history rooted in human experience — agricultural or otherwise — should not be taken lightly. Those who ignore their history are likely to face the penalty of repeating mistakes.

Agricultural people examining the story of their industry will see, also, those ingredients from which pride and inspiration generate. There was something refreshing and sparkling about the pioneer personali-

ty. There were courage and self-reliance and imagination that should be remembered.

Daniel Webster saw agriculture as the forerunner of all other arts, and farmers as "the founders of human civilization." In the early West of Canada, Webster's remarks would have been slightly in error because agriculture was preceded by the fur trade, that 200-year onslaught against beavers and other wild creatures whose skins were marketable. But the fur trade made practically no lasting impression upon the face of the country and it was still for agriculture to furnish the civilizing force.

Old World agriculture was already mature, with some thousands of years behind it when the first crops were planted in the Canadian West. When and exactly where the first cultivation and planting were conducted is not clear. It appears likely that Stone Age Man's decision to quit his primitive reliance on the hunt in favor of a more settled existence supported by cultivation was made about 7,000 years ago. Historians believe that the earliest attempts were made on the fertile soil between the Euphrates and Tigris rivers in Mesopotamia — marked by today's Iraq — or on the valley lands of the Nile in Egypt, where silts from annual floods contributed perpetual enrichment. It is possible, also, that the initial exercises in Mesopotamia and Egypt were conducted simultaneously as well as independently. No doubt the new way of living which allowed the former nomads to settle down was instantly popular and agriculture became the sustainer of the human family.

The Old Testament tells much about the growing importance of agriculture. "Abel was a keeper of sheep, but Cain was a tiller of the ground." Abraham became a rancher operating on a large scale and Joseph gained a rank like that of a deputy minister and chairman of the National Wheat Board under the Egyptian king. By this time, good food fare included bread, meat, milk, butter, cheese, and honey.

Agriculture was introduced from Western Europe to ancient Britain at least 3,000 years ago with the bringing of domestic livestock and seed grains which were planted in small circular fields. Plows of primitive kind were in use for some time before the Roman occupation. The British farmers demonstrated a special skill in animal improvement and their little islands came to be recognized as the livestock "seed-farm" of the world.

It was for Britain to make the biggest contribution to agriculture in the new land west of the Atlantic — largely through British breeds of livestock — although Canada's first farmer was a Frenchman, the former apothecary, Louis Hébert, who was with du Monts and Champlain at Port Royal on the south end of Nova Scotia in 1604 and twelve years later brought his wife and children from France to settle on land at Quebec. There Hébert, starting with no implement except a spade, grew grains, vegetables and fruits and kept livestock. More French settlers came to occupy long and narrow riverfront farms and agriculture gained importance and prominence.

Upper Canada or Ontario was the next to be caught up in farming, receiving its big impetus from the coming of the United Empire Loyalists. But in the western country known as Rupert's Land where "Fur was King," agriculture was still as dormant as an unsprouted acorn. Thus it remained until the coming of the Selkirk settlers, more than two centuries after Louis Hébert's historic decision to pursue the life of a St. Lawrence farmer.

The movement westward was slow and the vast country beyond Red River remained undisturbed to ultimately qualify as the last major farm frontier. Occupation was slow because most people, including those residing there, were slow or reluctant to catch the vision of the mighty food-producing potential. For many years, the detractors were more numerous and certainly more vociferous than the hopeful supporters. But that, too, added a touch of interest to the ultimate success story.

Finally, the rush for homestead land was under way and a great chapter was being written. England's Industrial Revolution deserved its place of prominence in history but westerners who watched the changing scenes between the Red River and the Rocky Mountains will wonder if prairie Canada's Agricultural Revolution was less important. The transforming forces which would enable a single worker to multiply, product output by twenty or twenty-five times must be seen as revolutionary.

Speaking personally as one who spent much of his life practicing and teaching agriculture after being raised in a pioneer farm home which my father built soon after coming to the West to farm in 1889, I wanted to see the preparation and publication of a well-illustrated history of western agriculture. Of this hope, I made confession in the presence of Rob Sanders, manager of Western Producer Prairie Books, on April 29, 1978, and was encouraged by his instant enthusiasm and suggestion that such a book could be an appropriate dedication to the seventy-fifth anniversary of the birth of two of Canada's leading agricultural provinces, Saskatchewan and Alberta, to be celebrated in 1980. Happily most of the needed illustrations were already in my files although other pictures were acquired later and for them, I express my very sincere thanks.

Grant MacEwan

Chapter 1

THE "UGLY DUCKLING"

Agriculture has been recognized as the world's first industry but in prairie Canada it was second. It was a slow starter, having been preceded and held back by the fur trade. It was the country's "ugly duckling," the object of insults and rebuffs until the "young bird" began to acquire its "feathers" and "swanlike shape."

The fur traders, who loved the wild, free life which allowed them to make their own laws as the occasion demanded, and take and discard native wives without formality, convinced themselves that their adopted area had been consecrated by the Maker Of All Things for furs and furs alone. Many of them remembered the dull toil of thinning turnips, picking potatoes, shearing Scottish Blackface sheep, and mucking out the byres at home and were glad to be far away. The very idea of introducing such operations to Rupert's Land brought anger and, in some instances, violence. For more than a hundred years the trade in furs stood alone and unchallenged. Until the time of the 5th Earl of Selkirk, nobody on either side of the Atlantic displayed the imagination and courage to advocate a farming venture.

Prompted by the derogatory remarks from the traders, it became fashionable for others to speak scornfully about Canada in general and the Northwest in particular. Jacques Cartier started it when he referred to the country he saw beside the St. Lawrence River as "the land God gave to Cain." To Voltaire, the country which is now Canada was just "a few acres of

Captain Palliser was a tourist buffalo hunter on the American plains ten years before he led an expedition to determine the agricultural possibilities of the Canadian prairies. (from a watercolor owned by Judge Henry Patterson and given to the author by the judge June 4, 1964).

snow." And Madame Jeanne de Pompadour, on hearing of the fall of Quebec in 1759, was said to have dismissed the matter lightly, saying: "It makes little difference. Canada is useful only to provide me with furs."

Nobody was attempting to separate the good from the inferior in the new land. It was being treated as if it were all bad. If one part of British North America was more promising than the rest, no effort was being made to define it. If some section possessed an advantage for producing cattle or wheat or peanuts, nobody was in a hurry to prove it. Instead of trying to find its worth, men of prominence seemed to be striving to surpass each other in denunciation. Without knowing what he was talking about, Sir Archibald Alison, British lawyer and historian who died in Canada's year of Confederation, would blemish an otherwise good record of judgment by proclaiming that: "Probably seven-eighths of British North America are doomed to eternal sterility from the excessive severity of the climate which yields only a scant herbage to the reindeer, the elk and the muskox."

That statement, if given credence, would certainly destroy any thought of growing wheat for trading but, as far as is known, nobody challenged the author. He, of course, did not live long enough to be embarrassed by the discovery not many years later that the western part of that land "doomed to eternal sterility" had the resources with which to become one of the leading "bread baskets" of the world. To further bedevil the gloomy pronouncement, the same area was found to possess the world's biggest deposit of oil-bearing sands, the world's largest known reserves of potash, to say nothing of wealth in coal, forests, nickel, iron ore, uranium, grazing lands, and more.

The folly of drawing conclusions before the facts are established should be obvious and the best examples can be found in utterances by men of the fur trade. Alison's hasty assessment of the country will invite less surprise than statements from people who spent years in the country and should have had a better understanding, men like George Simpson of the Hudson's Bay Company and Bishop Alexandre Taché of Red River. Simpson, as governor of the company in Rupert's Land for almost forty years, rendered notable service, but when called as an expert witness before the Select Committee of the Imperial House of Commons in 1857, he did nothing to enhance an otherwise good reputation for judgment. The committee was sitting to consider the future of the country west of Red River and Simpson was one of the first to be called. His words, some of them unworthy of the man, survive.[1]

One of the first questions put to him was: "Will you have the goodness to give to the Committee an account of your impressions of the character of the Territory of the Hudson's Bay Company in point of soil and climate, particularly with reference to its adaptation for the purposes of cultivation and colonization?"

To this, Sir George made the surprising reply: "I do not think that any part of the Hudson's Bay Company's territories is well adapted for settlement. The crops are very uncertain."

Asked if this observation would apply to Red River, the witness replied: "Yes." And then he made the statement which might have made all the other errors committed during the hearings seem trivial. His questioner asked: "Why so?" and Sir George answered in words which should have haunted him: "On account of the poverty of the soil, except on the banks of the river."

The date was ten years before Canadian Confederation, twelve years before Canada bought the West from the Hudson's Bay Company for $1,500,000 and some concessions of land. The witness was the man who, after thirty-seven years in the Northwest, traveling much of the time, should have been the highest authority on the future of the country. But the Simpson heart was in the fur business and not in colonization and agriculture and at least part of the land to which he alluded in the remark about "poverty of the soil," namely the Red River Valley, inherited its richness in soil from the immensely deep silt deposits of ancient Lake Agassiz, and was recognized a few decades later as one of the most fertile on the continent — or in the entire world. It was an area so rich that one soil expert warned against the careless application of barnyard manure because it could "dilute" the existing reserves of essential plant foods.

George Simpson's performance as the virtual ruler of Rupert's Land for nearly four decades leaves no doubt concerning his skills and leadership. How then was his expert testimony so faulty? It may be merciful to attribute it to wishful thinking or an inherent loyalty to his life's work. Although he gave dutiful support to the Selkirk Settlement — sometimes quite grudgingly — his first love was certainly for the fur trade. He would have found it difficult to believe or accept that the industrial role of furs would so soon yield to the growing might of the new giant, agriculture.

But Simpson's pessimism about agriculture and settlement in the West was not the last to be voiced. Capt. John Palliser, who came to prairie Canada as a servant of the government in London later in the same year in which Simpson was appearing before the committee, gave partial support to the gloomy view. Reporting in 1863, he spoke favorably about farming and settlement opportunities in what he termed the Fertile Belt, that crescent-shaped band which was known later as the park belt. But of the more central prairie region, what he described as "an extension of the Great American Desert," he was guarded, even pessimistic.

"In the central part of the continent there is a region, desert or semi-desert in character," he wrote, "which can never be expected to become occupied by settlers. . . . Although there are fertile spots throughout its extent it can never be of much advantage to us as a possession. . . ."[2]

Palliser was correct in his favorable opinion of the so-called Fertile Belt, meaning in modern terms, Red Deer, Edmonton, Vegreville, Lloydminster, Prince Albert, Melfort, and Dauphin. The combination of precipitation, soil quality and general climate was to prove most favorable to cropping. But Palliser was only partly correct in his estimation of the prairie part. True, the prairies were to suffer from drought more often than the park belt but the same plains country was to produce wheat of the hardest and highest quality and in amounts that tended to contradict Palliser. Those prairies were to be the source of a strikingly high percentage of the entries of wheat and other grains winning world championships in the annual competitions.

More years passed without much change of sentiment for the western soil. As late as 1868 — one year after the official birth of the Dominion of Canada at Confederation and one year before Canada acquired

The decline of the buffalo because of wasteful hunting in the last quarter of the nineteenth century helped to focus attention on agricultural pursuits. (Ashdown Johnson photograph).

Thanks to conservationist efforts, buffalo herds were built up on preserves. This one is at Banff. (Canada Dept. of Northern Affairs).

the West by purchase from the Hudson's Bay Company — the respected Bishop Taché had something to say, confirming that the "ugly duckling" was still waiting for its coat of fine feathers. "For my own part," said the bishop, "as there are extremely great difficulties in the way of colonizing the few points in this vast territory capable of cultivation, I acknowledge frankly that I would as soon — perhaps preferably — see the country remain as it is, as see it change, if the changes are to be such as it appears to me, they would inevitably be."[3]

Although men of the fur trade rebelled at every suggestion of agriculture, the fact was that the first plantings of domestic seeds in the West were in gardens or garden-size plots at the traders' posts. It was not a case of the traders giving serious thought to cropping contrary to their principles; rather it was the expression of an instinct calling for some vegetable foods to break the tedium of a wild meat and pemmican diet. The men were thankful for that nearly indestructible blend of dried buffalo meat and melted fat — sometimes flavored with saskatoon berries — but they could not escape the longing for variety. The only tools available for cultivation consisted of spades and hoes and this fact, coupled with the absence of winter storage for vegetables like turnips, carrots, and potatoes, limited plantings to small plots.

Studies conducted by Prof. Arthur Silver Morton in the Hudson's Bay records revealed a committee minute from 1674 — just four years after the company

A homesteader's cabin on the Plains. Note log construction with mud chinking.

charter was granted — stating: "Ordered that there be provided . . . a bushel of wheat and rye, barley and oats, or a barrell of each in casks, and such sorts of garden Seeds as the Governor shall advise . . . [also] a Bible and a common prayer book."

There is no indication of where these seeds were planted or if they were planted. It can be presumed, however, that if there was a planting, it would be at one of the company's posts at the bottom of James Bay.

The first cultivation and planting within the boundaries of present-day Saskatchewan may have been by the pioneer French trader, Chevalier de la Corne at his trading post on the south side of the Saskatchewan River, due north of today's town of Kinistino. The Master who built there in 1753 ordered cereal and garden seeds from France and was said to have had turnips, potatoes, peas, carrots, and cabbage from his own soil in the following year — also a small amount of wheat which he would no doubt crush between two selected stones for use in making bread or bannock. Whatever the modest amount grown, it would be enough to qualify la Corne for the distinction of being the first grower of wheat in the proud Wheat Province of Saskatchewan.

The corresponding distinction in the Alberta area is in doubt but it may properly go to the rather notorious trader, Peter Pond. There seems no doubt that he was the first of the newcomers to plant garden seeds. The only doubt is in whether he planted wheat or other grains in addition to the garden varieties.

Pond, the Connecticut Yankee who served with the British in wars against the French and then took to

trading, went from the headwaters of the Churchill River over the Methye Portage, down the Clearwater River to where Fort McMurray stands today, and then north on the Athabasca River to build Pond's House for trading purposes about thirty miles from the river's outlet at Athabasca Lake. That was in 1778 and the amazing fellow, who is known as a successful trader as well as a pioneer planter, was the first white man in the area. In addition to being the first of his race in the Athabasca region where the furs were abundant and the first planter, he was the first white man to see oil seeping from the sands along the river, the first to build a place of residence with more permanence than a teepee in the area of Alberta, and the first white man in the area to be suspected of murder.

In any event, when Alexander Mackenzie came that way a few years later, he wrote in his journal that Pond's garden was as good as any he had seen in Canada. But when Pond's name was mentioned as one which might be considered in a search for a Patron Saint for the Alberta Seed Growers' Association, a historian was quick to point out that as a suspect in two murders and a participant in a couple of man-to-man duels with pistols, he would probably be the least saintly of all patron saints.

Alexander Henry the Younger harvested fifty bushels of turnips and eighty bushels of potatoes at a Saskatchewan River post in 1809 and the hens at Fort Edmonton began to lay on January 6, 1811. The traders would have refused to admit it but at more and more posts there was a faint hint of agriculture, enough to encourage those who were growing tired of pemmican.

But still, in the first decade of the nineteenth century, there was not in all the Northwest a single genuine farmer or genuine farming effort. That was soon to change but not without some major struggles and some bloodshed.

Chapter 2

THE BOLD SELKIRK EXPERIMENT

Were it not for conflict with the busy harvest season, August 30 should be marked for an annual farmers' holiday, especially in western Canada. It was on that date in 1812 that twenty-three tired men pulled their canoes from the Red River to pitch their tents on the east side, right across from the mouth of the Assiniboine, where the cities of St. Boniface and Winnipeg sprang up later. These men, the real couriers of agriculture in the West, spent fifty-five paddling days in traveling from York Factory and it was now more than a year since their departure from Stornoway at the top of the Island of Lewis on Scotland's west side. Leathery Miles Macdonell, as leader, and his men of the Selkirk work crew, hoped to travel right through to the site to be fixed for the

colony in 1811 but delays and frozen rivers necessitated wintering close to the inhospitable coast of Hudson Bay.

The arrival of this "advance guard" at Red River was the first local evidence of Lord Selkirk's bold plan to establish a farm settlement in the remote fur country, one that would aid evicted crofter folks from the Scottish Highlands and needy families from Ireland to rehabilitate. The same courageous scheme would test this untried western soil. The tall Macdonell with military stride, Scottish accent, and a clansman's stubbornness was there, first of all, to take possession on Selkirk's behalf of the huge land grant conferred by the Hudson's Bay Company.

There would be no official ribbon cutting or sod turning but Macdonell was determined that something should be done to prevent misunderstanding about his authority and Lord Selkirk's land claim as proprietor. It was particularly important that the men of the North West Company would understand and he took pains to invite the residents of the North West Company's Fort Gibraltar, located right across at the northwest angle formed by the union of the two rivers. Three Northwesters condescended to attend and Macdonell ensured a better audience by inviting a few freeman hunters and natives and insisting upon his hired helpers being present. At twelve o'clock noon on September 4, Macdonell assumed his stiffest military bearing and faced Fort Gibraltar to read the proclamation which confirmed Lord Selkirk as proprietor of the 116,000 square miles of territory to be known as

Fort Prince of Wales, Churchill, Manitoba. Historically this fort is one of the treasures of the century. Building started about 1740 and took 40 years to complete. It stands today as one of the relics of history.

Assiniboia. He then read the companion proclamation which appointed him the governor of the Selkirk Territory.

When the formality ended, Macdonell invited his guests to his tent where he produced a keg of spirits, hoping to make the fur traders forget their fears and accept the new order with good grace. But the men from Fort Gibraltar were not totally submissive. "What's the meaning of this?" they seemed to be asking with a touch of hostility which alcohol did not banish. "Is Selkirk serious in thinking that an agricultural settlement will succeed here in fur country, and what makes him think that we will surrender our trading posts that happen to be inside the land he claims?"

To grasp the full meaning, the North West Company men would have had to know Lord Selkirk, who was born on St. Mary's Isle at the mouth of the River Dee on Scotland's southwest, June 20, 1771, and christened Thomas Douglas. As the youngest of seven sons of the 4th Earl of Selkirk, there seemed no chance of this one inheriting the father's title and family estate, but one by one, the older Douglas sons died and then the elder Douglas passed on, leaving Thomas to become the 5th Earl of Selkirk. In the meantime, the young man attended University of Edinburgh and became friendly with other bright intellectuals like Walter Scott, who became Sir Walter. Another friend outside the university was Robert Burns who was twelve years his senior but shared concern about Britain's social problems. Such friends made him more stubbornly eager to help Ireland's disgruntled masses which had endured both famine and oppression, and Scotland's crofter folk who were being evicted from their small Highland holdings to make way for sheep pastures and deer runs. Angry because nothing was being done to help these people, the young earl proposed a government-sponsored plan to aid such Britishers to establish farm communities in the Colonies. There was no interest.

He had not seen Rupert's Land where the Hud-

The arduous work of harvesting by hand as in the days of the Selkirk settlement.

son's Bay Company claimed monopoly trading rights conferred by Royal Charter from King Charles II in 1670, and the North West Company claimed the right of free men to trade where they chose, but from imperfect maps and conversations with former traders, he became convinced that land "out there" would be suitable for a farm colonization scheme. Almost instinctively he was gazing at that area marked on maps by Red River. Taking a request for a grant of land in that part to the Imperial Government, he received no encouragement but was told that only the Hudson's Bay Company could act on it. The old company, with primary involvement in furs, had no interest in agriculture or colonization and Selkirk's proposal was rejected, abruptly, as though it was heresy.

Unable to secure land in Rupert's Land, Selkirk became interested in the Sault Ste. Marie area and returned to the British government with a plan. He would finance a colonization undertaking to that part if the government would provide some assistance by granting him the mineral rights on the north shore of Lake Superior. This the government refused to do but intimated to him at this point that he could purchase 80,000 acres on Prince Edward Island. Selkirk accepted the proposal and moved quickly to send settlers to the area. Halfway through 1803, some 800 men, women and children from Highland communities were on their way in three ships, the *Dykes, Polly,* and *Oughton.* Selkirk himself was accompanying, on the *Dykes,* and remained on the island to see his colonists making headway with building of log cabins, cultivation to allow for plantings in the following spring, and preparations for winter food supplies which would consist mainly of potatoes, porridge, and fish. When he left the island, it was with confidence that the settlement was almost certain of success. He was ready for the next venture, which happened to be the Baldoon Colony beside Lake St. Clair in Upper Canada. But because of crop failures, illness among the settlers, and deaths in the cattle herds, the Baldoon undertaking was a disappointment.

Through it all, however, the earl's original fascination with Red River as a place for a colony remained. Hudson's Bay Company policy was unchanged but the fur trade was experiencing slump and company shares fell from a high point of £250 to trade as low as £60. Selkirk was seized with the idea of buying his way into the company to gain a voice in its affairs.

In 1807, he married Jean Wedderburn Colvile who happened to have some rich relations and within a year, Selkirk along with Jean's brother and cousin were buying company stock. Andrew Wedderburn Colvile was elected to the executive committee of the company and, as disclosed by the minutes of meetings,

there was an immediate change in policy. Instead of refusing to consider a request from Lord Selkirk for a grant of land, a resolution approved on February 6, 1811, stated: "That Mr. Wedderburn be desired to request Lord Selkirk to lay before the Committee the terms on which he will accept a Grant of Land within the Territories of the Hudson's Bay Company . . ."[1]

Lord Selkirk must have chuckled. He was not long in responding. His new proposal was endorsed by the committee on March 6 and reached the shareholders at a general meeting or "General Court" on May 30 for a final decision. Voting was based on the value of shares held and shareholders holding £14,823 in stock voted against the proposed grant of land while shareholders with £29,937 in stock voted in favor. Among those voting for the grant were the Earl of Selkirk who was shown to have £4,087 in shares and Andrew Wedderburn Colvile with £4,474. And of those who opposed, Edward Ellis and Sir William Mackenzie were conspicuous as leaders in the North West Company. But the decision was definite enough and the earl found himself with some 116,000 square miles or roughly 74 million acres in a part of the world which he had never seen.

In accepting the grant, he was making a token payment of ten shillings and undertaking to find up to 200 men per year for company services. But his object was settlement and having anticipated the favorable outcome of the vote, he was almost ready to start recruiting workmen for the company and for his proposed settlement. He had two able leaders standing by, Miles Macdonell and Colin Robertson. Macdonell was sent at once to Ireland and Robertson to the Highlands to hire workers. The response was favorable until it was discovered that the North West Company men were campaigning to discourage both workmen and possible settlers from joining in any manner.

A long letter signed by "A Highlander" appeared in the *Inverness Journal,* a paper with wide circulation in the area from which Lord Selkirk hoped to draw workers and settlers. The letter was a warning to readers who might be interested that owing to "the nature of the country and the severity of the climate," settlement would be impossible. If the emigrants managed to get through to the point of settlement, "they will be surrounded by warlike savage nations. . . . If they escape from the scalping knife, they will be subject to constant alarms and terror. Their habitations, their crops, their cattle will be destroyed and they will find it impossible to subsist in the country."[2]

As discovered, the author of the letter was actually Simon McGillivray, brother of William McGillivray, the head man in the North West Company.

The recruited party was reduced by desertions

and weakened by dissension but finally departed Stornoway with Miles Macdonell in charge. The old sailing ship, *Edward and Anne*, took sixty-one days to reach York Factory and then, near the end of September, it was obvious that there would not be sufficient time to get through to Red River before the rivers were frozen. The only logical decision was to winter at or near York Factory. As it turned out, the ensuing winter was rough. In addition to extremely cold weather, Macdonell's men encountered food problems, with the constant threat of scurvy. To add to the unpleasantness, there was quarreling, Irishmen quarreling with Scots, Presbyterians quarreling with Roman Catholics, and everybody quarreling with Miles Macdonell.

As soon as the Hayes River was free of ice in the spring, the men were on their way, an estimated 700 miles to the mouth of Red River. Progress was slower than Macdonell expected because much of the journey was against river currents. At Oxford House, about one-third of the distance to Red River, the party made a notable discovery, a pair of young cattle, a bull and a heifer. Having yielded to expediency, Macdonell left eight young cattle behind at Stornoway rather than tax the ship's space with the amount of feed and fresh water that would be needed for a voyage of two months. Here were two cattle that the settlers would need and Macdonell named them Adam and Eve and took them along, with or without permission from the fort's official. Teaching the two cattle to step into and out of the canoe was not easy but Macdonell persevered and believed he had the only representatives of their species in all of Rupert's Land.

Macdonell was not unmindful of Lord Selkirk's instructions about choosing a site for the settlement. By premonition, the earl favored Red River and mentioned Pelican Ripple — known later as St. Andrew's Rapids — but if Macdonell failed to find a good farming location on the Red River, he was to examine Dauphin River or Little Saskatchewan as it became known. From advice at York Factory, Macdonell concluded that Red River had more to offer and, as though following a guiding star, he paddled directly to it.

He knew that the first contingent of genuine settlers was likely to come all the way in 1812 and might arrive at any time. If he was to make even the slightest preparation for them, he would have to hurry. As soon as the formality of reading the proclamation was completed, he set out by canoe to re-examine downstream sites for the settlement. Before returning three days later, he fixed firmly upon the land at and near a bend in the river to become known as Point Douglas, just a mile north of the Assiniboine. The soil was obviously rich and fires had served to reduce the job of clearing trees. At once he instructed a few of the

men accompanying to begin cultivating a plot of ground to receive a bushel and a half of precious seed wheat which he had carried from Scotland, winter wheat as it happened.

A bigger decision called for attention. If 50 or 100 men, women and children, the first of the real settlers, were to arrive within days or weeks, how and where were they to be accommodated? Macdonell might have started to erect log cabins which would be habitable by the onset of winter but homes would be rather useless if they were not within reach of food for the occupants. The rivers would furnish fish but that was not enough. Writing to the earl, he expressed his displeasure that "notwithstanding all the orders the Company posts in this quarter might have had to provide for our arrival, there was not one bag of pemmican or other article of provisions reserved for us."[3]

The decision was to send all the settlers south to Pembina — another sixty miles — as soon as they arrived. There, where the Pembina River entered the Red, the wintering conditions would be better; both the Hudson's Bay Company and the rival company had posts and hunters would not have as far to go for buffalo meat. Holding only a few of his men to plant the wheat, Macdonell sent the others to Pembina with

Renovated grave of Lord Selkirk, May 24, 1978. (courtesy Neil J. McMillan).

instructions to get logs for cabins and start building. He joined them in a few days but after receiving a message notifying him that the settlers were soon to arrive, he hastened back to the Forks where, on October 27, with winter chill in the air, he welcomed the amiable Irish leader, Owen Keveny, and seventy weary but hopeful settlers. They had been traveling for about four months, which included sixty-one days at sea. But all had survived. Indeed, they had completed the ocean voyage with one more passenger than they had had at starting, Mrs. MacLean having given birth to a daughter en route.

Macdonell's hunch in ordering his men to cut more prairie hay than Adam and Eve would eat was a good one because the Keveny party was arriving with twenty-one sheep — seventeen ewes and four rams — certainly the first of their species in the Northwest. They were not ordinary sheep but, rather, members of the golden-fleeced Merinos of Spain, selected by Lord Selkirk with thought to the possibility of an export trade in superior wool.

It was a long winter at Pembina and the hunters had trouble in maintaining the needed supplies of buffalo meat. But with the coming of spring, the colonists were none the less eager to return to the Point Douglas location to begin building on their long riverlot farm allotments being marked out by the Hudson's Bay Company handyman, Peter Fidler from Brandon House.

The first full summer on the Red River farms brought only moderate progress. The winter wheat planted in the autumn of 1812 was a total failure, and with insufficient horses and no oxen and no plows, cultivation was still limited to what could be accomplished by hand. Lord Selkirk's advice about capturing buffalo calves and domesticating them for use like oxen resulted in only one heifer surviving. To people with British ideals in mixed farming, the near total lack of livestock was a serious disappointment. And to add to the season's disappointments, the big group of settlers expected from Kildonan in Sutherlandshire was obliged to winter near the mouth of the Churchill River and did not arrive until midsummer of the next year, 1814.

Lord Selkirk had special admiration for the Kildonan people but luck failed them and they suffered greater delay and more hardship than any previous group. First, there was ship's fever or typhus during the voyage and the man who was both leader and medical doctor was one of the earliest to be removed by death. The ship's captain, impatient and visibly provoked by the constant smell of sick people, sailed to the port at Fort Prince of Wales instead of York as planned. Left stranded, the resourceful people built cabins beside the Churchill River and subsisted for the winter on fish and ptarmigan. Before the snow

had melted in the spring, all who had the strength for it began the long walk toward York Factory where they still had to wait for the rivers to lose their ice before tackling the long and hard trip to Red River.

Although relieved to be at journey's end where Macdonell was ready with farm allotments on the west side of Red River, downstream from Point Douglas, the Sutherland men and women were disturbed to hear of an increase in tension between the North West Company traders and the settlers. The trouble was largely of Miles Macdonell's making and became known as the Pemmican War. Ill advised, Macdonell had on January 8, 1814, issued his famous Pemmican Order intended to force the retention of all available food supplies for the use of the settlers, but it convinced the men of the North West Company that it was a subtle device intended to destroy their business.

The proclamation, after defining the borders of Selkirk's 116,000 square miles known as Assiniboia, ordered in legal terms that no person "shall take out any provisions, either flesh, fish or vegetables procured or raised within the territory, by water or land carriage for twelve month from the date hereof."[4]

Men of the North West Company were angry and when Macdonell, who happened to possess the better stock of guns, undertook to enforce the order by seizing pemmican intended for use by the fur brigades traveling eastward and westward, they were ready to resist with all the force they had. Pemmican, as everybody knew, was needed to keep "the wheels of the fur trade" in motion. Brigades on the long "lifeline" between Athabasca and Fort William couldn't operate without it.

Most of that essential pemmican came from the good buffalo country westward along the Assiniboine and Qu'Appelle rivers and when Macdonell's men tried to intercept supplies being brought down by canoes and later forced their way into Fort Souris to seize 479 bags of pemmican, 93 kegs of grease and 865 pounds of dried meat, there were immediate signs of warfare.[5]

When officers and wintering partners in the North West Company met for the annual discussions at Fort William a few weeks later, the chief topic concerned ways of ending the menace of the Selkirk farm colony, especially the governor. How could that purpose be achieved? Two methods were considered and approved. Duncan Cameron's responsibility would be to convince the settlers that an agricultural colony could not succeed in this fur country and to encourage them to desert, and Alex Macdonell of the Qu'Appelle area would be expected to work on Métis emotions with the idea of fomenting a direct attack upon the colony.

Both measures proved to be effective and men of

the Montreal company chuckled with satisfction. By the spring of 1815, these North West Company traders were the obvious aggressors. They seized the colony's surplus guns and after making Miles Macdonell their prisoner, they were sending him to Montreal to be tried for theft of pemmican. At about the same time, 134 men, women and children from the uneasy colony lined up to accept Duncan Cameron's offer of free transportation by canoe to Upper Canada and food provisions for the trip. Only about fifty people remained in the settlement and before many days these saw forty Métis riding in from the west to burn homes, trample crops, and shoot livestock, enough to send the remaining residents fleeing for their lives.

The Northwesters beamed with satisfaction, exclaiming: "At last! We'll have no more trouble with the farmers." But Selkirk's colony, although seriously wounded, was not dead. Colin Robertson came that way and persuaded the fifty refugees who fled to return to their holdings beside the river. Toward the end of the year, another group of settlers under the leadership of a new colony governor, Robert Semple, arrived from the Old Land to bring colony numbers back to approximately 200. Semple had Imperial Army experience and lacked nothing in courage and confidence. But the North West Company men were not ready to give up and resolved to make colony destruction more complete next time. The climax came on that awful day, June 19, 1816, the day of the Battle of Seven Oaks which saw a brief but bloody clash between settlers following Governor Semple and half-breeds following Cuthbert Grant. In a matter of minutes, Semple and twenty of his followers were dead on the field of battle, with one man dead and one wounded on Grant's side.

Again the distraught survivors of the colony fled to the north to take refuge at Jack River, convinced that they would never return to Red River. Again the Northwesters who plotted colony destruction felt the thrill of triumph. The pioneer farm colony, costly to Lord Selkirk and disappointing to those who joined it, appeared to be at an end. But it was not at an end. Lord Selkirk, although unaware of the fateful Battle of Seven Oaks, was on his way from Montreal to see his Red River colony for the first time and encourage his settlers. With him were 100 hired soldiers and when the sad news of battle and colony destruction reached him at Sault Ste. Marie thirty-five days after the clash, he changed his course and traveled directly to the North West Company's post, Fort William. There, using his authority as a justice of the peace, he seized the fort and arrested the company leaders who happened to be present. He may have exceeded his authority but his anger at those who plotted the destruction of his colony was understandable.

The taking and holding of Fort William brought delay to the plan to visit Red River. But while still at Fort William, he sent some of his men ahead to recapture Fort Douglas and persuade the shocked and reluctant refugee settlers hiding at Jack River to come back for one more trial at Red River. The promise of better protection for the settlement and of a personal visit from the earl was enough to persuade the peace-loving people to try again. Some of them, on returning, were building cabin homes for the third time but were cheered when, on June 21, the news spread from home to home along the river, "The Earl has come." It was one day after his forty-sixth birthday and although he looked worn and sad, he brought reassurance to Point Douglas residents. He spoke softly and expressed sympathy for those who had suffered much. He promised to do all in his power to prevent repetition of the aggressions. The people listened attentively, clinging to every word as he announced that all their land debts to him were being canceled and he had various plans for their betterment. It was his intention to secure a substantial herd of cattle for the colony, establish an experimental farm, arrange for the making of bridges and better roads, and to the Kildonan people, he added: "Here I offer you a site of ground for your school and over there another for your church and manse."

Yes, he promised, he would come again. But he did not come again because soon after leaving to face the courts in the East on charges of seizing and occupying Fort William, he was returning to Scotland, a sick man, and then to southern France, to die.

The earl's death in 1820 marked the end of a frustrating and disaster-ridden chapter but not the end of the Selkirk influence in pioneer agriculture. The experimental farm Selkirk promised was started in 1818 with William Laidlaw in charge and the cattle he said he would obtain arrived after several attempts, two years after the earl's death. And best of all, the colony proved a point of lasting importance to the future of Canada, that contrary to the opinions expressed so freely by the Lords of the Fur Trade, the Northwest was indeed capable of supporting an extensive and vigorous agriculture and a broad program of colonization.

Moreover, had the biased views of the fur traders prevailed without the Selkirk demonstration at Red River, the Canadian government's 1868 indifference toward the Hudson's Bay Company lands might very well have left the way open for the United States, pursuing its policy of Manifest Destiny, to buy the West from its acknowledged proprietors, just as Alaska was bought from Russia a year earlier. Had such a transaction been completed, what is now one of the great "bread baskets" of the world could be shown on modern maps as three or four more states of the American Union.

Chapter 3

AN EXPERIMENTAL FARM AND THE FIRST PIGS

Experience — either one's own or another's — is an essential for agricultural success. Lack of it can be costly. The colonists to Red River understood Scottish and Irish farming but were strangers to Rupert's Land soil and weather. Miles Macdonell's selection of winter wheat for the planting on freshly turned sod in the autumn of 1812 was an example and the poor cropping record for the next eleven years was due in part at least to human errors. If the crops of 1814 and 1817 had been planted earlier in the spring seasons, they might have escaped the disastrous fall frosts, and if the settlers understood grasshoppers, they might have employed cultural methods that would have minimized the crop damage in 1818 and 1819. Not until 1824 did crop returns express the real worth of the Red River Valley soils. Wheat in that latter year was said to have yielded forty-four bushels per acre on plowed ground and sixty-eight bushels per acre on land cultivated by hand, thereby encouraging the inexperienced conclusion that the new thing called a plow would never be satisfactory. The debate was long and loud and there was nobody within a thousand miles to whom the settlers could turn for advice based on either science or practice. The immigrant farmers would be obliged to learn by the ancient expedient of "trial and error," but it would be wasteful of human resources if every mistake had to be repeated on every farm at Red River or elsewhere. Hence there was the strongest case for an experimental farm and Lord Selkirk recognized it.

Canada's Experimental Farm system of recent years had its beginning when Hon. John Carling was minister of agriculture in Sir John A. Macdonald's government. He asked William Saunders, a London, Ontario, druggist with a flare for plant breeding, to conduct a survey of experimental farms in the United States and prepare a recommendation for a Canadian program. The Saunders report, tabled in the House of Commons on April 15, 1886, was well received and parliament acted quickly to give it effect. Saunders was appointed to be the first director and in line with his recommendations, a Central Experimental Farm was started at Ottawa and plans were drawn for other farms at Nappan, Brandon, Indian Head, and Agassiz.

Canadians took justifiable satisfction from their experimental farms and experimental stations but they should not have forgotten that the West had an experimental farm, in name at least, sixty-seven years before the equivalent plans were made at Ottawa. It was an all-western institution, the dream of Lord Selkirk. Nobody will argue that the Hayfield Experimental Farm of 1818, half hidden in trees west of Fort Douglas, was a great success. It came far short of measuring up to its founder's expectation but that did not detract from the Selkirk reasoning which inspired it or the dedicated effort of William Laidlaw who managed it under the most trying conditions.

The earl chose the occasion of his visit to Red River in 1817 to announce his intention and before leaving a few weeks later, he selected the site for the first experimental farm in British North America. It might have been seen as another measure of the man who was to be described as a prophet, a philanthropist, colonizer, and empire builder. It would have been appropriate to add the descriptive term, scientist.

The recognition of need for an experimental farm was in itself an evidence of scientific instinct. He had the scientist's approach to the introduction of new crops and the challenge of hybridizing cattle and bison for the benefit of the colonists. Indeed, the technique prescribed in starting the first flock of high-grade sheep gave him the glow of a modern Professor of Animal Science. Having selected the flock of Spanish Merinos with the idea of developing a highly specialized export trade in premium wool, he issued the appropriate instructions. Both ewes and rams were to be given individual identifications by means of a system of notches in the ears. Then, for the purpose of determining the most useful animals for the breeding program, all fleeces were to be weighed and identified at shearing time and sent for separate appraisal by the best wool experts in Britain. As in more modern experimental farm projects for wool improvement, the hope was to establish strains of breeding animals possessing the greatest possible concentration of genetic or hereditary factors for the qualities desired.

The farm which was intended to feature dairy cattle and dairying, did not achieve much in that line and reason was not hard to find; namely, a lack of dairy cattle, for which nobody connected with the colony could have been blamed. The farm's best claim to fame came from its place in relation to the introduction of pigs and its pioneer struggle to obtain power for work in the fields.

Although Selkirk announced the experimental farm plan when he was at Red River in the summer of 1817, the fact was that he had already taken steps to engage the man who was to manage it, William Laidlaw, who, in arriving at the settlement during the early part of the ensuing winter, made agricultural history at once by bringing with him what may be seen as the first pigs in the vast area of Rupert's Land; hence the abiding bond between the first experimental farm and the future pork industry.

Inasmuch as Laidlaw was making the trip anyway, he and the earl agreed that he should bring some needed livestock. The decision was to take seven pigs, probably two months old at the time of sailing, and five or six months old with weight of 100 pounds each at time of arrival at destination.

Accommodating seven pigs on the sailing ship going to York Factory presented no obstacle because pigs were often carried on long ocean voyages as a matter of routine, partly to consume waste from the galleys and partly to provide fresh pork during travel.

The major transportation problem began when leaving York Factory and men and pigs were obliged to share the same canoes. At first the pigs were crated and loading and unloading could be carried out easily, but, like all healthy swine, Laidlaw's were becoming bigger and heavier by the day. Worse, the canoes were traveling late in the season, facing the danger of being caught at some midjourney point by frozen lakes and rivers.

Sure enough, the fear was realized. At the north end of Lake Winnipeg, Laidlaw encountered winter conditions; ice brought the canoeing season to an abrupt end. "Now what?" Laidlaw probably asked himself while breathing regret at having allowed himself to be the official escort for a small herd of pigs. But he knew that this was his first major test in Selkirk's employment and was determined to complete the delivery, no matter how unfriendly and unco-operative pigs and weather might be.

The only hope now was to obtain sleds and dogs to pull them. This he did, but there was increasing danger of the pigs freezing to death while riding on the sleighs and to avoid the hazard, each of the unwilling pigs was wrapped in buffalo robes and tied to the floor of sleds. The squeals from the protesting swine could be heard for miles in the wintry weather and left the sleigh dogs drooling for a taste of fresh pork. Laidlaw found it necessary to muzzle the dogs in order to safeguard the pigs.[1]

When the supply of characteristic pig feed carried from Scotland was exhausted, Laidlaw fed the pigs on fish caught along the way. By his instructions, the fish were to be cooked before feeding but orders were not carried out and three of the seven pigs died from what Laidlaw believed to be the eating of frozen fish. Remaining were four healthy pigs and these, delivered at Point Douglas, were the first livestock of any kind at the new experimental farm and the first of their species in half a continent. Their delivery was a triumph in resourcefulness and patience, and in terms of human effort, they must have been the most expensive pig stock in history.

Having delivered the porkers, Laidlaw could turn his full attention to the farm and needed buildings. His first impression of the farm won his enthusiasm. The location was ideal and the soil appeared to be excellent. "There is an immense quantity of the best natural hay I ever saw in my life, which induced me to call it Hayfield," he wrote.[2]

While winter restricted other activities, Laidlaw took some experienced woodsmen to Pembina to cut building logs and drag them to the river's edge to be floated down to the settlement in the spring. A big and handsome log house took shape in the summer — too big and too handsome because it overshadowed the main purposes of the farm and brought ridicule.

Laidlaw could not be held responsible for the lack of milk cows on the so-called dairy farm but the lack of headway in breaking ground for crops was more difficult to explain. As of July, 1818, he had only six acres of new breaking done with a wooden plow. His biggest handicap was shortage of draft power and next to that was the unsatisfactory plow. He resolved to make a better plow from iron carried from York Factory, and did. But a plow — any plow — needed much pulling power, especially in the Red River gumbo sod.

S. A. Bedford, appointed in 1888 to be the first superintendent of the Brandon Experimental Farm. Upon retirement from the Experimental farm, he became professor of field husbandry at the Manitoba Agricultural College.

Early in 1818, he had four small Indian horses for the plowing — until they strayed away. Weeks were lost in hunting for them and three were recovered. Hoping then to make up for lost time, Laidlaw outfitted two plows, one to be pulled by the three remaining horses; for the second he was harnessing the only three cattle on the farm, two cows and a bull. The cattle, he reported, made the better plowing outfit.

By the next summer, while still waiting for the stock cows to be brought from St. Louis to make his place look more like the dairy farm it was supposed to be, misfortune continued to plague him. Fire destroyed the handsome log house and grasshoppers were eating every green thing in sight. And contrary to his hope, the farm power situation had not improved. By harnessing and working his three horses, two cows, one bull, and one domesticated bison heifer to perform the field work, he must have had the strangest assortment of draft animals in experimental farm history.

He had reason to expect the cattle from St. Louis in 1820 and traveled to Big Stone Lake on the United States side of the border to meet them, but they did not come. Gradually, Laidlaw was becoming discouraged and he left the post. The experimental farm for which Lord Selkirk held such high hopes was sold to be operated as a private holding. It had survived six years without fulfilling expectations but nobody could criticize the original concept or say that Laidlaw had not tried to make it a success.

That first experimental farm passed into history but the principles were not forgotten and the general idea was revived to produce a second experimental farm at Red River in 1830 and a third one in 1838, which would be two years after the Selkirk land empire known as Assiniboia was sold back to the Hudson's Bay Company for £84,000.

The second experimental farm, approved by Governor George Simpson, was charged with the special responsibility of rearing sheep and discovering the best techniques for the preparation of such products as tallow, wool, hemp, and flax for export to the British markets. The location of that farm was, according to Robert Campbell who worked on it from its beginning as assistant manager, on the north side of the Assiniboine River and about three and three-quarter miles west of the Red.

Again, the experimental farm performance was not brilliant except for its part in furnishing a base for the founding flock of sheep driven from Kentucky in 1833 (and treated more fully in another chapter), and a home for the famous breeding stallion, Fireaway, brought from England in 1832. The experimental farm may have derived more credit than it deserved from the horse's leaping reputation but that was exactly what it needed.

As the settlers discovered, they could obtain horses in small numbers from the Plains Indians but they were never impressed by them. Laidlaw's trouble in obtaining the number of draft horses he needed illustrated part of the problem. The Indian stock, strange to tell, traced to the aristocratically bred horses of Spain but after living for a few generations as wild mustangs and more generations in the ownership of the tribesmen, deterioration was strikingly clear. It suggested a reversal of the evolutionary processes which had brought primitive North American horses from the diminutive Eohippus to sizes and shapes resembling modern breeds, then to become extinct on the Americas — extinct until reintroduced by the Spaniards coming after Columbus. The horses the settlers were able to get from the prairie natives were small, dejected, and generally thin, and the immigrant farmers longed for Clydesdales, Shires, and Thoroughbreds.

The Hudson's Bay Company officials may have been moved by a desire to do something useful and visible for the second experimental farm or they may have heard the private prayers uttered by the settlers.

In either case, a communication from Deputy Governor Nicholas Garry early in 1831, announced: "We will send a stallion of proper breed by the ship to York Factory. We should think the Experimental Farm at Red River the best place to commence raising horses for the service."[3]

What the company officer meant by "proper breed" was not clear and settlers at Point Douglas speculated eagerly, each one hoping the new horse would conform to his favorite British breed. There was still the problem of delivering the stallion by sailing ship to York Factory and then over the 700 difficult canoe miles to Fort Garry. The earlier tasks of conveying sheep and pigs and even young cattle by canoe or the bigger edition known as York boat was acknowledged to be difficult but to move a mature stallion by the same means would have seemed frightening if not impossible to most people. But miraculous as it appeared, the stallion, bearing the name of Fireaway, was delivered at the experimental farm at Red River without mishap.

A band of selected brood mares was assembled and settlers from far up and down the rivers admitted their interest by rushing to see this "wonder horse" and exercising every horseman's prerogative to pass judgment and make critical remarks about hocks, feet, fetlocks, withers, action, and so on.

At once most of the questions about Fireaway were answered. There he was, a handsome bright bay, standing sixteen hands in height and a representative of the old Norfolk Trotter breed which implied that he carried Arabian blood in his veins. It was the strain from which England's fashionable Hackney breed emerged. Robert Campbell who was working on the experimental farm at the time, called the horse a Hackney.[4] The animal had a proud bearing and was winning friends for himself and the experimental farm from the moment of his arrival. He possessed a superb quality of bone which caught the eyes of the Scots with Clydesdale ideals and his trotting record of something over fifteen miles an hour, impressed everybody. Even those who had been skeptics admitted that he was "quite a horse."

George Simpson was pleased to see the public acceptance of the stallion, also the new prominence coming to the experimental farm. Reporting to the governor and committee in London, he stated: "The stallion sent out last year reached the settlement in perfect safety and in high condition, and will soon give us a better breed of horses. He is looked upon as one of the wonders of the world by the natives, many of whom have travelled great distances with no other object than to see him."[5]

One of the problems created by the possession of a horse of acknowledged superiority at that period was

This bull and mule hitched together represents a rare scene from the depression period. This 1936 photograph depicting the transport of firewood was taken near Craik, Saskatchewan.

Canadian Experimental Farm, Morden — approximately 1940. (Canada Dept. of Agriculture).

in protecting it from theft. Horse stealing was the great native pastime and the prize of a horse like Fireaway could be a constant temptation. It was considered necessary at times to keep an armed guard with Fireaway twenty-four hours a day.

There was no doubt concerning the excellence of the stallion's conformation and quality and after a year in the country, he was being seen as an outstanding sire as well. The Fireaway offspring possessed the hardiness and durability of the native mares and much of the size, refinement, and speed of the sire. These half-breed horses made the best buffalo runners the country had known and the most useful work animals the settlers had driven. Fireaway, by every measure, was a great success and the experimental farm which had adopted him, enjoyed the benefit of reflected glory.

That second experimental farm, however, like the first one, failed to live more than what looked like the "allotted span" of six years. But the need for something of the kind was not in dispute and the third farm was initiated by the Hudson's Bay Company from its London office and was established on the north side of the Assiniboine, close to the Red and

close to Upper Fort Garry. It was the most expensive and the most elaborate of the three farms, with Capt. George Carey, a Londoner, engaged to manage it. The logic of bringing a Londoner to direct an experimental farm at Red River would be questioned, of course, and there was criticism. As Alexander Ross told it, the workmen brought from England were "notorious beer-drinkers" and their appetites for food were no less immense. It seemed to take all that the farm could grow to keep them supplied.

If lack of experience was a serious handicap in farming, it was no less true about running experimental farms and the third of these farms, lacking the attraction of a pioneer flock of sheep or a wonder horse like Fireaway, needed something with similar appeal. Apparently the basic experimentation which would have been most useful was neglected and the third experimental farm, like its predecessors, was short lived.

It is significant that none of the three farms made a glowing record. The motives were good and Lord Selkirk's contention that testing and research were essential for success in any agricultural program was never questioned. There was something seriously wrong with the interpretation of purpose but nobody could deny the Red River experimental farms the distinction of being Canada's first.

Chapter 4

THE STRUGGLE TO GET CATTLE

"It's no' a proper farm wi'oot a coo," a Kildonan man said, expressing the British ideal brought to Red River. As Selkirk's colonists discovered, they could get dogs and small horses of inferior shape from the prairie Indians but the native people of the West had never seen cattle, sheep, pigs, or domestic cats. They had not seen domestic poultry until Alexander Henry the Younger brought two hens and a rooster from Fort William to Pembina in 1807.[1] The newcomers, hoping to become successful farmers, wanted representatives of all these species but knew they would be extremely difficult to obtain.

Of the various good things they were obliged to leave behind when sailing to the new world, cattle and sheep would rank next to relations and friends. Inasmuch as cattle could supply milk, butter, cheese, meat, leather, and oxen for draft purposes, they represented the local need mentioned most frequently in family prayers and in conversations up and down the river. True, Miles Macdonell had the good fortune to find, unexpectedly, two young cattle at Oxford House, which he brought to Red River in 1812, partly compensating for the eight young cattle he was obliged for practical reasons to leave behind when departing from Stornoway in the previous year.

With the Oxford House pair, to be known as Adam and Eve, in their possession, the newcomers to Red River supposed that they had all the cattle in the western part of the continent. In this they were wrong; three more cattle — a bull, a cow and calf — were in the possession of the North West Company post at the mouth of the Souris River and these were bought by the Hudson's Bay Company's versatile servant, Peter Fidler, for £100 and brought to Point Douglas when he came down to survey the elongated riverlot farms for the settlers in 1813. With these, the men and women of

the settlement could count five cattle, two bulls and three females, few enough with which to build the herds of which the settlers dreamed.

But there was cattle trouble ahead and herd

John McLean was a Scot who arrived by riverboat in what is now Manitoba in 1862. He was the first farmer on the Portage plain and his family has remained in the Portage district through to the fifth generation.

building proved to be grievously slow. First, the bull bought from the North West Company became viscious and was slaughtered for beef. With Adam remaining to fill the noble position of herd sire, the other bull seemed superfluous anyway, but bulls are unpredictable critters at any time and Adam created a minor crisis by yielding to masculine curiosity and straying from the home pasture. Settlers searched diligently for the essential fellow, without success. Nothing more was seen of Adam until the following spring when his lifeless carcass was observed floating down the Red River as the ice was breaking up. Presumably, the stray bull had gone onto the ice in quest of water and had broken through and either drowned or become mired.

The cattle in the settlement now numbered three, with no bull. This had to be a hopeless way to start a cattle industry. The only remaining solution to the problem was in the chance that Eve, then pregnant, would drop a bull calf. This she did, but the colonists were growing impatient at the long delays, at least until the early part of 1817 when Selkirk's paid soldiers marching from Fort William to recapture Fort Douglas, brought five cattle — one bull, one ox, and three females — found at the North West Company's post at Rainy Lake which was seized en route. Five new cattle would help to meet the urgent need at Point Douglas but the benefit was fleeting because the commissioners appointed to restore peace between the two warlike trading companies ordered the restoration of all confiscated property and when the Northwesters repossessed their cattle, they did the spiteful thing and shot them under the gaze of the shocked settlers. To colonists longing for the security which only cattle could bring, it was the most despicable act they had

The buffalo once claimed all of the immense grazing lands of the prairies. They were later replaced by cattle.

witnessed since the Battle of Seven Oaks. Thus, by late 1817, the colony had more domesticated prairie buffalo than cattle, and fewer cattle than in 1813. It raised a question: would the colonists have been better off if they had followed Lord Selkirk's advice about capturing and taming young buffalo in larger numbers and without waiting for cattle? Apparently there was a resurgence of interest in domesticating the wild kind because John Pritchard in writing to Andrew Colvile in 1820 could report eighteen domestic buffaloes in the settlement, "as tame as European cattle."[2]

Selkirk retained his interest in using the plains buffalo but was not giving up in his determination to bring cattle to the settlement. While negotiating for a substantial herd of cattle from the United States, he was arranging at the same time, in 1819, for a shipment of four yearling heifers from Scotland. Because "the cattle at Red River have been so much destroyed in the various attacks made by the N.W.Co.", he was instructing a Scottish friend to select and buy four Orkney heifers, noting: "The Orkney cattle are not handsome [but] are spoken of as good milkers which is the most essential point for our purpose."[3]

The young cattle were well fed and well attended on the ocean voyage and reached York Factory in good condition but their late arrival dictated the necessity of wintering there. Two of the heifers died before spring, leaving only two for delivery at Point Douglas.

It proved again that cattle in such meager numbers would never match the need. Nothing short of a big drive of cattle from the American south, where they were said to exist, would satisfy the Red River demand and Lord Selkirk, who was well aware of it, was making the necessary plans. Business discussions about a possible drive from St. Louis, far south on the Mississippi, began as early as 1814 and progressed slowly at first. The earliest inquiry was for "one hundred young milk cows and four or five bulls but not to exceed one thousand pounds for the whole expense including purchase and the expense of driving."[4]

Hearing of Lord Selkirk's interest in ordering such a herd, Joseph Rolette, of Prairie du Chien, wrote in early 1817 to inform the earl that he considered himself to be "the only man in this country who will undertake such a job."[5] Having expressed the good opinion of himself, he assured Selkirk that he was prepared to make delivery in July or August of the next year of 200 cows and one or two pairs of oxen at $100 per head. It proposed a bigger expenditure than Selkirk was willing to make but when the earl was returning from Red River to the East in the autumn of 1817, he traveled via Prairie du Chien to see and talk with Rolette who appeared to be insisting upon a $10,000 order — still a bigger deal than Lord Selkirk saw fit to authorize.[6]

Shortly thereafter, Lord Selkirk made contact with a Michilimackinac trader, Michael Dousman, who was prepared to accept an order according to the Selkirk specifications and drive the cattle from some point near St. Louis. Selkirk made it clear by letter that he hoped to obtain 100 young cows and 4 or 5 bulls for a total price not to exceed £1,000 delivered.[7]

Having made the proposal and intimated the maximum price he was prepared to pay, the earl then left matters of contract and delivery arrangements to his agent in the region, Robert Dickson. A contract was drawn and signed by Dickson but it was for 120 cattle priced at $80 per head for cows and $100 per head for oxen, making for total costs far above what Selkirk indicated a willingness to pay. On this point, Selkirk was angry at Dickson but it was too late to change the terms because Dousman had both a signed contract and a cash advance.

But Dousman, for reasons best known to himself, chose to escape from his obligation and instead of asking to be released from the contract, he sold it to another Michilimackinac man, Adam Stewart, for $1,800.[8] The latter, considered a responsible fellow, appeared to be taking the contract seriously. He was certainly not overlooking the Selkirk gesture of a bonus at the end of a successful drive, a 500-acre farm at Red River for the person directing the operation and 100 acres to each of the drivers.

Late in 1819, Stewart was taking steps to secure the necessary cattle at or near St. Louis, with the idea of driving them as far as Prairie du Chien to winter and be ready for the final drive to Big Stone Lake where men from the settlement would meet him and take formal delivery in the spring. Selkirk was unhappy about the Big Stone delivery point which Dickson had allowed to be written into the contract because loss of the herd between the lake and the settlement would still be possible.

The people at Point Douglas had nothing to do

A prize of fat cattle at Winnipeg.

with the terms of the agreement but accepted faithfully, and William Laidlaw who was in charge of the Hayfield Experimental Farm and needed milk cows urgently led a party to Big Stone Lake to meet the incoming herd at the date proposed, May 10, and escort it to the settlement. Patiently, the Laidlaw men waited for weeks in that summer of 1820 but no cattle came and no message from Stewart. What Laidlaw did not know was that feed supplies laid in at Prairie du Chien had been totally inadequate and nearly all the Stewart cattle died from starvation during the winter.

The loss of the cattle was a loss that Stewart would have to bear but it was, nevertheless, another setback and disappointment for the settlers. They wondered if Stewart would take his loss and give up on the contract. But Stewart was not a quitter and returned to St. Louis to obtain another herd which he proposed to drive right through to Red River in the 1821 season. He would not be caught by another winter of feed shortage. But as he was soon to discover, there were other trail hazards capable of being no less deadly.

Although the second herd was making commendable speed, it had the misfortune to encounter a band of hungry Sioux Indians, eager to try cow beef as a change from bison beef. The natives happened to be nursing more than the usual number of grudges against white men at that time and quietly helped themselves to the cattle until Stewart's second herd intended for the settlement was entirely liquidated.

There is no record of Stewart's words but his patience must have been strained and his good humor exhausted. Certainly nobody expected him to try again. But Stewart clansmen had a reputation for tenacity and in the next spring, sure enough, he and his men were starting from St. Louis with the third herd, hoping for better luck. Starting earlier and following a different course, they did benefit from the experience of two previous years and unbelievable as it seemed to those who had grown weary of waiting, the herd of 170 cattle reached the settlement on August 28, 1822, to make it one of the most

Cutting wheat with oxen at Sturgis, Saskatchewan in 1938.

Oxen on the J. G. Miller farm, Craik, 1906. This unusual picture of a team of six oxen demonstrates the power that could be harnessed. (Mrs. Charles Hay, Willowdale, Ont.)

memorable days in Red River history. The number of animals was more than enough to satisfy the contract, but as Stewart knew, there would be no trouble in finding buyers for the surplus.

It was too bad that Lord Selkirk had not lived to see the day and witness the rejoicing. The Swiss sang their native songs; the Scottish majority celebrated by dancing, and the Germans drew upon their limited stores of beer.

Even before the precious cattle were allocated to the settlers, Andrew Bulger, who was then in charge of the colony, reported to Andrew Colvile: "It will be gratifying to you to hear that the cattle, 170 in number, have at last reached Red River, and in very good condition. 120 head we are bound by contract to take, the remainded being brought on speculation and will be disposed of, I suppose, by auction. I am at a loss how to distribute those which belong to us, there being very few persons here able to pay for them and all being equally anxious to be supplied."[9]

Colvile, as an executor of the Selkirk estate, inherited the earl's displeasure at Dickson for contracting to spend far beyond the earl's wishes and instructions but, nevertheless, Adam Stewart, on November 1, 1823, acknowledged the receipt of payment totaling £2,520 for the 96 milk cows, 1 bull and 23 oxen delivered.

After admitting his concern about an equitable means of distributing the contract cattle, Bulger explained how he did it: "In distributing the cows I began with the married men of the de Meurons who had Lord Selkirk's promise of cattle in writing; next I considered the Scotch families who had been the longest in and had suffered the most for the country, and then the married Canadians who had come from Montreal under engagements with his Lordship. These being served, I was induced in consideration of what the Swiss had suffered and in the hope of reconciling them to the country to give a cow to each of them that had a family. I also supplied the three German families and then the unmarried men of all countries who appeared to have the strongest claim on Lord Selkirk. No one was allowed to choose. I adopted a kind of lottery that no man might say I had been partial to another. I have in this way given 91 cows but there are still some settlers ... who required to be supplied. . ."[10]

In any case, that August 28, 1822, the day the cattle came, marked the beginning of a new chapter in pioneer agriculture. After waiting for ten years, the settlers would have milk, butter, cheese, and curds for their tables, meat without the necessity of chasing buffalo for it, ox-power for their farms, and the sight of grazing cows to satisfy a longing. They would have a degree of security not previously possible to them since coming to Red River. It was also enough to make those who were administering the Selkirk estate hope for more self-reliance on the part of the Red River farmers. In writing to the colony governor, in the second year after the cattle came, Andrew Colvile warned: "The settlers must now walk alone, and having a stock of provisions from their good crops and plenty of cattle, they may do very well if they are industrious. If they are not industrious, they must endure the whole consequences as they best can."[11]

Chapter 5

THE SHEEP DRIVE FROM KENTUCKY

The triumphant delivery of the cattle from St. Louis brought rejoicing, of course, but there was a further wait of eleven years for the survivors of the big flock of sheep started from Kentucky. Although the trail losses were extremely heavy, the 251 head that completed the historic journey were enough to produce more rejoicing.

Nothing in the animal kingdom would have appeared more foreign to the Rupert's Land scene than sheep. Nothing resembling them existed there in the wild state and Indian tribesmen, seeing them for the first time, looked for cover in case these strange creatures were ferocious. But sheep were particularly close to Highland hearts. With most peasant people, nothing would take the place of wool for spinning and making homespun clothes. Lord Selkirk knew it and hoped to see sheep well established at Red River, first of all to meet the local needs and then to support his dream of a profitable export trade featuring the world's finest wool. It was with export in mind that he selected twenty-one of the best Spanish Merino sheep available to be sent forward with the colonists emigrating with Owen Keveny in 1812. Amazingly enough, the sheep made the long journey with only one death but the record of survival was too good to last. Red River coyotes, hungry Indians and semi-domesticated dogs, after getting a taste of mutton, made inroads, and natural causes accounted for more losses until none of the Merino bluebloods remained.

A bigger flock was needed to establish the species on the new soil and keep the family spinning wheels busy. When the Upper Canada settlement at Baldoon was failing, the earl proposed driving 200 sheep from there to Red River. It would have been a 1400-mile drive by way of Chicago but the War of 1812-14 intervened and with American and British troops overrunning the area, so many of the Baldoon sheep disappeared to become unauthorized army rations that the idea of the ambitious undertaking had to be abandoned.

Although the Merino breeding project of 1812 ended in failure, it was not forgotten and was repeated in the year after Lord Selkirk's death. Fifteen carefully chosen Merino ewes and five rams were delivered safely as far as York Factory and there suffered a new variety of disaster. Taking what the York Factory servants of the Hudson's Bay Company believed to be the surest precaution against loss from dogs, wolves, and other predators, they went to the trouble of placing the five rams and an equal number of ewes on a small island at the mouth of the Hayes River. There they seemed to be isolated against all outside dangers. But unexpectedly, the river rose to flood level, obliterated the island and drowned the ten valuable sheep, including the entire population of rams.

The survivng ten head — all ewes — reached Red River in November, 1821, to bring only slight encouragement to those people with dreams of a prospering trade in wool and mutton. If the rams could be replaced, there was still hope and a request was forwarded to the Hudson's Bay Company. But nothing helpful for Red River ever happened promptly and not until midsummer, 1824, was a ram delivered by way of Fort William. By this time, most of the ewes were dead and much of the former enthusiasm for this small project was dead also. The ram was for all practical purposes wasted and was sold. The colony at this time had fewer sheep than it had twelve years earlier when the initial small band of Merinos came with the settlers.

But interest in a larger scheme was not dead.

Stubborn men formed the Assiniboia Sheep and Wool Company, with Colin Robertson as manager. Robertson, whose record of success was unimpressive, seems to have achieved this latest position more or less by default. The company did not survive long enough to have its own sheep but with George Simpson's help, another company was formed and a drive of sheep from the south was authorized. The flock was started but it was halted by a band of Sioux Indians and the animals went no further.

As with the big herd of cattle that was delivered at the settlement on the third major trial, so it was the third effort that produced a sheep drive from the south. Again Simpson was one of the backers, and through him, the second experimental farm was committed to provide a home for the flock.

William Glen Rae, a clerk in the Hudson's Bay Company service, was named to be the leader of a party to travel south to purchase the sheep and drive them to Red River. I. P. Burke, a former company clerk, and Robert Campbell, who was already serving as an assistant manager of the experimental farm, were

Ten thousand sheep at Maple Creek in 1889. The big flock had just been trailed from Idaho and Montana to stock Sir John Lister Kaye's farms and ranches. The buffalo bones in the foreground are awaiting shipment. (Photo courtesy of the Glenbow-Alberta Institute).

accompanying as Rae's chief aides. Campbell, having grown up on a Perthshire sheep farm, probably knew more about sheep than any of his traveling companions. Fortunately, he kept a record of the journey.

Leaving Point Douglas on November 8, 1832, the party consisted of ten men with two carts for carrying supplies and eight saddle horses. It was late in the season to be starting such a trip and winter was setting in to make traveling slower and more difficult than usual.

Hoping to escape Sioux Indian eyes after leaving Pembina, the men adopted unusual traveling hours, starting about three A.M., having breakfast about nine A.M. if wood and water were convenient, halting briefly for the evening meal and then moving "some distance off before lying down for the night in case the smoke from our fire would be seen by the Indians and draw them down on us."[1] The Indian danger was believed to be very real and whenever the travelers were serenaded by night calls from wolves, foxes, and owls, the more nervous of the men took the sounds to be from war parties signaling to each other. The men might have been closer to danger than they realized because Campbell heard when returning some months later that a war party did follow them for three days before giving up.

Before the end of November, the party was traveling in snow. The leaders had hoped to reach St.

Peter's Post on the upper Mississippi in time to catch the last riverboat going to St. Louis. In this they failed and in order to cope with the new winter conditions, they exchanged their carts for sleighs and pushed on. But when weather moderated and the river appeared to offer good boating, they left their horses and went on by canoe. But the moods of both the river and weather were hard to judge and when river ice became heavy, they had no recourse except to return to the land and travel on foot.

The party was at St. Louis on January 3, thus terminating, as Campbell noted it, "a journey of no ordinary danger and hardship, performed at a most inclement season in 56 days, the distance being about 1800 miles."[2]

For the next six weeks, Rae and his men toured the country around St. Louis and St. Charles, searching for sheep, without any encouragement. Often they were told they would have to go to Kentucky if they were to fill their needs but they "thought the distance too great." When it became apparent that, in Campbell's

The Chris Bartsch flock on its way to Dawson City in 1901. (Photo courtesy of Theodore Bartsch and Mrs. May Bartsch Alexander.)

A range band of sheep leaving camp near the Matador ranch.

words, "not a sheep was to be had for love or money," they carried the search into Illinois and finally, Kentucky.

At Versailles, the Red River men found sheep and bought 1,100 ewes and lambs, then 270 more. By the first of May, the sheep were sheared, marked, and counted, ready for the frighteningly long trek. The drive began the next day, with the flock of 1,370 head moving away at a speed of about ten or eleven miles per day. A few ewes and lambs became lame but that was to be expected and Rae and Campbell were able to sell them along the way. The more serious problem was one which the men had not considered, namely, speargrass. The hardships and difficulties of the trail were varied; there were rivers to cross; there were rattlesnakes which caused the death of as many as five sheep in one day; there was the normal cussedness of sheep that don't want to be driven, but all these faded into insignificance when the sheer treachery of the ripened speargrass spears was discovered.

It was after crossing the Illinois River at Peoria that the men found themselves facing this new enemy with which they could not cope. As the grass plants matured, the barbed seeds of "spears" were ready to

Bill Martin of Maple Creek was Canada's leading trainer of sheep dogs. A century earlier, dogs like his might have made the first sheep drives less onerous.

detach themselves from the parent stems and enter the wool and penetrate skin and flesh.

Hoping to reduce the speargrass annoyance, the sheepmen halted to shear the sheep for the second time in the spring season. It was reasonable that with less wool the animals would catch fewer of the javelin-like seeds. It didn't have much effect but proved a most nauseating experience for the men working with the festering animal bodies, made more repulsive by maggot infestation. But the men did their best, "shearing to the skin, picking out the prickly spears and doctoring the suffering animals as best we could."[3]

Rae sold the wool to local people but when they discovered that he could not take it with him, they reneged, thinking the wool would be left behind and they would have it at no cost. This annoyed Rae, naturally, who then tried to burn the wool, but one of the good features about woolen clothing is that it does not burn readily and Rae was probably not very successful.

The sheep losses continued to be heavy. By July 7, the flock, which had started out at 1,370, was down to 675 and by August 25, only 295 sheep could be counted. Looking back upon the speargrass destroyer, Campbell wrote: "If we had known its disastrous effects we could have avoided it by a detour or by waiting till the grass ripened and [the seeds] fell, and

thus our flock would have been spared much suffering."[4]

Late in the drive the sheepmen encountered a band of mounted Sioux Indians and remembered George Simpson's warning that they'd be lucky if they completed the expedition without losing their scalps. The confrontation, however, turned out better than might have been expected. Instead of falling savagely upon the sheep and the men in attendance, the natives accepted some presents and a further peace offering of dressed mutton and rode away.

Finally, on September 16, 1833 — almost a year after leaving the settlement — the sheepmen arrived back at Fort Garry, driving 251 weakened sheep and lambs. The number represented less than twenty percent of the flock driven out of Kentucky and the men were criticized for driving too fast and for allowing losses to be so high. The loss was heavy indeed but the greater wonder was that sheep in any number came through alive. To the more understanding people at Red River, a flock of 251 sheep looked big.

Campbell was one of the first to admit that the "long, harassing and dangerous trip was most disappointing in its results. The most of our trouble and the sad diminution of our flock was brought about by the wild speargrass and our total ignorance of its existence. Had we commenced the trip with the knowledge and experience which, alas, we bought at so dear a price . . . the enterprise would have been an entire success."

The Kentucky sheep were delivered, as planned, at the experimental farm where Robert Campbell was placed in charge. With the English stallion, Fireaway, the Kentucky sheep, and the Scottish shepherd to relate the great and tragic adventure, all occupying the experimental farm at the same time, the place assumed its highest state of public prominence and Campbell — like Fireaway — gained fame.

The Kentucky sheep recovered quickly from the exhausting journey and did well, with the result that the Red River community and then the province of Manitoba were never again without sheep. Red River sheep by 1856 numbered 2,429 and by 1871, the first census year for the province of Manitoba, the old settlement area had 12,288 head and the province had 25,228. It seems reasonable to presume that nearly all of these traced to the small surviving band — portraying "survival of the fittest" — from the famous drive from Kentucky.

Chapter 6

PALLISER, THE AGRICULTURAL EXPLORER

In spite of the truly great experiment in farming and settlement at Red River, prejudice generated by men of the fur trade persisted and the future of Rupert's Land remained in doubt. The evidence reaching London was contradictory and as the time approached for the aging Hudson's Bay Company to make its periodic application for renewal of a trading license on the vast Indian territory lying beyond Rupert's Land, questions of colonial policy were being raised. Members of the House of Commons were familiar with official company desire to maintain the status quo but they were also sensing a widespread impatience on the part of people asking: "Must Rupert's Land and the rest of the British Northwest be kept forever to serve only the fur trade?" With an admission of confusion, the parliamentary decision was to appoint a Select Committee to study the matter and make a recommendation.

The resulting committee, with the Right Honorable Henry Labouchere as chairman, would conduct public hearings and invite all informed citizens to give evidence. One of the first to take the stand was Sir George Simpson, the man with the best-known name in the entire fur trade. Appearing on February 26, 1857, with his usual air of dignity and confidence, his answers to questions were short and abrupt. He was there, of course, to advocate a renewal of the lease which would give the Hudson's Bay Company complete control over all the country to be known later as Western Canada for another twenty-one years. His principal message seemed to be that the land "out there" had no practical future except for furs, and his crowning expression of prejudice or error in judgment was when he was asked why the country except for riverbanks would never be useful for agriculture, he replied: "On account of the poverty of the soil."[1]

To the next question: "Have you an equally unfavorable opinion of the country on the Saskatchewan River?" Sir George replied: "Yes; the climate is more rigorous and the crops are less certain on that river; the scarcity of timber also is a great bar; there is little or no wood in the country."

One of the witnesses who followed was the

Captain John Palliser and Dr. James Hector in 1860.

brilliant Alexander Isbister, born at Cumberland House on the Saskatchewan. After serving as a clerk with the Hudson's Bay Company, he went to England to further his education and remained there. He made it clear that he left the company on good and friendly terms but believed company policy was generally unfavorable to the development of the area. Practically contradicting Sir George Simpson, Isbister expressed the view that "agriculture can be carried on . . . in all the country intervening between the Great Lakes and the Rocky Mountains."[2]

With such a glaring conflict in testimony, the committee members were more confused than ever and reacted approvingly to a suggestion that they should engage and send their own representative or investigating body to the distant land in question, to make an objective study and early report.

While the hearing was still only a few weeks old, Rt. Hon. Henry Labouchere, as chairman, was writing to Capt. John Palliser as the appointed leader of the proposed expedition, giving him the essential instructions. There were various views about how Palliser obtained the important appointment, among them that he went seeking the job without waiting for the committee to seek him. Whatever the technique, it was effective, and nobody questioned his qualifications.

As a forty-year-old Irish bachelor, an engineer, a redhead and one with a known love for adventure, he was moderately conspicuous in the circles in which he traveled. Already, his hunting adventures had taken him to many parts of the world, including the buffalo country of prairie North America. Exactly ten years before the beginning of the fact-finding expedition ordered by the Select Committee, Palliser was sailing from Liverpool "to visit that ocean of [North American] prairies extending to the foot of the Rocky Mountains."[3] His particular mission was to hunt in the buffalo country and for much of the ensuing year he was indulging in his favorite sport along the upper reaches of the Missouri River.

Although he wrote a book about his buffalo-hunting year, it is not clear that he was or was not hunting at any time on the British side of the international boundary. In any case, he retained a desire to engage in exploration on the north side of the border. All things considered, he was probably an excellent choice for the role of leader.

By the instructions which went to Palliser from the secretary of state, he was to explore "that portion of British North America which lies between the northern branch of the River Saskatchewan and the frontier of the United States, and between the Red River and the Rocky Mountains." The essential objectives, as set down, were to record "the physical features of the country through which you will pass, noting its principal elevations, the nature of its soil, its capability

for agriculture, the quantity and quality of its timber, and any indications of coal and other minerals."[4]

The party was to start as soon as possible and travel by way of Sault Ste. Marie and Fort William to Fort Garry. The instructions cautioned Palliser about the importance of exercising economy, but in providing the leader with qualified assistants, the government seemed generous enough. Dr. James Hector, in whom Palliser found his greatest strength, had trained to become a medical doctor and then turned to pursue his greater interest in geology and biology; John W. Sullivan filled the dual role of astronomer and secretary, and Eugene Bourgeau was the specialist in botany. And Lt. Thomas Blakiston, with experience as a surveyor, was to sail directly to Hudson Bay and join the expedition at Fort Carlton, at the end of the first season.

Palliser, accompanied by Hector, Bourgeau, and Sullivan, traveled as instructed by way of Fort William and Fort Francis and saw Fort Garry on July 11. There, where Lord Selkirk's servants and settlers had come forty-five years earlier, agriculture had made modest progress but there was much to see and note. Although still dominated by the fur trade, this, as Palliser would realize, was still the only farming community in the entire Northwest. The recent census had shown the human population to stand at 6,523, and to give some idea of the size of farming operations, the same survey showed 2,799 horses, 2,726 oxen, 6,527 other cattle, 4,674 pigs, 2,429 sheep, 585 plows, 730 harrows, 2,045 carts, 16 windmills, 2 reapers and 8,371 acres of cropland.[5]

For ten days after arrival, Palliser and his aides were engaged in assembling supplies and hiring helpers for their main thrust into the land of controversy. James Beads, who had been George Simpson's personal servant, was transferred to become Palliser's servant and twelve others were hired, giving the leader a very mixed crew which he described as "Gentlemen, Scotch halfbreeds, French Halfbreeds, Americans and one colored man, Dan Williams."

Having acquired two American wagons, six Red River carts and twenty-nine horses, the cavalcade set out boldly to explore the future farming country of the West — and make history. The course from Fort Garry led south on the west side of the Red River to Pembina, then west to Turtle Mountain and northwest to Fort Ellice, close to the junction of the Qu'Appelle and Assiniboine rivers; they reached the latter place twenty-five days after leaving Fort Garry. From Fort Ellice, the party made a side trip to see the strange rock formations on the Souris River, known as La Roche Percée. There, Dr. Hector examined the local deposits of soft coal but probably did not grasp their extent and importance.

Back at Fort Ellice, the men took note of a plot of

ground growing potatoes and pasture for a few head of Hudson's Bay Company cattle. From there, the course of travel was westward to Qu'Appelle post on the plains, then north to the mission at the present site of Fort Qu'Appelle where the party was welcomed by the Church of England missionary, Mr. Charles Pratt, described by Dr. Hector as "a pure Stoney Indian by birth" and by Capt. Palliser as "a pure Cree educated at Red River." Anyway, he was growing potatoes, barley, Indian corn and some other vegetables with what appeared to be surprising success.

For the captain, with a secret love for the ancient pastime of horse trading, the highlight of his stay at the mission might have been his dealings with the parson, giving occasion for an entry in his journal: "Mr. Pratt gave us a very fine mare in exchange for two wretched horses, one of which is not likely to live long." He might have been accused of taking advantage of a churchman but ministers and missionaries had the reputation of being well qualified to take care of themselves in horse trades. A few days later, the captain was trading again, this time with Cree Indians, but with no boastful entries in the journal, it can be surmised that the tribesmen were more than a match for him.

Continuing on westward, Palliser was receiving many reminders that he was close to the traditional battleground of Cree and Blackfoot, "where none go to hunt for fear of meeting enemies." He knew, also, from scarcity of grass and the absence of trees that he was in dry country. He saw it as good buffalo pasture and possibly useful for grazing cattle but he could not imagine the arid plains being good for other forms of agriculture.

The explorers saw the "creek where the bones lie," meaning Wascana Creek where the city of Regina was to be located, then Moose Jaw Creek where they felt the growing uneasiness of proximity to Blackfoot hunting ground and reversed the direction of travel to proceed toward the Elbow of the South Saskatchewan. Along the route, they saw wild game in abundance, herds of bison, of course, antelope, deer, elk, and even grizzly bears. From the Elbow, the party drew a course toward Fort Carlton which had been designated for winter headquarters. The captain, after issuing instructions for certain winter activities, rode away eastward to make a winter visit at Montreal and further the arrangements for the next season's operations. He completed his trip from Fort Carlton to Fort Garry in twenty-one days but when riding south toward St. Paul, he lost his horse and was obliged to continue on foot.

Dr. Hector remained to spend the winter in the country, and used his time to advance his studies of the area. On a westward trip by dog team, he was at Fort Edmonton on December 30 and recorded a good description of that place with its great involvement in the fur trade and trivial involvement in agriculture. "Edmonton," he wrote, "which is quite as large as Fort Garry, is wholly built of wood and is furnished with strong bastions and palisades. . . . It stands on a high steep bank immediately overhanging the river, about 100 feet above the water. Along and below this point are large flats of rich land, only 40 to 50 feet higher than the river. . . . Both of these were at one time under cultivation to a considerable extent; but now the farm attached to the establishment, though the only one in Saskatchewan, is of very small size, not exceeding 30 acres. On a hill behind the fort stands a windmill in which the stones were made by splitting a granite boulder that was found near the spot and these as may be supposed, are not very serviceable. However, they manage when they get a gale of wind, to grind some tolerable flour, quite enough to prove that if the business was properly conducted, it might be a valuable source of support; nine-tenths of the little flour that is consumed in the Saskatchewan, is brought either from Red River or all the way from England. As it is, the boats for navigating the Saskatchewan are mostly built [here], 10 or 12 new ones being turned out every year," necessitating a large staff of tradesmen and servants. "In all, they have about 50 employees here and the usual population within the fort is about 150 souls. These are all fed on buffalo meat, and if there happens to be a good crop, they get a certain small allowance of potatoes. The consumption of meat is enormous, amounting to two buffalos a day on the average."[6]

Palliser was back at Fort Carlton on June 4, 1858, and the second season's studies, mainly between the north and south branches of the Saskatchewan River, began a few days later. But with somebody in England having raised a question about a railway being built at a time in the future, both Dr. Hector and Lt. Blakiston were to make sorties into the mountains to search for passes. Being a practical fellow more than a dreamer, Palliser showed more interest in a pass that would accommodate horse-drawn carts than in a railway route which might never be needed. Nevertheless, the straws of change were in the wind and before the end of Palliser's third season in the West, the citizens of Fort Garry were surprised to hear the toot of a steamboat on their Red River and then see the sternwheeler, *Anson Northrup*, splashing its way downstream to gain recognition as the first of its kind. Although looking more like a warehouse on a raft than a genuine riverboat, it was its owner's answer to a challenge issued by the St. Paul Board of Trade and backed with a prize of $1,000. After being launched at Georgetown, Minnesota, it made its appearance at Fort Garry on May 19. Dr. Hector while discovering the

Kicking Horse Pass might have been muttering: "A steamboat today, a railway tomorrow."

The Palliser party spent the second winter at Fort Edmonton and the third and final summer in exploring what can now be defined as southern Alberta. While Hector was penetrating the foothills and mountains, Palliser was going from the general region of the Elbow's entrance to the Bow River, to the distinctive Cypress Hills with which he fell in love, saying: "A perfect oasis in the desert we have travelled." And then, toward the end of 1859, with return to England in mind, Palliser and Hector bade farewell to the prairies and took separate routes to the Pacific Coast; Palliser took the Columbia River route to the ocean while Hector followed the Bow to cross the Rockies and then to the forks of the Fraser and Thompson and on to meet Palliser at Victoria on January 16, whence they sailed together for England, there to prepare the report.

The famous report was presented to the Colonial Office on April 4, 1862.[7]. It was a sizable document with more of detail than most readers wanted but it was as exhaustive as anybody at that time could have made it.   What most people wanted to know was Palliser's opinion about the general suitability for agriculture and settlement of the country upon which the men of the fur trade were reluctant to relax their ancient grip. Did the far-flung country hold any real hope for farming and settlement? Having crossed and recrossed the country in question, having dug holes at innumerable places to see the depth and appearance of the soil, having done it all in a scientific manner, Palliser was certainly in the best position to bring a reliable answer. That did not mean that he was correct in all his judgments, but he was helpful to those who were inquiring.

Palliser was cautious — of course he was. In the light of the experience of later years, he was overly cautious. He did recognize the country which he came to study as being extremely variable; prairies and parklands, for example, were so different that they should not be treated together.

In his assessment of the park belt — or what he termed the Fertile Belt — he was justifiably enthusiastic. There he found the evidences of fertile soil, relatively heavy growth of grass, and enough precipitation to ensure crops. There were trees to provide building logs and fuel, lakes and rivers offering fish for the settlers. He could see a farming population living in security on that black soil band forming a crescent around the prairies. But for the plains areas, he had warnings. The central prairie region, he believed to be an extension of "the Great American Desert" on which he had hunted the buffalo just a little more than a decade earlier. Historians will speculate that Palliser happened to be on the Canadian

plains in one of the recurring drought periods, like that of the nineties in the last century and the thirties of the present century. Such is possible and it may be, also, that he brought certain preconceived notions about prairie zones from the time of his buffalo hunting in Montana. It may be proposed with some reason that Palliser was inclined too readily to judge the worth of soil by the volume of vegetation growing on it. Perhaps he did not realize fully that the added nutritional value of the short grass on the dry plains is at least partial compensation for the lower yield.

But he was emphatic, saying: "Whenever we struck out on the broad prairie, we generally found the soil worthless, except here and there." The fact was that prairie soil, as he saw it, was dry but much of it was highly fertile. It was easy to say later that the dry prairie soils under cultivation needed nothing more than irrigation or seasons of above-average rainfall.

In defining the prairie area with the worst record for drought, Palliser and Hector were remarkably accurate. The British portion of the continent's arid prairies was seen as a triangular region with apex reaching to the 52nd parallel and its base, applied along the international boundary, extending from 100 degrees of longitude to 114 degrees. The base of such a triangle sketched on a modern map would extend from Waterton Park on the west to a point on the international boundary south of Brandon, and the apex would be somewhere at the level of Saskatoon. The report conceded that the area contained many varieties of land, some of them being very good; "but on the whole, it must be described as deficient in wood, water and grass," using Hector's words.

Palliser would have approved the plains region for grazing or ranching but he would have found it unbelievable that the soils would someday produce the world's best and hardest wheat. Among the winners of world championships for wheat were Henry Holmes of Raymond, J. C. Mitchell of Dahinda, R. P. Robbins of Shaunavon, Fred Hallworth of Taber and others who operated within the Triangle.[8] The record of crop reliability would not be as high as in Palliser's Fertile Belt but the quality of wheat would be higher.

Palliser's errors in judgment became clear enough, but as the first to be called to make a comprehensive assessment of the big country, his performance deserved praise.

It can be argued, of course, that Palliser and his party making the famous survey in 1857 were not entirely alone. As it happened, the Province of Canada was entertaining an interest in annexing a portion of Rupert's Land and appointed Henry Youle Hind, professor of chemistry and geology at Trinity College, Toronto, and S. J. Dawson, engineer, to determine in part if the area was worth acquiring. Hind's party did not travel as far as Palliser's and remained in the field only two years, but within the area now marked by the provinces of Manitoba and Saskatchewan, it visited many of the same places as the British group.

Hind's engrossment with the Qu'appelle Valley was especially significant. His visit at the Elbow of the South Saskatchewan awakened an interest in the possibility of diverting the south branch of the Saskatchewan at that point and sending the water down the Qu'Appelle Valley and into the Assiniboine to furnish a water course from the foothills to Fort Garry. With such a means of transportation, there would be less need for a railroad and Hind had a vision of a dam of some 85 feet high, situated, interestingly enough, about where the big Gardiner Dam was built to 210 feet in height almost exactly a century later.[9]

Hind and Palliser saw the West quite differently. Palliser after his three summers of exploration could not bring himself to believe that the very dry parts would ever be useful for cropping; they might therefore be a handicap to the country. Hind, on the other hand, after two summer seasons, was optimistic and believed that the country could and would become a great producer of wheat and other grains. One was needlessly pessimistic, the other overly optimistic. In their different ways, they directed attention to the agricultural capabilities of the fur country and their respective reports remained useful.

Chapter 7

HOPE AND HOPPERS IN THE SIXTIES

When the dashing John Palliser, looking slightly worn after three seasons of exploration, was preparing to sail back to England from Victoria, Vancouver Island, at the end of 1859, settlers and others at the Red River side of the country were quietly welcoming the first issue of the first newspaper to be published between Upper Canada and the Pacific Ocean. William Coldwell and William Buckingham — known in some quarters as the "Two Bills" — had successfully oxcarted the dead weight of a printing press over the 500-mile trail from St. Paul, Minnesota, and the first copy of the Nor'Wester made its inauspicious appearance on December 28. It was a fitting landmark for the end of one pioneer decade and the beginning of another.

The editors in the first issue — as all starting editors would choose to do — declared faith in "the agricultural capabilities of the country and the facilities for commerce." Then, growing more eloquent, they added: "For hundreds of miles beyond [Red River] stretches one of the most magnificent agricultural regions in the world, watered abundantly . . . a sufficiency of timber . . . vast prairies of unsurpassed fertility . . . and a climate as salubrious as it is delightful. Such a country cannot now remain unpeopled. . . . The printing press can hasten the change."[1]

The two young editors had never seen the distant expanses about which they were raving but there had to be something genuine about their faith when they would give expression to it by being among the first in their generation to come with the intention of making their homes. "We came persuaded that the time has arrived when this fertile and magnificent country [should be] thrown open to the people of all lands."

It was indeed difficult to understand how such an area possessing agricultural potential had continued to be treated with slight and scorn. True, a few thousand people were obtaining their food needs from it but the striking fact was that the annual buffalo hunt or hunts contributed more to local food demands than the farm fields.

The Nor'Wester's description of one of the hunting parties at that time would aid to understanding of the magnitude and importance of the operation. "The return of the White Horse Plains brigade enables us to give the interesting statistics of their expedition," it was written. "They started out on the 10th of June, intending to go to the Grand Coteau, but turned off at the Dog House and found buffalo enough near Turtle Mountain and Big Head River to save them the trouble of a longer journey. The party numbered 154 families, including 210 men able to carry arms (of whom 160 were buffalo runners) and 700 non-combatants, women and children. They took with them 642 horses, 50 oxen, 6 cows, 522 dogs, 533 carts, 1 wagon, 232 guns, 10 revolvers, 21,000 bullets and 270 quarts of gunpowder. They made 12 runs in which they killed 3,270 buffalo — 1,151 bulls, 1,893 cows and 226 calves. The carcasses produced 1,964 bags of pemmican, 2,429 bales of dried meat, 15,120 pounds of marrow fat, and 9,600 pounds of tallow. . . ."[2]

The big and exciting annual hunts which helped to ensure local security in food probably hindered agricultural development. As long as food could be taken by the hunt, there was less incentive to grow it. Agricultural products were traded near home but, except for furs, nothing was being exported. The prices quoted for staples bought and sold at the end of 1859 and beginning of 1860, gave a good indication of what farmers were growing and the general character of Red River commerce:[3]

Wheat	4 shillings, 6 pence per bushel
Potatoes	1 shilling per bushel
Beef	2½ pence per lb.
Butter	1 shilling per lb.
Cheese	9 pence per lb.
Buffalo meat	2 pence per lb.
Pemmican	4 pence per lb.
Wine	1 pound, 4 shillings per gallon
Brandy	1 pound, 10 shillings per gallon
Beaver skins, large	3 shillings, 6 pence each
Buffalo skins, dressed	8 shillings each
Firewood	5 shillings per cord

The *Nor'Wester* did succeed in winning eastern and overseas interest in the West. Without waiting for Palliser's report, the editors called for the establishment of a Crown Colony or some form of elected government, no matter how much the Hudson's Bay Company might be opposed to the change. One of the public figures attracted by the message was Edward Watkins who in 1861 was president of the Grand Trunk Railway. Determined to employ expansion to revive his rail company, he gave his attention to the Intercolonial Railroad which was to connect Quebec and Halifax. A successive dream was of a railway to the west coast to catch the trade with China; if not a railroad, at least a wagon road.

But a western line of communication needed the approval of the Hudson's Bay Company over whose lands it would pass and it is told that the proposal, when taken to Governor Berens, provoked an explosive response. The very idea of an outside organization proposing to cut into the company's fur preserves, frighten away the buffalo, and admit all manner of immigrants to ruin the time-honored trade! It was preposterous. If these impostors were so ambitious to destroy the fur business, he was reported to have shouted, why wouldn't they buy the territory and then it would be within their jurisdiction to destroy it.

The Duke of Newcastle, colonial secretary at the time, having heard the governor's reaction, countered with a question about an asking price. To this the governor may have replied with ill-considered haste, saying: "a million and a half pounds sterling."

Less than two years later, the *Nor'Wester* carried what it described as "Important News. The International Financial Society has made arrangements for purchasing the property and the rights of the Hudson's Bay Company, by giving them £300 for every £100 share. The total capital of the Company is £500,000 and the total amount of purchase will be £1,500,000. A deposit of £1,000,000 has already been paid."[4]

The old company with its charter and territorial rights was taken over by the new body. But instead of producing spectacular change as expected, the company name remained and policy was scarcely altered. To the inhabitants of Rupert's Land, nothing appeared changed except the names of the governor and directors. And the idea of a railroad to the Pacific was soon forgotten.

Frontier agriculture was still having trouble in changing the pace of a slow start. Cultivation had not been extended greatly or rapidly and the implements in use until the early sixties were mainly those that could be made in the settlement. It was a matter of public interest, therefore, when the riverboat, *Anson Northrup*, docking at Upper Fort Garry on July 4, 1860, discharged one horse rake, one portable mill, one reaping machine, one threshing machine, one fanning mill and one iron plow.[5]

Farming, which had seemed frightened to leave the parental protection of the old colony, was only now — fifty years after the coming of the first Selkirk people — venturing westward and reaching as far as Portage la Prairie.

Archdeacon Cochrane and a few followers went to that point recognized as the prairie portage between Lake Manitoba and the Assiniboine River in 1853 but the unquestioned farm leader in the parade to the portage was the unflinching Perthshire Scot, John McLean. This dour fellow, with muscles to invite a blacksmith's envy and a readiness to match friendliness with friendliness or fight with fight, had come to Fort Garry on the same riverboat that brought the main party of Overlanders on the way to seek fortune in the Fraser River goldfields. The group, mainly from Upper and Lower Canada — and a few from England — numbered about 150 men, women and children. They had traveled to St. Paul, Minnesota, by rail, then by stagecoach to Georgetown, and the balance of the way to Fort Garry on the new riverboat, *International*, where the ship docked on May 26.

John McLean's grandchildren could retell the pioneer's story of a scene on the boat two days before reaching Fort Garry. The eastern passengers, with British loyalties, proposed marking May 24 by flying the Union Jack but the American captain, still on the United States side of the boundary, refused. To his surprise and horror, he discovered that his angry passengers, having been denied the use of the British flag, had raised the cook's dirty dishtowel on the flagstaff. The captain stormed, as captains are known to do so well, and proceeded to remove the greasy indignity but found John McLean and some others defending the base of the flagpole, refusing to allow the offending towel to be brought down until they had a promise that a Union Jack would take its place.

At Fort Garry, the Overlanders outfitted with horses, oxen and carts — forty dollars each for horses, and forty dollars for an ox with cart — and started west to travel via Fort Edmonton.

John McLean might have followed the Overlanders but he wanted to farm rather than hunt for gold. He couldn't take a homestead because he was ten years ahead of the Lands Act which defined homestead policy. As it was, the forty-six-year-old wandered westward and bought squatter's rights from a Portage la Prairie Métis, Rivere by name, paying him $375 in gold for about 120 acres fronting on Crescent Lake and extending back for roughly two miles.[6]

The Portage soil, as McLean found it, was rich and unbelievably productive. If he had troubles, they were not with soil but with the Indians, especially after the Sioux refugees with added hatred for white men came to the district following the Minnesota Massacre. Some 3,000 of them came with Chief Standing Buffalo in 1864 and worried the residents. McLean, it seemed, was involved in most of the conflicts, most of them involving guns, and miraculously, he was spared from serious injury.[7] He might be unpopular with the Indians but to the non-natives he was the man to whom they turned when they were worried. It was McLean who, in 1867, did most to frustrate the upshot Republic of Manitoba or Republic of Caledonia, the illegitimate brainchild of Thomas Spence, and after another year or two, he was among those taken prisoner by Louis Riel. When he died at the age of eighty-seven in 1902, he was described, very properly, as the first farmer in the Portage la Prairie district.

But there is always somebody ready to aim higher or travel farther and four years after McLean selected Portage la Prairie, Rev. James Nisbet, ignoring all precedents, was leading his small flock of Presbyterian followers — eight adults and three children — on an overland journey to a more remote place, to be known later as Prince Albert. He had been ministering at Red River for four years and in 1866 felt the urge to remove well beyond the rim of sinful civilization and start a farm colony. After a month on the trail, the Nisbet group came to Fort Carlton and there constructed rafts on which to float carts and oxen and humans to some favored location. The place of their choice was some thirty miles downstream, on the North Saskatchewan and there they proceeded to build log houses and a farm community. They did reasonably well, making pemmican, growing wheat, oats, and potatoes, and finding independence. Nine years after arrival, they imported a gristmill and sawmill, and in 1878, a threshing machine. The year of 1884 saw the formation of the Lorne Agricultural Society, with eighty-four people paying a dollar each to become members. Here were the evolutionary steps of a vigorous farming community and before the end of that year of organization, the new society staged an agricultural

fair, one of the first in the area of present-day Saskatchewan.

McLean was followed to the Portage district by some brother Scots, Kenneth McBain in 1864 and Kenneth MacKenzie for whom McLean acted as guide and counselor in choosing land near Burnside, a short distance west of his own location. As might have been expected, the first Caledonia Society west of Winnipeg was in that district.

Kenneth MacKenzie, who became one of Manitoba's foremost farmers as well as one of the first, was an Inverness-shire man who stopped to farm at Puslinch in Ontario before coming to the West in 1868. He was still ahead of the survey but with John McLean and the technical aid of a pocket compass, he marked out a farm of 1,800 acres on Rat Creek and, using McLean's ox team and walking plow, cut a furrow around it to remove any doubt concerning its claimant.

Having chosen his land, MacKenzie returned to the East to bring his family and then settled into the task of breaking new ground for crop purposes. When Miss Mary Ramsey traveled overland from Fort Garry to Fort Carlton in 1868, she saw no cultivation anywhere west of Portage la Prairie but when she was returning in the next year, according to her testimony remembered by Winnipeg grandchildren, some of the MacKenzie land was plowed and becoming the most westerly cultivation to be seen by travelers.

A couple of years later, 1871, when Kenneth MacKenzie's son, Adam — six feet, two inches and big in all proportions — came west to join his father and farm on his own account to become Manitoba's biggest farm operator, he drove a small herd of Shorthorn cattle all the way from St. Paul. They were the first purebred animals of their breed in the midwest of Canada and among them was a young bull, Baron Solway by name, whose later record in showrings and the MacKenzie breeding herd made him conspicuous in breed history in the country.

Clearly, the western scenes were changing. Agriculture was improving its standing but not without some painful warnings of western Nature's unpredictability and occasional meanness. It was all very well for editors like Coldwell and Buckingham to become fluent about "one of the most magnificent agricultural regions in the world," but there could be no reason for shutting eyes to that streak of cussedness which could try the patience of Job. There were frosts out of season, hail, droughts, floods, grasshoppers and other hazards and before the hoppers ran their course in the late sixties, the editorial boasting about farm opportunities was at least temporarily silenced. The effect of the hoppers upon the young industry was much like that of the dry and depression-ridden thirties in the current century

The grasshoppers appeared in moderate numbers in 1864 — the year of Kenneth McBain's coming — but instead of departing as suddenly as they appeared, they became more numerous with each successive year to make 1868 the most tragic crop year the settlers could recall. In a general way, it was the worst community disaster since the Battle of Seven Oaks.

While eastern people were celebrating — or bemoaning — the realization of Confederation as it embraced four provinces, the Red River residents were counting their losses and carting away the piles of dead and stinking grasshoppers from the walls of Fort Garry. Red River pigs feasting on dead insects were the only creatures to find benefit. The hopeful settlers said: "Next year will be better," but as it turned out, 1868 was worse, much worse, leading readers of the Old Testament to wonder if this infestation might be a punishment for sins, like the plagues which visited King Pharaoh in the years of Moses, when the insects "covered the face of the whole earth so that the land was darkened and they did eat every herb of the land and all fruit of the trees."[8]

"Within the whole colony," said the editors, "not one bushel of any kind of grain will be harvested. . . . We will reap nothing, absolutely nothing in the shape of wheat, barley, rye or oats."[9]

To further increase the risk of starvation, the great buffalo herds — also affected by the loss of native vegetation due to grasshoppers — remained far away, beyond the normal traveling distance of hunters from the settlement.

It was enough to humble the most ardent boasters and boosters and the *Nor'Wester* carried admission that "the total destruction of the crops by grasshoppers, together with the failure of the buffalo hunts and the fisheries, and the disappearance of the rabbits, usually so numerous in the winter season, have combined to produce this deplorable state of suffering and starvation. To meet the distress, the Governor and Council of the Settlement at an early date voted all the funds at their disposal, amounting to £1600."[10]

The Red River community was placed on an emergency footing and a Co-operative Relief Committee was appointed. A few doggedly self-reliant citizens departed to winter near the distant buffalo herds, hoping to obtain the food they required. By December it was estimated that 430 families, or 2,412 individuals, were depending upon relief, with more likely to surrender to the necessity. It was humiliating to be calling for charity but it had to be, and the response was good. The sum of $8,000 was received as a gift from the Hudson's Bay Company in London and $40,000 came from friends in eastern and United States cities. The people at St. Paul, Minnesota, were most generous.

The disaster did nothing to build confidence in western farming, and in a strictly agricultural sense, the entire decade did nothing spectacularly great for the infant industry. But having regard to the fact that it was the decade which produced Confederation in the East and then the Canadian decision to acquire the West from the Hudson's Bay Company, it became a period of the greatest political importance and agriculture was to feel the impact.

An interest on the part of the United States in gaining all or part of British North America brought a sense of urgency to the government at Ottawa and the Rupert's Land Act passed at the end of July, 1868, furnished authorization to buy the West. Soon thereafter, negotiations were opened with the Hudson's Bay Company and on November 19, 1869, the Deed of Surrender covering the company's land was signed. The territory was being surrendered to the Crown to be turned over to Canada at a paying price of $1,500,000, plus certain land concessions to the company. Transfer of the territory was set for December 1, 1869, but both the selling and purchasing parties had failed to recognize the feelings of the native people in the matter and before the transfer date, Louis Riel and his Métis followers were taking a belligerent stand at Fort Garry and the official plan suffered delay. The area was in the grip of insurrection for nearly a year; but it ended and Canada, by the purchase of the West, increased its holdings of potential farm lands by 300 percent, whether it was understood and appreciated at the time or not.

Chapter 8
A LAND SURVEY, THEN A HOMESTEAD POLICY

Kenneth MacKenzie could plow a furrow around the land of his choice and hope such action would, in the course of time, be enough to confirm his ownership, but a better arrangement was needed and it was for Lt. Col. John Stoughton Dennis to find it.

Dennis, who gained his rank by being a good army man, won his greatest fame from service in bringing an orderly survey to the western lands soon to be the scene of an invasion of homesteaders. Even before Canada's purchase of the West was negotiated, he was reminding men in authority that one of the first duties of government was "to devise and adopt a comprehensive scheme or system upon which to conduct the surveys of the country, and to proceed with the survey of such portions as were likely to be required for immediate settlement."

The government responsibility for the survey of the new territory was assumed by the department of public works and on July 10, 1869 — still more than four months before the Deed of Surrender was signed by the Hudson's Bay Company — the minister, Hon. William McDougall, was writing to Dennis of the provincial land survey staff, asking him to proceed to the Red River district for the purpose of "selecting the most suitable localities for the survey of Townships for immediate settlement," and to recommend "to this department the plan of survey you propose to adopt as soon as you shall have determined upon it."[1]

Fortunately, there was the United States experience with its western lands upon which the novice Canadians could draw for guidance. Developers in the neighboring country had faced similar land problems more than a decade earlier and were most co-operative in sharing their experiences. People on both sides of the boundary could see the advantage to be gained by a reasonable degree of uniformity, especially close to the border.

In his letter to Dennis, the minister admitted that the American system of survey appeared most suitable to the Canadian West except in the matter of section size. He was dropping a broad hint that sections of 800 acres each would serve the Canadian purpose better than the American section of 640 acres. His reasoning was that the first settlers, "and the most desirable," could be expected to be from Canada where the people were familiar with 100-acre farms and the 800-acre sections would subdivide into such units with ease. A 160-acre quarter section, on the other hand, would seem foreign to them.

Dennis obtained a supply of instruments and a few helpers and was at Fort Garry at mid-August, realizing, of course, that the big country was still totally without survey marks except for those made to define the riverfront farms on the Red and Assiniboine to accommodate the Selkirk settlers. Two weeks later, he was forwarding his recommendations to the minister, proposing a system of survey which was formally approved by order in council on September 23. The plan did indeed resemble the American system except that Dennis — for technical or political reasons — recommended square sections consisting of 800 acres each with an additional 40 acres or five percent of the area for public highways.

Recognizing the need for base or datum lines, he would use the 49th parallel or international boundary as established by the Internaton Boundary Commission for his east-west base; and for a north-south

Canada's appeal for homesteaders was promoted around the world.

starting line he would project the first meridian northward from a point on the boundary, ten miles west of Pembina. The reason for rejecting longitude 98 degrees west was not very clear. This would be the principal meridian, known also as the Winnipeg meridian.

While awaiting approval and further instructions from Ottawa, Dennis remained active, fixing the position of the first meridian and laying out some trial townships. The honorable minister had instructed him to keep busy during this interval, but unknown to both the minister and Dennis, trouble was brewing along the Red. The government had been grossly remiss in its failure to consult with or even advise the native people on matters pertaining to the proposed takeover. Rumors about the sale of land, which the native people regarded as their own, made them angry and when, on October 11, one of the Red River residents, André Nault, saw members of the Dennis survey crew working on land to which he exercised a personal claim, two and one-half miles back from the river, he hastened to inform them that they were on his pasture land and were to leave at once. His French words were wasted on the English-speaking surveyors and they ignored him. He hurried away to notify his friends, including a young fellow to whom he was related, Louis Riel the Younger, who had returned only recently after several years at school in Montreal. The young man had been sent to the East to train for the priesthood but had abandoned that calling and was ready to accept the way of life of his own people along

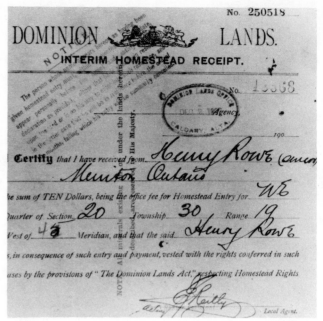

Homestead receipts such as this one were issued to thousands of new residents of the prairies.

John Sanderson, first man to file on a homestead in western Canada, farmed five miles from Portage La Prairie. (July 2, 1872).

the river. Possessing qualities of leadership, he was accepted immediately as the spokesman as eighteen French half-breeds accompanied Nault to the scene of the trespass. As Dennis reported the affair, the men were unarmed but they stood defiantly on the surveyor's chain and "made threats of violence." Their leader's message was to quit surveying at once and stay away from all lands to which the Métis people made claim, meaning all land south of the Assiniboine River.[2]

Dennis, wisely, suspended his surveying operations. But Métis belligerence increased. Riel and his followers stopped Hon. William McDougall at Pembina when he was coming to assume the office of lieutenant-governor of the North-West Territories at the moment of transfer, then seized Fort Garry and set up a provisional government, McDougall was glad to have the counsel of his friend, Dennis, during his long and futile wait on the American side of the border, but there was no more surveying in 1869 and none in 1870.

Riel's occupation of the community did nothing to further the cause of western agriculture but it ended as abruptly as it started when the small military force under Col. Garnet Wolseley arrived on August 24, 1870. The months of occupation were none the less important. Canada completed purchase arrangements for the West and the government displayed a surprising spurt in creating the new province of Manitoba which was allowed to take its place in Confederation on July 15, 1870. It was haste for which the insurrection could take the credit.

A new lieutenant-governor, Hon. Archibald Adams, arrived to serve both the new province and the North-West Territories, signaling the dawn of a brighter day. When surveying was resumed in 1871, Dennis held the rank of surveyor general of Dominion lands and was returning with a revised plan for the survey. The American idea of the 640-acre section was now accepted, thanks in large part to the support given to it by the new lieutenant-governor. But the initial work done by Dennis and his men was not all lost because the 49th parallel and the Winnipeg meridian were still the starting lines, this much having been confirmed by the passing of the Dominion Lands Act on April 14, 1872. Present-day travelers on the Trans-Canada Highway cross that principal or Winnipeg meridian a few miles west of Winnipeg where it has been identified and honored by a suitable historic marker.

Surveying, when resumed, confirmed also the plan to count and identify sections, townships, and ranges. Sections in a complete township would number from the southeast corner westward to section 6 in the first tier, eastward to section 12 in the second tier, westward to section 18 in the third tier, eastward

to section 24 in the fourth tier, westward to section 30 in the fifth tier, and eastward to section 36 in the sixth or top tier.

East-west rows of townships would number northwards from the international boundary, and the north-south rows or ranges of township blocks would number both eastward and westward from the principal meridian and westward only from all other meridians. The second meridian was placed at longitude 102° W; the third meridian at longitude 106° W; the fourth meridian at 110° W which coincided exactly with the Saskatchewan-Alberta boundary, and the fifth meridian at longitude 114°W.

With the resumption of surveying after the Red River trouble, there seemed to be added reasons for haste. Perhaps the government at Ottawa was anxious to recover its capital investment of one and a half million dollars in acquiring the West. Undoubtedly the entry of British Columbia into Confederation in 1871 was an incentive, because the clever representatives from the west coast negotiating a union won a big bonus in the form of a promise that the Dominion would build a connecting railroad within ten years. Certainly the sparsely populated Dominion, facing the necessity of building a transcontinental railway, could not afford to let a vast expanse of prairie land lie idle.

Certain areas qualified for survey priorities. Lands on which Hudson's Bay Company posts were located were to remain the property of the company and it was important that the exact locations be defined in legal terms at once. Beyond that, Dennis tried to concentrate the survey effort on areas likely to experience the earliest and biggest demands from homesteaders. The surveyed portions of the country might present a patchwork pattern but with as many as 400 men in the field, the workers succeeded in staying well ahead of the incoming landseekers. By early 1881, at which time the recently formed department of the interior was responsible for the survey program, it could be reported that 6,973,742 acres had been surveyed in Manitoba and 5,298,422 acres in the North-West Territories, making a total of 12,272,164 acres.[3]

A survey was an agricultural essential, as every observer would agree, but it was not enough. A land policy providing for homesteading and grazing leases was the next requirement and the Dominion Lands Act was passed to become law on April 14, 1872. The critics will say that it should have been broadened to prevent many of the mistakes in improper land use, but in the absence of soil surveys which came much later, attempts to extend the legislation would have been premature. Even as it was, the Dominion Lands Act was monumental in its importance. It confirmed the general plan of the survey, defined the land to be reserved for the Hudson's Bay Company and the

Educational Endowment plan, and prepared the way for homestead regulations.

In taking over Rupert's Land in 1869, the government of Canada was not only paying the Hudson's Bay Company a million and a half dollars in cash but was allowing the company to retain one-twentieth of all lands surveyed into townships in the area called the "Fertile Belt." How was this allotment to be made? Inasmuch as the number of sections and quarter sections in a township did not divide easily into twentieths, it was agreed and written into the Lands Act that the allotment would be satisfied by reserving to the Hudson's Bay Company one section and three-quarters in every township, and an extra quarter section to make two full sections in every fifth township. In consequence, all of section eight and three-quarters of section 26 or all of section 26 became the property of the company.

And inasmuch as it was considered "expedient to make provision in aid of education in Manitoba and the North-West Territories," sections 11 and 29 "in every surveyed township throughout the extent of the Dominion lands shall be and are hereby set apart as an endowment for purposes of education."[4]

The act's provision for homesteading was probably its most important feature. It did not produce an immediate rush for "free land," but that was understandable. Until there was rail communication and until the country could show reasonable provision for law enforcement, interested people would have reservations. But considered over the years of its existence, it is doubtful if any government measure touched the lives of more people or did more to give shape to Canada's future than the homestead provision.

The homestead regulations, reading very much like the United States regulations of ten years earlier,

appeared more and more like invitations addressed to the land-poor people in older parts of the world. The needy ones in remote sections of the world were slow in getting the message, but they got it and responded.

An individual did not have to be a Canadian citizen or a British subject in order to file on a homestead farm. Any person who was the head of a family or had attained the age of twenty-one years was entitled to enter for a quarter section of his or her choosing from "unappropriated Dominion lands."

Angus MacKay homesteaded at Indian Head in 1882 and became the first superintendent of the Indian Head Experimental Farm.

A homesteader packed for the trip to settle on his homestead. Typically, homestead oxen pull the heavy load.

The homesteader, on making entry at a Dominion land office, paid a filing fee of ten dollars and accepted the qualifying conditions which demanded certain named improvements such as a habitable home and a specified acreage of breaking, also six months of residence on the property in each of three years. Hence, three years was the shortest period of time in which a homesteader could get the patent on his homestead farm. If his performance proved to be less than satisfactory to the homestead inspector, it would take longer. Inspectors knew they had to be alert because deceiving them was not considered a sin. It was not difficult to cheat a little on the period of residence and there were cases where a shack capable of being mounted on wheels served each of several homesteaders for the periods when the inspector was likely to call.

During the early years of homesteading, no candidate could complain about lack of choice in land. Even after the exclusion of sections 8 and 26 claimed by the Hudson's Bay Company, sections 11 and 29 marked for school support, and all the odd-numbered sections remaining in the townships within twenty-four miles of the main line of the Canadian Pacific Railway set aside to satisfy the 25,000,000-acre grant to the railway, the lands were still varied and abundant. Anyone who was a connoisseur of soils could find quality to match every desire. And if the person was not a judge of soil quality, he or she could have the satisfaction of choosing between woodlands, parklands, open prairies, and hill country. Even the man who wanted lots of stones because he intended to build a stone house and stone stable should have been satisfied.

Nor could anybody accuse the government of Canada of being stingy in its land policies. The give-away took a score of shapes. The homesteader for whom a quarter section was not enough could purchase an adjacent quarter of Crown land to be known as a pre-emption, at the usual price of $2.50 per acre, knowing he could not obtain title or complete payment until after meeting all the conditions required to obtain the patent on his initial homestead quarter. Thus, it was impossible for a person to obtain the ownership of a pre-emption quarter unless and until he had fully qualified as owner of the homestead quarter.

For some years, also, it was possible for a homesteader who had "proven up" on his original homestead, to apply for a second. Some got a second homestead and a third, but the policy was not considered successful and was withdrawn.

The distinction of being Homesteader Number One in Western Canada went to a thirty-one-year-old Scottish immigrant, John Sanderson, who was the first in line when the Winnipeg Land Office opened for

W. R. Motherwell, shown with his son (right) and his grandson (left), homesteaded at Abernethy in 1883. He went on to become the first minister of agriculture for Saskatchewan and later became a popular minister of agriculture for the Dominion.

A. P. Stevenson walked from Winnipeg to his homestead near Morden and became a leading breeder of hardy fruits for western Canada. He developed western Canada's first orchard.

business on July 2, 1872. After listening to words of praise about the Portage la Prairie district where John McLean and Kenneth MacKenzie had settled ahead of both the survey and the Lands Act, Sanderson studied a land map and filed on the northeast quarter of section 35, township 12, range 7, west of the first meridian.[5] Then, having assumed a homesteader's obligations, he bought a pair of oxen and wagon and drove west to find the farm.

Having made himself familiar with the statutory survey system, he located the quarter without difficulty and settled down to perform the usual tasks like digging a well, building a log house, and breaking sod for the next year's crop. At first he was almost alone in the township but in the weeks following other homesteaders moved in around him and he had neighbors. Four weeks after his arrival, a covered wagon which had been driven a thousand miles from Missouri stopped on a quarter section three miles southwest of him and William and Jane Trimble and two children studied the quarter section on which they were to make their new home, and received a welcome from John Sanderson.

Farther west, in what was the North-West Territories and then the province of Saskatchewan, the honor of being the first person to formally enter upon a homestead was Thomas Kavanah who had gone from his native Ireland to the United States and marched with the Union Army during the Civil War. Coming to the Territories, he chose his homestead close to the Qu'Appelle Valley.

But the rush for the "free land" was not instantaneous. Applicants in 1874 numbered 1,376 and dropped to 499 in the next year, a trifling beginning for a program that saw 42,012 individuals filing for homesteads in 1906 and 44,479 in the peak year of 1911. Landseekers could, of course, obtain their land by simply purchasing it from the Hudson's Bay Company, the Canadian Pacific Railway, or a colonization company but for a decade or more, the typical western farmer was a homesteader possessing a shack, a pair of oxen, a walking plow, and the hope to qualify for the coveted patent at the end of three years.

Some of those who set out to gain the quarter-section prize failed the test and abandoned their homesteads. Most of them, however, persevered and became the undisputed owners of the land and then progressive and independent farmers who never ceased to speak with pride of their homestead years.

Chapter 9

CAME THE MENNONITES, THEN THE ICELANDERS

A land survey and a generous homestead policy set the stage for agricultural development on a larger scale and the government of Canada, hoping to attract immigrants from overseas, did not have to wait long for the Mennonites and then the Icelanders, both farm oriented but in quite different ways.

The German Mennonites, accepting a Russian promise of complete military immunity, had fled from Prussia a hundred years earlier. The Czar of that time was glad to have these industrious settlers to work and develop some of the more arid steppes where winters were severely cold. The immigrant people were permitted to educate their children in the German language and in their own schools and were contented until Russian policy changed. When the 50,000 Mennonite people then in the country were informed that military exemptions were being withdrawn, they concluded that they were bound by principle to look elsewhere for living space.

An inquiry reached the government of Canada, which responded immediately with an order in council dated April 26, 1872, providing assurances such as the Mennonite people wanted. Members of the pacifist and intensely religious sect were attracted and 1873 brought a small delegation to "spy out the land" in Manitoba and parts of the United States.

Manitoba officials were delighted with the opportunity of placing their province on display and promoting group immigration. William Hespeler who had just been appointed to the office of immigration agent acted as guide and interpreter and speaking on behalf of the premier, informed his visitors that they could go anywhere in Manitoba and stay as long as they liked. "Wagons, tents and every requisite for travelling would be provided for them at Government expense, and no effort would be spared to facilitate their movement in every direction."[1]

A few days later a letter was being written on instruction of the federal minister of agriculture telling the Mennonite visitors exactly what they wanted to hear, promising "entire exemption from Military service," a reservation of eight townships in the province of Manitoba for free grants on the conditions of settlement presented in the Dominion Lands Act, religious and educational freedom, and the right to affirm instead of taking legal oaths. Nor was that all; reflecting the official eagerness to secure these agricultural immigrants, the federal government was offering to subsidize traveling costs by furnishing "passenger warrants from Hamburg to Fort Garry for the sum of $30 per adult person," $15 for children under eight years and $3 for each infant under one year. And if still more inducement were needed, the same letter offered provisions of food for the immigrants from Liverpool to Collingwood.[2]

Members of the Mennonite delegation were indeed impressed by what they saw and what they heard and on leaving Manitoba hinted broadly that Canadians would see them again.

One year later, the first Mennonites came to stay. A riverboat docking at Fort Garry on July 31, 1874, discharged 325 men, women and children, the first of some 6,000 who were to adopt Manitoba in the next five years. Eager to see their farm land, the newcomers paused only briefly and went on to their reserve on the east side of the Red River, the area of which Steinbach became a center.

The head of each family was allotted a homestead quarter but the Mennonite way of life at that time demanded sharing, and communal villages sprang up. Everybody worked hard to get ready for winter. They built, dug, planted, and gathered fuel. An admiring editor, writing in November of that year, reported that some of these immigrant people had "already planted apple trees."[3] After two winters and one summer, another newspaper report recognized thirty-one villages in the East Reserve with a total of 414 families, each village having from six to twelve houses. "There are now 5,600 acres under cultivation," the report added, and "5,000 bushels of grain will be sown and 3,200 bushels of potatoes planted. The settlement has at present 1,160 horned cattle, 65 horses, 22 sheep and poultry at nearly every farm."[4]

By 1876, the Mennonites had outgrown the East Reserve and a West Reserve on the opposite side of the Red River was being added. There, centers like Altona and Winkler were born and there more communal villages appeared, many more, although the passage of years changed many customs and brought an end to the communal living plan. Likewise, the early isolation disappeared and more and more sons and daughters were choosing careers in business, the professions, and public service. But while being drawn into the mainstream of Canadian life, the Mennonites, more than most sectarian or ethnic groups, clung to agricultural traditions, rich traditions rooted in the bold Mennonite decision to reject the highly regarded park belt in favor of the prairie country. The demonstration of what could be done in farming the treeless plains brought immeasurable benefit to the

West. Many settlers, who were ready to accept Palliser's warnings about the prairies, saw what the Mennonites were able to do and followed their example, thereby putting the plains to earlier and fuller use.

Between the time the Mennonites were surveying the Manitoba scene and the date of their coming to stay one year later, the new West was witnessing another historic development in the coming of the North West Mounted Police. The Mennonites had not waited for assurances of safety from all frontier dangers but immigrant groups venturing farther west would expect a better guarantee of security than the North-West Territories could offer. Prime Minister John A. Macdonald's government was making a serious effort to improve public confidence by bringing an end to lawlessness in two areas about which people were talking. Street-corner stories had it that the gravest dangers were in the chance of Indian revolt where treaties had not been signed, with bloody massacre resulting, and the growing ruthlessness displayed by that breed of whisky traders operating in the prairie southwest where ranching gave a glimmer of promise.

The traders, using Fort Benton, Montana, as a base, encountered no opposition in carrying out their evil but profitable business. United States law made it clear to them that they must not sell liquor to American Indians but it did nothing to discourage the sale to Canadian Indians and the trade flourished. The stuff classified as trade whisky was as varied as the

A typical Mennonite house and barn combined.

men who drove north to peddle it. Each trader had his own secret recipe with ingredients such as turpentine, shredded tobacco, molasses, ginger, colic-cure, veterinary pain killer, red ink for coloring, perhaps some alcohol, and a generous amount of slough water. Its merit was in being able to generate a "kick" at small cost to the trader.

The effect upon the Indians was terrible. A report prepared by William Francis Butler advised a force of 100 to 150 police officers, one-third of them to be mounted. Another report, coming from Col. Patrick Robertson-Ross and presented to the prime minister in 1872, told of eighty-eight murders in the course of drunken brawls within the Blackfoot tribe alone in a single year, and recommended a force of 500 mounted riflemen to police the plains from seven different stations, Portage la Prairie, Fort Ellice, Fort Carlton, Fort Pitt, Fort Victoria, Fort Edmonton, and Fort Porcupine Hill.[5]

The Fort Benton-based traders were blamed for the Cypress Hills Massacre of Assiniboine Indians, about the beginning of May, 1873, resulting in the death of at least 20 native people, perhaps as many as 100.

News traveled slowly — bad news no faster than good — and by the time a report of the crime reached Ottawa, Sir John A. Macdonald had already introduced to the House of Commons what was described as "An Act Respecting the Administration of Justice and the Establishment of a Police Force in the North-West Territories." The bill advanced rapidly and became law on May 23, just twenty days after its introduction. But then, for reasons unknown, there was delay and the order in council required to permit recruiting was not passed until August 30, just days after the Mennonite delegation was completing its inspection in Manitoba.

The new force of up to 300 Mounties was for men between eighteen and forty years of age, able-bodied, able to ride and able to read and write in either English or French. Joining meant service for three years with a constable's pay of one dollar per day and board, and a sub-constable's of seventy-five cents per day. Those signing knew, also, that they might qualify for a grant of a quarter section of western land at the end of their term.

The first of the recruits went west before the end of the year, to winter at Lower Fort Garry, and on June 6 of the following spring, the main force consisting of 16 officers, 201 men and 244 horses left Toronto by special train. The United States authorities granted permission for this semi-military regiment to travel over American rail lines as far as Fargo, North Dakota — closest rail point to Manitoba — provided uniforms were not worn en route and all weapons were formally sealed.

From Fargo the men marched to Fort Dufferin, not far inside the Manitoba boundary, where they were joined by those who had wintered at Fort Garry and from which point on July 8, the great cavalcade,

A Mennonite community near Raymore or Quinton.

looking in part like an army maneuver and in part like an agricultural adventure, moved gaily away. Its 297 officers and men — strikingly close to the statutory maximum of 300 — 308 horses, 142 oxen, 93 other cattle, 114 Red River carts, 73 wagons, 20 Métis drivers and some assorted farm machinery, made it, by far, the most imposing parade the country had seen — and not a camera within a hundred miles. There was hardship and frustration along the way but three months and almost 800 miles later, the tired men and exhausted horses and oxen rested at the Oldman River where a fort was built and named in honor of Col. James Farquharson Macleod, the assistant commissioner who accompanied all the way.

The police acted promptly in routing the whisky traders and with the signing of another Indian treaty, the homestead country became measurably more inviting to landseekers, especially those coming from the east of Canada and who were more conscious of security than the ones from overseas. The first Mennonites had arrived twenty-three days after the Mounted Police began their westward trek from Fort Dufferin but their decision to come had been made months before the new force was a reality. Nor did the policing of the plains seem to be an important consideration with the Icelandic people who were to choose their location at a point on the west side of

Peter Asmundson ploughing with his oxen in 1905. He belonged to the Icelandic settlement near the Quill lakes in the Wynyard district.

Lake Winnipeg which was at that time in the North-West Territories, beyond the northern boundary of the "postage stamp" province of Manitoba. Their arrival in October, 1875, would coincide exactly with Mounted Police activity in building Fort Calgary and it would be several years before the new settlers witnessed much police action near the lake.

Their coming in 1875 made the Icelanders second only to the Mennonites in group settlement after the passage of the Dominion Lands Act. Like the Mennonites, these people of the same Norse stock that produced Leif Ericsson, came to farm although their concept of farming was very different. Farming to the Mennonite meant a pair of oxen, a plow, and an expanse of prairie land to cultivate and he found it in southern Manitoba. To the Icelander, farming presupposed a cow, a few sheep, an acreage close to waterfront, and a good boat for fishing; by accepting Lake Winnipeg as a substitute for the North Atlantic, he, too, found what he demanded for his idea of mixed farming.

Iceland had been experiencing hard times and many citizens of the tiny island felt compelled to emigrate. Of twenty-two going to North America in 1872, all but one went to the United States. That one, however, Sigtryggur Jonasson, became an effective promotor of Canada and was the means of inducing groups of his people to move to land in Ontario and Nova Scotia.[6] The areas chosen, however, proved less than satisfactory, and in the spring of 1875, Jonasson and a few representatives from the eastern colonies set

out to investigate settlement possibilities in the West. They had a large part of the continent from which to choose and might have found highly productive wheat land. Instead of searching for the best soil, they were thinking about conditions resembling those on the native island in the North Atlantic. They chose the homestead land on the west side of Lake Winnipeg which seemed to offer at least moderate opportunities for cultivation, plenty of logs for building, wood for fuel, a waterway to Winnipeg, and good fishing. The enthusiastic delegates returned to the East to report and on October 11 of the same year, Winnipeg welcomed the 285 men, women and children from eighty-five families, arriving on the riverboat *International*.

"They will leave tomorrow for their reserve on Lake Winnipeg," an editor commented. "They will immediately engage in the erection of a village which will doubtless be the nucleus of a future large town."[7]

In the next few days the hopeful people guided their flat-bottom boats down Red River and across Lake Winnipeg to the place where the village of Gimli was to arise, in the district to be known as New Iceland. It was late in the season. They lost no time in locating their homesteads and starting to build.

It was, of course, too late for planting but they broke up small plots of ground to receive potatoes and vegetables and seed wheat in the next spring. They

erected stables as well as houses and acquired a few cows, then used scythes to cut the tall-growing, low-quality marsh grasses for hay. They bought hens, hoping for winter eggs, but their main item of diet in that first season was fish.

More settlers came directly from Iceland to share the pioneer hardship. Winter weather in the first years was more severe than the people expected and late in 1877 the colonists felt the cruel attack of smallpox. The epidemic left fifty people dead. But more Icelanders came and new settlements were started at Riverton, Arnes, and Hecla Island. The people of the area organized a local government with a constitution. Perhaps it had no legal legitimacy but the so-called "Republic of New Iceland" with Gimli as capital, served a useful and practical purpose until the Manitoba boundaries were extended to embrace the Icelandic settlements.

New colonies sprang up in each of the midwestern provinces and Icelandic Canadians became leaders in many walks of Canadian life to give the story a still more distinctive character. When those of Icelandic descent celebrated the fiftieth anniversary of the coming of the first contingent to the West, they could count eighteen of their people sitting as members of provincial legislatures, nineteen university professors, two Rhodes scholars, forty lawyers and forty doctors, to say nothing of distinctive individuals such as Vilhjalmur Stefansson who was born near Gimli in 1879 and became an Arctic explorer of international fame.[8] And time added impressively to the list.

The home of Peter and Gudrun Asmundson, Wynyard district, 1915-16.

Chapter 10

MAKING WHEAT AND CATTLE HISTORY IN 1876

October 21, 1976, offered an occasion for a centennial anniversary which deserved recognition by Canadians everywhere. As it was, only Winnipeg citizens celebrated that 100th anniversary of the movement of the first wheat shipped out of western Canada, in this case to Toronto. It was the initial "trickle" of what was to become a "torrent" of wheat exports.

No spectators were more surprised by a sale of wheat for export to the East than the Manitoba farmers who furnished it. They, better than any others, understood the long record of adversity left by those who showed determination to grow wheat in the new country. They knew how the Selkirk settlers planted for twelve successive years before getting their first big crop return in 1824. They were familiar with the destroying floods and frosts, and then the grasshoppers attacking in the sixties and again in the seventies to leave the Red River community virtually without flour and without seed. They were very conscious of the partial loss of wheat from hoppers in 1874 that sent men and women into the fields to glean one head of surviving wheat at a time, hoping to recover enough to furnish seed for 1875. It was well known, also, that the insects in the latter year did not leave anything, not even straggler heads to be gleaned, thereby forcing a delegation of local men to travel as far as Wisconsin early in that year of 1876 for the sole purpose of buying seed wheat to be rafted back to Manitoba when the water was high in the spring. The wheat was duly bought and delivered and drew the Red River comment that it was harder and redder than kinds grown formerly. But when the Manitoba growers called for the name of the new variety, members of the purchasing delegation were vague beyond recalling that they had heard it called Fife.

What the Red River people did not know at the time was that this Fife or Red Fife wheat actually began as a Canadian variety with a storybook quality about its history, and its introduction to Red River was to have a big part in shaping the farming future of the new country.[1]

The variety's discoverer was David Fife whose family from Perthshire, Scotland, settled on the fourth concession of Otonabee Township, a short distance east of Peterborough, about 1820. When son David took over the family farm, one of his first efforts was a search for a more suitable variety of spring wheat. The kinds known in the district were low yielding and low in quality. In the course of the search, David Fife, with the imagination of a good research worker, sent to Scotland for some untested kinds but time proved them no better than varieties previously in use. His stubborn nature drove him to try again, this time to ask a friend working as a clerk in Glasgow to obtain a sample or samples of plump wheat, preferably from cargoes arriving from northern Europe.

The Glasgow friend, anxious to help, went strolling on the dock on a Sunday afternoon and noticed a shipload of wheat, just in from Danzig. Fife, he was sure, would be interested in obtaining a handful of that wheat but how was such a sample to be obtained in the face of tight dockside security? In relating it later, members of the Fife family told that the Glasgow friend found an excuse to walk on the deck of the boat and, while strolling there, his hat fell into the hold containing the wheat. Accidents will happen. Nobody could criticize him for trying to recover a perfectly good piece of headgear and boldly he descended into the hold where his garment was lying in plain view, on the grain. An observer might have noticed that the struggle to regain the hat was more muscular than would be expected and more strenuous than necessary. Inevitably, the recovery effort resulted in some kernels of wheat becoming lodged in the lining of the hat, there to remain in temporary hiding when the hat was returned to the clerk's head.

In the isolation of the Scottish home, the trapped kernels of Danzig wheat were removed from the hat, placed in an envelope and mailed to David Fife, Peterborough, Upper Canada. Fife welcomed another chance to find a better wheat and planted the most recent sample in a row in his garden. Most of the new seeds sprouted but grew indifferently and Fife was disappointed again — until he noticed one individual plant showing more vigor than the rest. It stooled to furnish five stalks with five heads. Hopefully, David

David and Mrs. Fife, Peterborough, Ontario. He was discoverer of Red Fife wheat, the strain of wheat that brought fame to western Canada.

and Jane Fife studied these heads, the product of a single seed.

But when these beautiful heads of golden grain were almost ready to be harvested, one of Fife's insensitive oxen broke into the garden and was in the act of devouring the experimental wheat when Mrs. Fife, who happened to be preparing the noon meal for her family, saw what was happening and dashed from the kitchen to frighten the ox away and survey the damage. Sure enough, the ox had reached the plant which had become the center of interest and had consumed four of the five heads. The Fifes were saddened but they were not abandoning hope and proceeded to erect a special barrier to safeguard the sole remaining stem of promising wheat. In due course, they harvested the seed from the lone head and placed it in an eggcup to await the 1842 planting season. There was enough wheat from that head to plant a full garden row and again the wheat gave a good account of itself.

The neighbors came to see for themselves and

remained to plead for a few seeds to give them a start with this new variety. The wheat was a rich red in color and so was Fife's hair and they called it Red Fife wheat. It spread across the spring wheat belt of Ontario, into Michigan, then Illinois and Wisconsin, and in 1876 it was brought to Red River where only club wheats and unnamed kinds were grown previously. There it was to find the soil conditions it fancied and there help to demonstrate the real wheat potential of the old fur country.

When time and transportation were considered, the cost of the Wisconsin wheat delivered at Fort Garry was high. But the farming people admired it and planted it with more hope than confidence in its chance of escaping the destroying grasshoppers. Happily, natural forces intervened and dealt a blow at the insects. The crop of 1876 grew and yielded well. Red River, instead of facing another year of virtual famine, produced beyond local needs.

This year, for a change, it was Ontario that experienced crop failure. Between a dry growing season and a wet harvest season that wheat crop was so poor that seed firms faced a shortage of supplies for their customers. Members of the Toronto firm of Steele Brothers, troubled to know where to look for stocks, received a report about a good crop in the distant West and asked some logical questions: "How would one get there to buy it? How in the absence of a railroad, could it be delivered if it were purchased?"

R. C. Steele, then a junior member of the firm and later its president, volunteered to travel that way with the idea of making a substantial purchase. His transportation ticket would allow him to make the journey by rail to Chicago, St. Paul, and Fisher's Landing, and from the latter point to Winnipeg — recently given its new name[2] — by river steamboat. As he soon discovered, river transportation was extremely slow and, with visions of the river freezing over before he could get the needed wheat and have it shipped out, he abandoned the idea of river travel and hired a wagon and team of horses and drove into Winnipeg.[3] The last 150 miles were covered in thirty hours although there is no information about the number of times the horses were changed.

The Winnipeg press of October 13, 1876, notified its readers: "Mr. Steele, of Steele Bros., Seedsmen, Toronto, arrived last night . . . for the purpose of obtaining 5,000 bushels of Manitoba wheat for seed in Ontario. . . . Any person able to facilitate the matter will please notify Messrs. Higgins and Young, the Free Press or Mr. W. Burrows."[4]

Upon arrival at Winnipeg, Steele made the acquaintance of David Young of the firm of Higgins and Young, "Dealers in Boots and Shoes, Crockery and Glassware," and assigned to him the responsibility of buying and assembling the 5,000 bushels of wheat

or as close to that amount as possible. From October 13 to 21 the *Free Press* carried the Higgins and Young announcement: "Cash for choice wheat to export to Ontario . . . 80 cents a bushel."

For Higgins and Young there was a purchasing commission of 5 cents per bushel making Steele's first cost 85 cents per bushel. In addition, there was an inescapable cost of 26 cents each for new cotton bags and finally the freight charge of 35 cents per bushel.

For years the local farmers had used wheat as a medium of exchange, much as beaver skins had been used still earlier. They had traded wheat for pemmican, wheat for horses, and wheat for Hudson's Bay Company credit, but never before had wheat been sold for cash — Toronto cash at that. Without delay they assessed their wheat stocks to determine how much could be spared. While Manitoba wives and mothers held the white cotton bags made to hold two bushels each, the men shoveled to fill them. All trails then led to McMillan's Mill beside the Red River at Post Office Street — later Lombard Street — where the bagged grain was weighed and piled for loading on a river-boat.

No single farmer had a lot of wheat to sell and it was soon evident that the big country could not furnish 5,000 bushels for the simple reason that it did not have that much. The biggest single contributor was G. R. Miller of Kildonan who delivered 204 bushels. Next in volume of sale was H. Soar of St. John who was paid for 154 bushels. Others making delivery were "Mr." Black, Springfield, 102 bushels; D. McDonald, Springfield, 94 bushels; J. W. Carleton, Clear Spring, 80 bushels and 10 pounds; John Spear, Springfield, 44 bushels; John Reich, St. Paul, 40 bushels; F. Dick, Springfield, 35 bushels; Alex Gibson, Springfield, 33 bushels; T. B. Robinson, Rockwood, 32 bushels; Neil McLeod, Victoria, 22 bushels, and John McIvor, Greenwood, 17 bushels and 40 pounds.[5]

The wheat collected and bought totaled 857 bushels and 10 pounds, far short of the desired 5,000 bushels. It was all that could be obtained in that season six years after the province of Manitoba was formed, that year in which the Indian treaty with the Cree was signed at Fort Carlton and Fort Pitt, that year in which Sitting Bull and his Sioux warriors completely wiped out the American cavalry force following Gen. George Custer in the Battle of the Little Big Horn in Montana.

On that important date, October 21, 1876, the river boat *Minnesota*, carrying Steele's wheat in 412 cotton bags, drew away from the Winnipeg dock to paddle upstream, just hours before a shore-to-shore crust of ice ended river navigation for the year. But Steele's wheat reached Fisher's Landing ahead of the ice at that point and was moved from there to Duluth by rail, then to Sarnia by lakeboat and Toronto by rail.

There, at its destination, the Manitoba wheat brought surprise. It was superior wheat and admiring spectators asked questions: "What's the variety name? Can the West produce more like that? When will we have a railroad to that wheat country?"

It is probably correct that interest in the wheat did have something to do with the increased pace of railroad building.

An event as important as that first shipment of wheat deserved a historic marker of some kind and got it. Visitors at the legislative building in Winnipeg were able to see a tangible reminder in a bronze plaque hanging in the hallway. There was an earlier and more visible marker in the form of a plaque attached to a riverside boulder close to the site of McMillan's Mill, unveiled when the Canadian Seed Growers' Association held a convention in Winnipeg in 1932, but vandals could not resist and the metal plate was damaged or destroyed on at least two occasions. And then the big stone, having lost its metal identification, lost its public appeal and became the victim of burial under the dike constructed to protect that part of the city from floodwater in 1950.

But a mounting trade in wheat became the best possible monument to the historic shipment of 1876. In the next year, while Lieutenant-Governor David Laird and Mounted Police Commissioner James F. Macleod were negotiating with Blackfoot, Blood, Piegan, Sarcee, and Stoney tribesmen far to the west and proceeding toward the signing of Treaty Number Seven on September 21, eastern buyers visiting Winnipeg were contracting for bigger amounts of wheat, this time for 20,000 bushels. And on October 17 — the same day exactly that found Gen. Alfred H. Terry of the United States military forces meeting Sioux chief Sitting Bull at Fort Walsh in a futile attempt to persuade the latter to return to the United States side — the wheat left Winnipeg by riverboat to follow the same course as Steele's wheat to Toronto. Significantly, some of that wheat had been bought to fill an order from Barclay and Brand of Glasgow, Scotland, and would be the first grain of any kind to leave the West for shipment overseas. In being sent to Glasgow, this Red Fife wheat was being returned to the place where ancestral seeds had become caught in the lining of a Scotsman's hat to be sent to Canada and in time to become a major force in setting a great industry in motion.

The year of 1876 had still more for the students of agricultural history. It was the year in which Thaddeus Harper drove south from his British Columbia range with 800 head of cattle, intending to take them to market at Chicago but revised his objective while en route and actually drove into San Francisco some eighteen months later.[6] It was the year also in which cattle were given the opportunity to demonstrate their ability to winter outside on the Canadian range.

In the second year after the coming of the North West Mounted Police, John B. Smith, of Sun River, drove a herd of fourteen cows, ten calves and a bull to Fort Macleod. At some time in the autumn, the herd of twenty-five cattle was acquired by Constable Robert Whitney of the Force. It seemed improbable that a full-time policeman with neither farm nor ranch land would be buying cattle and the reason for the ownership remained obscure for many years until a pioneer ranchman, who wanted to remain unidentified, whispered that Whitney won the cattle in a poker game. Having neither feed nor shelter for the cattle and with winter coming on, Whitney was properly worried. In his dilemma, he did the only thing possible; he turned his cattle on the open range, knowing very well that his friends were correct in warning of almost certain disaster for the herd. If the cattle did not freeze to death in the Northwestern winter, and if the Indians did not shoot them down the way they killed buffalo, they would likely drift away with the buffalo and end up in Texas.

But there was no alternative and the cattle were released on what was regarded as the inhospitable range. Whitney tried to forget about them, at least until spring when, yielding to curiosity, he rode out to look for fresh bones or other evidence of the herd's fate. But to everybody's astonishment, he rode back into Fort Macleod a couple of days later, driving his twenty-five cattle and every cow had a calf following. It might have been seen as the first roundup on the Canadian range and also as the demonstration of what John George "Kootenai" Brown of Waterton Lakes had been saying, that where buffalo had lived and lived well, cattle would do the same.

Just as Steele's shipment of wheat signaled the beginning of the wheat industry, so Constable Whitney's unplanned cattle operation, at the same time, provided a starting point for ranching as conducted on the Great Plains.

Chapter 11

CATTLE WHERE BUFFALO GRAZED

Ranching on the Canadian Great Plains was a logical successor to the mighty buffalo herds and a proper companion for the emerging wheat trade. Domination of the prairie scene by the buffalo had ended with dramatic suddenness. Bison numbers had been so great that Rev. John McDougall standing on Nose Hill, within present-day Calgary, in 1874, saw what he believed to be half a million of the big animals; but two years later, when Constable Whitney released his twenty-five domestic cattle to test the prairie winter, the wild herd was under heavy hunting pressure and after another four years it had, for all practical purposes, disappeared.

The homesteaders were coming but not rapidly and cattle seemed to offer the best means of filling a vacuum left in the wake of the buffalo, especially in the grassy southwest which was favored by those warm, dry chinook winds capable of moderating winter temperatures and removing snow to facilitate grazing. Even the cynics who inferred that Montana's good grass and favorable ranching climate must end at the boundary could not halt a northerly expansion.

Western Canada's agriculture inherited its breeds of domestic livestock from England and Scotland, its ideals in dairying from the East and its ranching customs and traditions from the south. Texas was the cradle of North American ranching and its first cattle were those of Spanish origin which came in from Mexico. The Texas plains suited the Spanish stock and the cattle multiplied and became a distinct race, characterized by long horns, long legs, racehorse speed and mean dispositions. Texas, at the end of the Civil War was believed to have three and one-half million of the wild critters, unbranded, unclaimed, and unloved. But with a growing population and market for meat in the Northeast, the Texas stock could not

escape the interest of men seeking fortune and believing they could cut out a herd of a thousand or three thousand longhorns and drive them to a railhead somewhere to the north.

About a quarter of a million cattle were driven out of Texas in 1866, most of them being directed to Sedalia, Missouri, and Baxter Springs in Kansas where they could be loaded on freight cars and shipped to St. Louis. The next year found most of the trail herds being driven to Abilene, Kansas, where the enterprising McCoy Brothers from Springfield, Illinois, built a stockyard to accommodate 3,000 cattle, provided a scale for weighing cattle, erected a hotel, and then dispatched riders to intercept the northbound herds and invite the cattlemen to come Abilene way. Thirty-five thousand head were loaded out of that terminal in its first year, 350,000 in its second year and 700,000 in 1871. A few years later, Dodge City,

The Cochrane Ranch bunk house, west of Calgary, built in 1882. This was, until it was recently demolished, the only surviving ranch house of this period.

Kansas, gained supremacy as a loading point and was said to have shipped out almost seven million southern cattle in a period of fourteen years.

Trailing, which was the means of bringing the foundation stock for western Canada's ranch herds, became a highly specialized operation, requiring all the known cowboy skills. A trail outfit, in addition to the cattle, required a chuckwagon, cook, horse wrangler, trail boss or captain, about six cowboys for every thousand cattle, and from six to ten stock horses for every cowboy. A trail day began at sunrise and for the first couple of hours the herd was allowed to graze as it was guided leisurely in the proper direction. This was followed by harder driving until noon when there was a rest period for two or three hours, and finally more grazing as the herd was eased forward at its own speed until time to settle down for the night. Cattlemen hoped to cover fifteen miles each day but had to be satisfied with ten or twelve at most times.

The trails knew stirring times and cowboys had to be ready to deal with stampedes, raiding Indians, swollen rivers that had to be crossed, and the familiar cattle rustlers weighted down with guns.

John Ware, famous Negro cowboy and rancher who came with the N.W. Cattle Company drive in 1882, shown with his family. (Glenbow Institute.)

The first Texas trail herds were intended for slaughter at some distant point like St. Louis or Chicago, but growing numbers were being sought for breeding purposes in founding ranch herds in Wyoming, Dakota, Idaho, and Montana. And then, from these northern states, a few years later, trail herds brought ranching across the international boundary to western Canada.

The British Columbia interior had ranch cattle earlier than the Canadian foothills or plains. These began with surplus or leftover cattle from the Fraser River gold rush. Jerome and Thaddeus Harper, who had driven herds from Oregon to Barkerville in 1862 and 1863, recognized an advantage in raising cattle in the area and about 1865, chose a ranch location a few miles east of Kamloops, where they adopted the "ℋ" brand taken from Jerome's initials.

East of the Rockies, the small McDougall herd of twelve cattle — eleven cows and a bull — driven from Fort Edmonton to Morley on the Bow River in 1873 would represent the first in what is now known as southern Alberta but these were mission milk cows more than ranch cattle and it was a few more years before the first cattle were driven to Fort Macleod or before George Emerson and Tom Lynch drove a few hundred head to the Highwood River, mainly for resale. But ranching began in earnest in 1881 when the first big herd was trailed from Montana to Big Hill, west of Calgary, to found the Cochrane herd.

The Canadian Lands Act was amended to allow grazing leases on areas up to 100,000 acres with lessees required to pay annual rental of one cent per acre. It was a time when ranching in Texas and other western states was attracting investors on both sides of the Atlantic and gigantic ranches were being started, among them the Capital Syndicate or "XIT" and the

A shorthorn steer at a time when heavy beef was popular. This one, owned by C. W. Parsons, Pibrock, Alberta, weighed 4000 pounds at six years of age.

Matador, the latter with Scottish capital. It was hoped that the new Canadian leasing policy would attract eastern and overseas investment capital. It did.

Hon. M. H. Cochrane of Compton, Quebec, set out to see for himself. Coming to Fort Benton in the spring of 1881, he bought a democrat and pair of driving horses and drove north. On his way, he met John George "Kootenai" Brown, who had been in the country for fifteen years, and received the reassurance that the buffalo which had disappeared so recently was an excellent judge of grass and found the Canadian grazing very much to its liking.

Cochrane located a ranch setting in the vicinity of Big Hill — later marked by the village of Cochrane — west of Calgary, and when on his return to the East, he stopped at Fort Benton long enough to contract for the purchase of 3,000 Montana cattle and to arrange with the I. G. Baker Company for their delivery in the autumn. But the cattle suffered misfortune. They were driven too fast and arrived at the ranch headquarters in thin condition, poorly prepared to enter the winter. As might have been anticipated, the winter losses were heavy but Cochrane had courage and ordered another big herd for 1882 delivery. Again the area experienced a winter of storms and severe cold and again losses were heavy.

Having encountered two winters with heavy loss of cattle, Cochrane believed he had chosen the wrong district and proceeded to obtain a lease between Waterton and Belly rivers and move the herd to that more southerly part. But ill luck followed and in the next winter season, the snow conditions were reversed with open grazing around Big Hill and heavy snows on his southern range. Cattle drifted around Waterton Lakes and were starving until Frank Strong of Fort Macleod, for a consideration of a thousand dollars, undertook to open a course through the snow by which the cattle could escape from their winter trap. The ingenious Strong rounded up 500 horses from the Blood reservation and forced them through the drifts,

A roundup on the Matador Ranch, north of Swift Current, about 1908.

taking two days to do it but, sure enough, opening an avenue through the snow over which the Cochrane cattle escaped to areas offering winter grazing.

They were difficult and costly pioneer experiences but the Cochrane enterprise survived the misfortunes and became a rangeland leader, enjoying such eminence until the ranch was sold in 1904 to the Mormon Church.

The North West Cattle Company, known later as the Bar U Ranch, was the next of the ranching giants on the prairie side of the mountains and the one which surpassed all others in its long record of performance. Backed by the Montreal Allans of the Allan steamship line, the site on the Highwood River was chosen by the man who promoted the company and managed the ranch, Fred Stimson. Carrying out an initial task, Stimson bought a foundation herd in Idaho and instructed Tom Lynch, undisputed "King of the Canadian Cattle Trails," to drive it to the Canadian foothills. As it turned out, that drive of 1882 brought not only the first cattle for the Bar U — 3,000 head — but was the means of bringing the great Negro cowboy and cattleman, John Ware, perhaps the most skillful rider of his generation.

George Lane, whose name became indelibly linked to that of the ranch, came in 1884 in response to Stimson's order placed with the Sun River Stock Association in Montana for a ranch foreman, the best man obtainable at a wage of thirty-five dollars per month. But before long, Lane had cattle of his own and was leaving the Bar U to devote himself more completely to his ranch affairs on the Little Bow and then Willow Creek. Just after the beginning of the present century, Lane heard that the Montreal owners of the Bar U were considering selling the ranch and made a special trip to the East to learn more. As he discovered, the ranch was for sale but the price of almost a quarter of a million dollars seemed forbidding. The discussion was not lengthy and after the price which would include 5,000 cattle and 500 horses, was named, Lane was given only three days in which to produce the money and make payment. He approached the well-known cattle dealers and exporters, Gordon, Ironside and Fares, and convinced them to become his partners. The deal was concluded with the same dispatch which characterized all Lane's business transactions.

There were good times and bad ahead for the ranch. The winter of 1906-7 dealt a near-crippling blow, when almost half of the 24,000 Bar U cattle counted in the autumn perished before spring. But Lane persevered and became one of Alberta's "Big Four Cattlemen," sharing the distinction with three friends, Pat Burns, A. E. Cross, and Archie McLean. He became an importer and breeder of high-class Percheron horses, became a friend of the Prince of Wales, and one of the West's distinguished citizens. After Lane's death in 1925, the Bar U was bought by his staunch friend of many years, Pat Burns, for the sum of $403,001, plus $50 per head for the cattle on it and $40 per head for the horses.

After the delivery of the first herd for the North West Cattle Company, the chinook belt proliferated with new ranches, some big, some small. The Oxley with the "OX" brand was organized in 1882 by one of the most able cattlemen of his time, John R. Craig, who found his financial backing in England. Craig managed the ranch until there was disagreement but the English influence was so pronounced that, according to hearsay, the Oxley saddle horses refused to respond to the usual commands unless they were delivered with an Oxford accent.

The Winder Ranch was next, bearing the name of its founder and owner, Capt. William Winder — brother-in-law of Fred Stimson — who had recently taken his retirement from the North West Mounted Police. He started with 1,200 head of cattle, making

The Duke of Windsor, then H.R.H. the Prince of Wales, standing with the Big Four Cattlemen who backed the first Calgary Stampede of 1912. From left to right, Pat Burns, George Lane, The Prince of Wales, A. J. McLean and A. E. Cross.

him neither very big nor very small in the business. Several big ones were started in 1883, among them the Walrond which took the "WR" brand and brought together two of the noted personalities of that period, Dr. Duncan McEachern who instigated the enterprise and Sir John Walrond who represented the British investors. McEachern who assumed the ranch management was probably a better veterinarian than diplomat and the ranch saw troubled times. Because of an alleged hostility toward squatters and settlers in the area of the Walrond lease, McEachern was at the very center of a drawn-out conflict between ranchers and homesteaders in general.

The next year, 1884, saw the coming of another big English company, the Quorn, to locate on Sheep Creek with headquarters not far from the Big Rock, west of today's Okotoks. The ranch organization was most unusual inasmuch as the original support came from members of the Quorn Hunt Club of Leicestershire and the first purpose was to raise hunter horses for the Old Country market. Two hundred selected hunter type mares and about twenty high-class Thoroughbred and Cleveland Bay stallions were imported. The Thoroughbred stallion, Eagle Plume, generated special ranch pride and may have been the best of his breed in western Canada during his time. The half-bred progeny from the superior Quorn horse

stock failed to capture the United Kingdom market but proved popular nearer home when army remounts and Mounted Police horses were wanted.

In the year of the Quorn's beginning, 1884, according to the department of the interior, forty-one lease holders controlled 2,782,000 acres of grassland and the Cochrane Ranch was still the biggest in operations, followed by the I. G. Baker Company, the North West Cattle Company and the Walrond Ranch Company.

Starting with a big herd of Montana cattle and a 100,000-acre lease required considerable capital but beginning in a small way was relatively easy. The Queen's grass was practically free and if an aspiring cattleman did not have a formal lease, he could brand his cattle and turn them loose on the open range, hoping they would be recovered in the general roundup. For the person with no scruples about branding another man's animals or those unidentified critters known as mavericks, the opportunities were unlimited.

For all operators, big and small, watering resources were as crucial as grass. As soon as barbed wire came to be used for fencing, there was an immediate rush to gain possession of good waterholes and approaches to streams, especially on the plains

where the value of grass was often limited by shortage of water. Homesteaders found that there was no easier way of making themselves unpopular than by fencing a good spring or waterfront on their land.

The biggest general roundup in those early years of ranching was in 1885 — Rebellion year. Cowboys gathered at Fort Macleod on May 25 and named James Dunlap, foreman of the Cochrane Ranch, to be roundup captain. A hundred cowboys with 500 horses rode out to comb the country in all directions and conduct the sorting. Some 60,000 cattle were gathered but the area proved to be too big for a single roundup and it was agreed that ensuing roundups would be conducted on a district basis with the various districts maintaining liaison by means of delegates or "reps."[1]

But with the adoption of fencing by the ranchers as well as the farmers, the great roundups passed into history. The range was changing. The terrible winter of 1886-87 which caused the deaths of an estimated forty percent of the cattle between the Red Deer and Missouri rivers hastened many changes. A few ranch operators canceled their leases and became homesteaders. Others, realizing the importance of having reserves of winter feed, bought haying machinery and vowed to use it. Thoughtful operators could see the day approaching when they would be obliged to fence their grassland, whether it was deeded or leased, and exercise better control over their herds, winter and summer. Another ranch-land byproduct of that disastrous winter was an increased interest in horse

The E. P. Ranch, which became the property of the Duke of Windsor, is located in the Alberta foothills.

breeding and sheep raising because horses and sheep survived better than the cattle.

It took a few years but adjustments were made and the optimism of the earlier period largely returned. At the end of 1890, according to the annual report of the department of the interior, 129 lessees held 2,288,347 acres of Crown grazing land, although almost half of that acreage — actually 1,009,714 acres — was held by only eight big ranch operators with familiar names. The Walrond Ranch Company and Sir John Walrond had two leases of 100,000 acres each; the New Oxley Ranching Company had three leases totaling 242,934 acres; the Cochrane Ranch Company had 166,500 acres; the North West Cattle Company had 147,960 acres, while A. B. Few and W. G. Conrad were shown with 100,000 acres each, and the Glengarry Ranch with 52,320 acres.[2]

Sheep were slow to establish themselves in the Canadian ranch country, partly because they appeared less glamorous to investors and largely because of a traditional antipathy on the part of cattlemen. Sheep grazed close to the ground and left nothing for cattle. Conflict between the two rangeland factions was known in the western states to flare into range warfare.

Nevertheless, nothing short of prohibitory legislation would keep the sheepmen out. Alexander Begg had a few of the "woolies" at the mouth of the Highwood River and there must have been other bands possessing unimportant numbers. In 1881, when the first Cochrane cattle were being delivered, the total sheep population of the North-West Territories was only 346. But that population figure received a sudden boost when, in 1884, a flock of 8,000 was driven from Montana to the Cochrane range west of Calgary. When these sheep, which cost three dollars per head in Montana, were forced across the Elbow River at Calgary on a late September day, they had been on the trail for more than two months, making, on the average, about six miles per day.

It was at this point that the federal government's policy makers resolved to try, in the interest of peace on the range, to restrict sheep ranching to the grass on the north side of the Bow River. It was a restriction which did not survive for long.

Sir John Lister Kaye, whose exploits with range sheep were spectacular if not profitable, appears as one who discovered the mutton and wool interest after noting the heavy cattle losses in the killing winter of 1886-87. It was in the latter year, while most ranchers were stll counting their dead cattle, that Sir John organized the Canadian Agricultural, Coal and Colonization Company, better remembered as the "76" and declared his intention of importing a big flock of sheep. First he located ten farms or ranches of 10,000 acres each between Balgonie on the east and Calgary on the west. He bought breeding cattle carrying the "76" brand from the Powder River Ranch Company and then took steps to import sheep. Two years later, 10,000 head were trailed from the point of purchase in Montana to Maple Creek where they could be divided into smaller flocks for distribution to the various ranches. In the next year the company sheep were consolidated at Swift Current, Kincorth, and Gull Lake and when John Oman in 1892 joined the "76" as an experienced shepherd, the company's sheep count stood at 30,000.

Every industry has its "ups and downs" and the years between 1893 and 1897 were remembered as the time of "The Great Sheep Depression." Sheep scab appeared and mutton and wool prices failed. Some of the pioneer flock owners quit, but by the beginning of the new century, the sheep business was reviving and owners appeared to be enjoying better returns than the range cattlemen. Flocks were assuming greater size as well as greater importance. The enthusiasts could point to the Jesse Knight flock at Raymond, numbering 46,000 head and prospering.

The ranch cattlemen, by this time, had new problems. One of them was the 1892 embargo against Canadian cattle intended for the British market, all because of some alleged cases of pleuropneumonia reported in animals exported from this country. If the disease was correctly diagnosed, it was fairly certain

Steers arriving at Dawson City, Yukon in October, 1901. These steers were purchased at Cochrane, N.W.T. by Chris Bartsch. (Photo courtesy of the Bartsch family.)

that the affected animals were from Ontario, but the western cattlemen were major sufferers. And then, while the sheepmen were fighting scab, the cattlemen found themselves with the costly and stubborn problem of mange. Perhaps the parasite was present for a few years before it was detected but in any case, the cattle ranchers came to the end of the century organizing unhappily for an involved and prolonged program of dipping. They grumbled at the inconven-

ience but co-operated with government veterinarians in building long and narrow dipping vats at convenient roundup points. The dipping necessity was hateful to man and beast alike. Certainly the range cattle, which did not welcome human interference with their lives at any time, hated the warm, soupy sulphur dip and the men pushing them into it. But dipping was carried out with such thoroughness that the ranges were ultimately declared free of the scourge.

Chapter 12

FARM FAIRS ON THE FRONTIER

Winnipeg and Portage la Prairie held agricultural fairs before the coming of the North West Mounted Police. Citizens of Fort Macleod organized for their first while the big southern herds were still moving on the Whoop-Up Trail toward the Canadian range, and Fort Edmonton, Prince Albert, Saskatoon, and a score of other places saw fit to conduct fairs before they had railroad communications with the outside, all of which seemed to acknowledge a value surpassing that of entertainment in those earthy institutions.

The fact was that fairs and exhibitions of one kind or another were almost as ancient as agriculture itself, sounding a conviction that competition brings incentive to most enterprises. Agriculture, even in its frontier form, was sure to benefit.

The Old World had fairs from Biblical times. The Prophet Ezekiel noted the trade fairs of Tyre and mentioned the appearance of "lambs, rams and goats," also products like wheat, honey, silver, iron, and tin. Apparently Tyre had something resembling a Women's Work Section, too, "with emeralds, purple and broidered work and fine linen" being displayed.[1]

England had fairs from the time of King Alfred the Great, at least, the most famous of which was that of St. Bartholomew at Smithfield, dating to 1102. If it is of any comfort to modern fair managers, such early events did not escape the familiar midway problem of "robberies committed and done . . . in booths." But the ancients gave the miscreants no chance to repeat their sins, it being enacted that those found guilty would suffer death in "such manner and form as for robberies committed in dwelling houses, and without benefit of clergy."[2]

Canada's first fair, at Windsor, Nova Scotia, was also North America's first. It was conducted under Royal Charter in 1765, with a butter churn offered as the prize for the best cow, a pair of shears for the best sheep, three yards of English broadcloth for the biggest display of cattle, a buggy whip and pair of spurs for the best horse, and a lace hat as first prize in the wrestling competitions.[3]

In the Canadian West the distinction of organizing and conducting the first agricultural fair could be claimed by Victoria, British Columbia, for an achievement in 1861. And in the midwest, the honor would go to Fort Garry or Winnipeg for a noble effort without success in 1871. Charles Napier Bell, who had come to Red River with the Wolseley expedition sent to quell the Riel insurrection in the previous year, served as secretary and manager. Entries numbered 500 and they were being assembled in the best fair-morning manner on October 4 when rumor reached Fort Garry that the rebel Irishmen known as Fenians were embarking upon a raid from the United States side of the boundary at Pembina. Exhibitors lost interest in the fair and promptly collected their cows, bulls, show horses, and sheep tied to fence posts and went home. The fair was over before it was really started.

After that collapse at Fort Garry, Portage la Prairie's successful effort in the next year established the latter community as the unquestioned western leader in the conduct of fairs. Ultimately, there were bigger fairs across the country but no town or city community in Manitoba, Saskatchewan, or Alberta could rob Portage la Prairie of its long-range distinctions through summer fairs and related events.

About the time the parliament of Canada was passing the Dominion Lands Act in the spring of 1872, Portage la Prairie pioneers were getting together to organize the Marquette Agricultural Society and elect stalwart Kenneth MacKenzie as president. Forthwith, members began planning for a fair to be held on September 25, a date which had to be changed to October 16 because of weather conditions. The town at the time had a population of 300 and a stagecoach service to Fort Garry; but otherwise, the Portage la Prairie communication with the rest of the world was dismally poor and the *Manitoba Free Press* in its very first issue,[4] apologized for failure to report more fully on the Portage la Prairie fair, saying: "We sent for a prize list for publication in this issue but it has failed to reach us as yet." As it turned out, readers had to wait for seven weeks to get a report of the fair and learn that there were 400 entries, with quality which "would reflect credit upon many an old county in Ontario."[5]

Among the exhibitors were numerous settlers with names having a familiar ring for students of agricultural history, personalities like the president, Kenneth MacKenzie; the pioneer breeder of purebred Shorthorns, Walter Lynch from nearby Westbourne; the country's first homesteader, Jock Sanderson; the local member sitting in the first Manitoba legislature, Francis Ogletree, and pioneer breeder of show sheep, Donald Stewart. Even the secretary of the fair, Charles Mair, was an exhibitor and won the prize for the best buffalo robe tanned at home.

By bringing together the earliest breeders of purebred Shorthorn cattle in Manitoba, the beef cattle classes carried special historical importance. The two farm leaders, Kenneth MacKenzie and Walter Lynch, divided the competition honors rather evenly. Mac-Kenzie was the winner in the classes calling for three-year-old heifers, yearling heifers, and bull calves, while Lynch scored first prize for mature bulls, mature cows, and heifer calves. There was then added interest in the outcome of the herd class, in which Lynch triumphed and MacKenzie was second. The same two stockmen found themselves competing for the awards in classes for heavy horses.

As if trying to prove something about the goodness of local soil, the society's president was again

A herd of prize-winning Holsteins, the property of A. B. Potter, Montgomery, Assiniboine. The herd is headed by Gretique Montgomery Prince, third prize two-year old bull at Winnipeg and first at Brandon, 1898. One of the two-year-old heifers is first prize winner at Winnipeg and Brandon.

among the prize winners for butter, cheese, grains, vegetables including watermelons, and potatoes of no fewer than four varieties.

For rather obvious reasons, neighbors described this as the "MacKenzie Fair." But it was indeed a great Portage la Prairie show and the Agricultural Society went on to do bigger things. In the next year, 1873, there were almost 700 entries with emphasis on dairy products and home industry. Every settler could milk a few cows and every farm wife considered herself as an expert in making dairy butter. On this occasion some 60 entries were brought forward for two classes, calling respectively for fifty-pound tubs or firkins, and five-pound rolls.

In the "do-it-yourself" competitions, prizes were awarded for such articles as homemade cloth, home-grown vegetable seed, Manitoba-made maple syrup, Manitoba-made salt, home-produced vinegar, wooden plows, homemade fanning mills, Red River carts, harness from farm-tanned leather, and so on.

It was a tribute to the demonstration of local enterprise when the provincial board of agriculture awarded to Portage la Prairie the privilege of staging the Provincial Exhibition in 1883 and voted a grant of money to help make it a success. Eight thousand dollars — an unheard of amount for a western fair — was offered in prizes and the community reacted with enthusiasm. Hotels, instead of doubling their rates as some have been known to do for fair week, reduced them to half and citizens turned out to help lay plank sidewalks and clean up the town. Again the purpose was clear, first to promote better quality and more diversity in agriculture and, second, to encourage the pioneer virtues of resourcefulness and self-reliance with more competitions for farm-made wares and articles.

Many other districts were following the Portage la Prairie example. The new province of Manitoba, on February 21, 1872, passed the Agricultural Societies Act which allowed for the organization of a provincial agricultural society and county agricultural societies. By 1882, Manitoba had nineteen agricultural societies, with seventeen of them holding fairs — one of them being at Brandon.

Of the early midwestern fairs which became big city exhibitions, there were Winnipeg, which had a

A livestock parade at the Virden Fair in 1898. Every farmer
was a horseman.

The stock parade at the Winnipeg Exhibition in 1902.

Some of the prize-winning cattle at the Winnipeg Industrial Exhibition, as they were lining up to take part in the Live Stock Parade on the evening of Friday, July 14, 1899.

faltering beginning; Fort Edmonton, which registered boldly in 1879; Brandon, starting with the utmost of humility in 1882; Regina, trying to prove that the unkind remarks being published by Winnipeg papers were false, and making its beginning with fairs in 1884, and both Calgary and Saskatoon, getting into the same act in 1886.

The Fort Edmonton initiative was especially courageous. The fort had long existed as the Saskatchewan River Capital of the Fur Trade and agriculture received only scornful attention. Members of John Palliser's staff visiting there early in 1858 saw only thirty acres in cultivation and when the first detachment of the Mounted Police came in 1874, the extent of farming had changed only a little and reliance for food was still on the buffalo herds. But as buffalo numbers declined, interest in farming increased and an agricultural society was formed in 1879, with Inspector W. D. Jarvis of the NWMP named as president.

The new society had no money and no prospect of getting a supporting grant, but it had vigor and ideas. By public subscription, members collected $323 and decided to mark half of it for the purchase of good seed for distribution and the other half for prizes at an agricultural fair they proposed to hold. Chief Factor Richard Hardisty offered the use of two big rooms in the fort for table exhibits and all the outside space needed for livestock. The chosen day was October 15, 1879, and classes were offered for teams of horses, yokes of oxen, fat steers, brood mares with foals, stallions and saddle horses, but, as might have been

expected, the livestock entry was small. But the inside exhibits of ladies' work, leather goods, woolen home-spun, grains and vegetables made imposing displays and gave the exhibitors something about which to boast.[6] Neither Calgary, Winnipeg nor Toronto would be able to better the demonstrated size of Edmonton carrots, measuring four inches in diameter and twenty-four inches in length, or the latest yield of Edmonton potatoes, said to be 1,300 bushels from less than two and one-quarter acres of land.

The contest inviting the greatest local interest was for the "Best Collection of Vegetables" for which the first prize was the astonishing sum of five dollars, plus two dollars' worth of garden seeds donated by Patrick Gammie Laurie's *Saskatchewan Herald*, published at Battleford.

As seen from the vantage point of a hundred years later, it was a modest effort, but it was 1879 and the fair was doing exactly what a pioneer fair was supposed to do.

All the leading fairs and exhibitions began in unpretentious ways. Brandon's first show carried a prize list offering only $200 and of the twenty head of livestock competing, about half were horses which hauled their owners' buggies and wagons to town that day.

The formation of the Calgary Agricultural Society in 1884 — year of the town's incorporation — was the forerunner of a world-famous Exhibition and Stampede. The first fair followed two years later and was held where Claxton's Star Rink could furnish shelter for the inside exhibits and an adjacent lot could accommodate the livestock. But in the meantime, the site that became Victoria Park and the permanent home of the Exhibition and Stampede was acquired at a cost which made it one of the most profitable real estate transactions in agricultural history. Maj. James Walker, who came west with the original Mounted Police, was the president of the society and much aware of the need for a permanent location. As the fates decreed it, A. M. Burgess, deputy minister of the interior, happened to be riding a capricious horse while inspecting Crown lands in the Fish Creek area. Without warning, the horse assumed an ugly mood and unseated the rider, leaving the eastern bureaucrat sitting on the prairie with a broken collarbone and some injured pride. It then happened that James Walker, like the Good Samaritan of old, came that way, rescued the injured man and compassionately took him home to recuperate.

While the deputy minister was in the poorest possible position to argue with his host, Walker hinted how the new agricultural society could use a piece of land for a fair grounds and inquired coyly about ninety-four acres of government-owned land nestling in a bend of the Elbow River. The helpless civil servant, in no position to give any other answer, promised to use his influence in the society's behalf and a short time thereafter, the Calgary Agricultural Society bought the future Victoria Park, ninety-four acres at $2.50 per acre, subject to only one restriction, that it would not be subdivided. The total cost to the society was $235.

Saskatoon held its first fair only four years after the original Temperance Colonization Society settlers came to the place and, like Edmonton, some years before it was served by a railroad. The fair, which was planned explicitly to bring incentive to the agricultural community, was held on the east side of the river and according to one of those who attended, Joseph Caswell, the absence of a grandstand and the lack of fences and gates to the grounds created handicaps, but every settler brought something for the competitions and a good show resulted. He could relate, too, that his brother Robert qualified for the reward of a diploma and a dollar for having the best herd of Durham cattle which had been brought very recently from Ontario. To complete their journey from the East, the cows had been driven over the trail from Moose Jaw and the bull, as if deserving better treatment, was transported by wagon.

Fairs were popular and by 1895, the West had them big and small, imposing and unimposing, all being directed with more hope of winning public recognition for their exhibitors and their communities. Portage la Prairie people had welcomed the opportunity of staging the Manitoba Provincial Exhibition in 1883 and Calgarians were happy to be having the Dominion Exhibition of 1908 and the substantial government subsidies that went with it. In the same spirit, Regina seized upon the idea of organizing and presenting the biggest agricultural exhibition program seen in the West to that time, the Territorial Exhibition of 1895.

Nothing even remotely like it had happened to Regina and citizens for several decades used the year of 1895 as a sort of datum-point in time; everything bore a "before" or "after" relationship to the Territorial. Regina, with fewer than 1,000 of population, was at the "awkward stage" in its growth and needed something to give it direction and purpose. It needed the Territorial. The town had been holding fairs since 1884 when 150 people attended the first one and progress had been satisfactory but not spectacular. The idea now was to organize for an exhibition along the most handsome lines. The government of Canada agreed to contribute $25,000 provided its purpose was to serve the agricultural interests of the entire North-West Territories. At the same time, the Territorial government and the Regina town council promised $10,000 each. The CPR would make its contribution by providing free transportation for exhibits. Such generous backing made it possible to offer the

Aged Clydesdale stallions in the ring at Brandon, 1906.

unprecedented sum of $19,000 in prize money. It would be the biggest prize incentive ever offered west of Toronto exhibition.

Lieutenant-Governor C. H. Mackintosh gave ready endorsement and followed by giving much of his time to planning and management. Regina citizens were immediately and enthusiastically behind the program.

Land was obtained on the west side of the town and there the Regina exhibition was to have a permanent home. Stables, grandstand, racetrack, and other appurtenances were needed, in a hurry. Some Regina services may have suffered but the buildings for the shelter of livestock and visitors were ready when needed.

Agricultural men of prominence across the West were pleased to accept invitations to serve as exhibition directors, Angus MacKay of Indian Head, Fred Stimson of the Bar U Ranch, William Cochrane of the Cochrane Ranch, Thomas McKay of Prince Albert, Maj. William Bell of Bell Farm, Indian Head, Michael Oxarat of Cypress Hills. The West was beginning to find an agricultural elite.

Pomp and ceremony were not overlooked. Lord Aberdeen, governor general of Canada, came to officially open the exhibition and with him were Lady Aberdeen and Mackenzie Bowell, prime minister of Canada. They made speeches, attended banquets, mingled with the Indians, and conducted themselves generally as though they were genuinely enjoying the show.

Such an exhibition demanded entertainment, of course, and it was provided adequately with music and games. Seven bands attended and in the category of entertainment were horse races, polo, baseball tournaments, walking races for horse teams hitched to wagons, Red River jig competitions, Mounted Police Musical Rides, bronco riding, trap shooting and an elaborate Carnival of Nations arranged by a church ladies' group. There was something for everybody, as an experienced exhibition administration is supposed to provide it.

Livestock, properly at the heart of an exhibition, filled the new stables and presented a rather new study in breeds. Breed suitability was not yet established and the Territorial brought out many kinds which visitors were seeing for the first time, also more breeds than could have been justified in agricultural practice, including eight breeds of pigs, and eight of sheep. But if eight breeds of pigs seemed like many, it should have been noted that the poultry section of the show brought out forty-nine breeds and varieties, not counting turkeys, ducks, geese, and pigeons.

It was a time when heavy horses dominated every fair or exhibition and the Territorial was no exception. The Belgian breed had not yet made its appearance in the West but the prize list contained classes for

A livestock parade at Edmonton, 1919.

Clydesdales, Percherons, Shires, Standardbreds, Hackneys, and Thoroughbreds. Moreover, the heavy horses qualified for the biggest prizes. The first award for stallions in one of the draft breeds was thirty-two dollars, generous to be sure. In the saddlehorse classes, there was a subtle stipulation that all entries winning prizes were to become the property of the North West Mounted Police at $125 per head.

In dairy cattle, Holsteins, Jerseys, and Ayrshires were bidding for popular favor. The leading exhibitor of Holsteins, A. B. Potter, whose address was given as Montgomery, was one with a name destined to remain prominent in breed circles for the next fifty years. In the section for beef cattle, most exhibitors were showing Shorthorns, just as most farmers were breeding Shorthorns. But William Sharman from Souris was there with Herefords and giving many visitors their first opportunity to see specimens of the breed. Likewise, the Aberdeen Angus breed was being introduced to many farmers through the show herds of J. D. McGregor from Brandon, Walter Clifford from Austin, and Joseph Glen of Indian Head.

It was becoming fashionable to preach mixed farming and dairying was receiving much encouragement. It was evident at the Territorial. Competition butter came from fourteen creameries and scores of farms. Yorkton's new creamery won the butter championship but the big cheese from Innisfail won most attention. It weighed 1,300 pounds and was said to be the biggest ever made or exhibited in the West.

The mixed farming ideal inspired two special classes, one for individual farmers, the other for agricultural societies. For the individual farmer, each entry had to consist of:

two bushels of wheat
two bushels of oats
two bushels of barley
two bushels of peas
½ bushel of flax
one male and two female cattle
one male and two female pigs
one male and two female sheep.

Similarly, the agricultural society class carrying a first prize award of $100 required for each entry:

five draft horses
five general purpose horses
four pedigreed cattle, one of which to be a bull
four grade cattle
four ewes and one ram
five pigs
two bushels of Red Fife wheat
two bushels of feed barley
two bushels of black oats
two bushels of white oats
two bushels of two-rowed barley and two bushels of six-rowed barley.

They were novel classes and one could only pity the officials who were obliged to judge them.

The scope of the program, the large response in exhibits, and the prestige it enjoyed, made the Territorial Exhibition a proper climax in an effort of two decades to employ the fairs and exhibitions as the "show-windows of agriculture." Bigger shows followed, of course, but not many big ones with an equal emphasis upon agriculture.

Chapter 13

THE BIG FARMS ON THE FRONTIER

Individuals who aspired to ownership of the biggest barns, the biggest herd bulls, or the biggest farms were not uncommon. Apart from personal gratification, they did not achieve much and were frequently the first in the neighborhood to face bankruptcy. In most instances, they contributed more to public entertainment than to leadership. But they did add something to history.

It might have been reasoned that if a small or homestead-size farm were worth while, a bigger farm would be proportionately more rewarding. It did not necessarily follow but the theory had to be tested again and again. Others who struggled to become spectacularly big as farmers may have craved attention more than anything. But neither ambition for wealth nor desire for popular recognition explained the Adam MacKenzie motivation. His extensive operations brought him notoriety but not because he sought it. Coming to the West a couple of years after his notable father, Kenneth MacKenzie, he admitted to an inherent fondness for land, as some people had for stylish clothes or good horses, but he would have been happy to be left alone to enjoy his farm holdings, unobserved and unmolested.

He was big, muscular, energetic, and economical with both money and words. He was a man of action more than of talk and when he did speak, it was with a bluntness that made him seem gruff. After three years in Manitoba, he married and he and his bride set out with a team of horses in the general direction of Arden, spending honeymoon nights under the democrat and days searching for land. He was carrying requisitions for Half-breed Scrip, each one good for a quarter section of government land, and if he couldn't get enough that way, he had another idea; he was carrying a walking plow in the back of the democrat

and being just a few steps ahead of the surveyors, he believed he could stop and plow a furrow around the land he wished to claim.

There was speculation about the amount of land that Adam MacKenzie ultimately owned. Nobody seemed to be sure but in the years when farmers were allowed to defray part of their municipal taxes by roadwork at the rate of one day with man and team for each quarter section, Adam MacKenzie complained that his quarter sections exceeded the number of working days in the summer season. Even when he was known to be Manitoba's biggest farm operator, he continued to buy land. Often he bought at tax sales and was known to bid on and buy quarters that were already his registered property because he had forgotten or lost the record of them.

Being well established when the settlers were coming, he was in a good position to sell them horses, oxen, breeding cattle, or freighting services between Minnedosa and Winnipeg or Minnedosa and Edmonton. Neighbors remembered when he had twenty-five wagons on the trail, hauling flour to Edmonton.

In 1881, MacKenzie extended his farming enterprise in the direction of Carberry Plains. It meant more machinery, more horses, more hired men. It might have meant more bookkeeping but it didn't. For payday he brought home the needed money in a grainsack and often, after making sales, he took cash to the bank in the same way. When he drove to Carberry on one of these occasions, he was delivering his democrat team at the livery stable and, as if it were routine, hung a bag tied with binder twine on a harness hook. But when the stable attendant proceeded to empty the contents of the bag in the horses' oat boxes, MacKenzie became excited, shouting: ''Halt, ye fool; it's no' oats, just a wee pouckle of money for the bank."

About 1908, MacKenzie sold his Manitoba land and moved to Victoria, B.C., but he was restless there and went to Cuba to embark upon business with plantations and cattle, and ran up 3,000 livestock, eventually returning to Manitoba where he died in 1926.

John Willian Sandison was an aspiring farm giant and leader of a very different kind. He was the young Scott working on a farm at Carberry when Adam MacKenzie was at the zenith of his farming career and fame and felt inspired to build an agricultural empire of similar size and character. He tried, and although he never became an operator on the scale of MacKenzie, he furnished no less interest and amusement for the citizens of Brandon community, which might have been one of his purposes.

He came to Manitoba in 1884 and after working at Carberry, married the boss's daughter. Then, with the backing of his father-in-law, he bought his first land on Brandon's northwest side in 1886. Brandon businessmen welcomed him as they would any spender, while amused farm neighbors were asking: "How long will he last?" With 400 acres of land in crop in his first year, he had nearly 4,000 acres plowed in 1890; of this amount of land in cultivation, 1,500 acres were in wheat, 300 acres in oats, 200 in summerfallow and 800 of new breaking being backset by ten teams and walking plows.

As he spent money freely, writers and editors thought they saw a great success story. A local editor held him up as a shining example, explaining that just "eight yeas ago, Mr. Sandison came to Manitoba as a farm laborer." Now, as reported at the beginning of 1892, "the Wheat King of Brandon district, ordered 13 new binders from the Massey-Harris firm and also paid the land commissioner of the Canadian Pacific, $22,000 for land which he proposes to add to his extensive farm."[1]

As the local farmers were quick to note, Sandison was a showman and a boaster. He was indeed an eccentric, progressive in some ways. He kept good horses, was ardent in weed control, and was among the first to take steps to prevent soil erosion. Unfortunately, his commendable qualities were overshadowed by his folly, like his custom of sending his shirts and collars back to Scotland to be laundered to his taste.

One of his chief extravagances was in farm machinery, especially binders. Every new machine model proved irresistible with the result that he was unconsciously performing an experimental farm service with new kinds, thus sparing neighboring farmers the inconvenience and high cost of buying faulty implements. His crop of 1891, for example, was seeded with one of the new "gatling gun" broadcasters mounted on the back of a wagon and capable of spreading seed on 100 acres per day. Most farmers, after seeing Sandison's demonstration, decided that the "gatling gun" broadcaster was not for them.

When the binders ordered early in 1892 were unloaded from freight cars at Brandon, there had to be an orderly parade to the farm, with each new binder spaced carefully behind the one in front and the proprietor on a stylish Thoroughbred or Hackney, in the leading position, like a cavalry officer leading his troop to war.

He became a self-appointed promoter of immigration to western Canada and apparently impressed some Britishers when he gestured at Old Country gatherings, holding up his jewel-laden hands and proclaiming: "If you want to wear diamonds on all your fingers, you must decide to farm in Manitoba."

But he hadn't fooled the farm neighbors. They recognized from the beginning the superficial side of the Sandison farming. His creditors were sensing it and when he returned from Scotland in the spring of 1893, he found them waiting to serve him with demands. Before the seeding operations of that spring were completed, the famous farmer disappeared and Brandon people saw him no more. It was reported that a Scotland Yard detective was trying to catch up with him.

Creditors seized what they could and the farm auction sale conducted in June was the biggest the country had seen, lasting two full days. The big stone house remained as a landmark and the Sandison stories were told and retold, partly for entertainment, partly for the lessons they conveyed, chiefly that spending more than one makes is a sure way to farm bankruptcy.

Just as Manitoba had MacKenzie and Sandison, so the Territories had Maj. William Robert Bell and Sir John Lister Kaye and others, colorful, conspicuous and entertaining, probably contributing more to western

The circular stone barn on the Bell Farm at Indian Head.

agriculture through their mistakes which wouldn't have to repeated, than through their successes.

Major Bell, known around Indian Head as "Major Billy," was from Brockville, Ontario, where he was born in 1845 and at which place he joined the army to fight invading Fenians. Leaving military life, he was in Winnipeg and then walking west from the end of the railway at Brandon, in 1881, "just looking around." Studying soil as he traveled, he was impressed by what he saw at a point marked only by an Indian skull suspended on a post and later called Indian Head. There he caught a vision of large-scale farming and he returned to Winnipeg to talk about it. Both Winnipeg and English investors were interested in Bell's concept and within a year the Qu'Appelle Valley Farming Company was formed and Bell's choice of land was a block of 100 square miles which included that point at which the town of Indian Head would be located. He secured much of the land from the CPR and Hudson's Bay Company at one dollar an acre, while making an arrangement with the government of Canada for the homestead land in the block — all except what was held by two stubborn squatters.

Bell, as managing director, organized the farm workers about the way he would have planned a military field force. Under him was a superintendent, then a foreman, eight assistant foremen, and the army

A rare photograph of workmen on the '76 ranch during the 1890's.

of workmen. Men with walking plows and oxteams were put to work with the least possible delay and 2,700 acres were broken and made ready for the first crop.

Twenty-two five-room cottages for married workers were built in 1883, also a fine stone house and stone stable at the headquarters site. And there was more breaking. In June, 30 three-horse sulky plows were sent to the fields, to bring the total of plowed ground to 6,000 acres. Some of the furrows plowed in that season were so long that the teamster made only one round per day, taking all forenoon to plow in one direction and all afternoon to plow back to the starting point.

The crop of 1883 was moderately good — twenty bushels of wheat per acre — and two threshing machines were in use. To the company directors, it sounded well, with a promise of dividends. But an early frost in the next summer damaged the crop and blighted the prospect of dividends. Nevertheless, Bell, like Sandison, had a flare for farm machinery and forty-five "self binders" were placed in the fields at one time during the harvest and seven steam threshing outfits were ready to recover the grain, 130,000 bushels of it in spite of the early frost. It seemed like a lot of grain but the frost damage had left it to grade no higher than feed. Directors were displaying a change of outlook and saying that too much money was being spent in relation to revenue.

Before the crop of 1885 was planted, Bell was

sending all available men and teams to serve the military transport conveying supplies to the scene of the Northwest Rebellion, and going along in person to serve as transport officer. The ten dollars per day which a man and team could earn at freighting was more than the big farm was likely to earn for the shareholders and practically no crop was planted. But the land that was permitted to lie fallow that summer had more moisture and hence more crop in 1886 and the practice of summerfallowing was born on the prairies.

Ever imaginative, Bell in 1885 was proposing the founding of an agricultural college on his premises. A college building was erected that summer and an invitation was extended to a prominent British authority to accept the position of principal. The person in question may have been Primrose McConnell who was known to have paid a visit to the Indian Head farm that summer.

But the big farm which had been western Canada's showpiece and a compelling point-of-call for every Britisher who crossed the continent was losing money rather steadily and retrenchment was necessary. The brilliant and personable Bell remained in management until 1895 when, instead of retiring, he simply turned

his great energy to other challenges, gold mining, coal, the development of peat bogs in Ireland, and so on. Gradually, the big farm was converted to smaller farms — which was logical.

The bumptious little Englishman, Sir John Lister Kaye, was very different from Bell in his farming performance. His mistakes were bigger and more costly. Westerners saw him for the first time in 1885 when he was associated with Lord Queensbury in a 7,000-acre farming venture near Balgonie. There, Sir John sent thirty walking plows to the field at one time but it was not big enough for him and later in 1887, with plenty of British capital, he organized the Canadian Agricultural, Coal and Colonization Company, better known as the "76," and obtained ten blocks of prairie land at points along the main line of the Canadian Pacific Railway between Balgonie on the east and Langdon on the west, each block consisting of 10,000 acres. Most of the land was bought from the government of Canada and the CPR.

Sir John would show Canadians how to grow wheat and cattle and while doing it, he would be bringing British families to work for him and then settle on half-section units of his land. That much of his land was within the Palliser Triangle did not seem to worry him in the least.

One who knew the man said that Sir John could only count in terms of thousands and millions. The ten spreads totaling 100,000 acres suited him well. In 1888, he was awarding a contract for two million board feet

Farming with oxen power in Saskatchewan. Thirty-five oxen breaking sod on J. E. Miller's farm, Lumsden, 1906. Two acres were broken with every round of the field with 960 acres broken in a season.

Eight binders cutting a field of wheat in southern Alberta.

of lumber for farm buildings.[2] He ordered 500 Clydesdale mares in Ontario, 50 for each of the ten farms. In the same year, he bought the 7,000 cattle from the Powder River Ranch Company and was talking about driving 30,000 sheep from Montana.

No time was lost in breaking prairie sod for wheat but drought was acute and crops failed. Sir John blustered. He had no intention of letting weather defeat his purpose and he placed an order with a Winnipeg factory for forty-four pine tanks of a kind that could be fitted on wagons and by means of which he could sprinkle the thirsty wheat land.[3] The tanks were eleven feet long and two feet high and each one would hold about 155 cubic feet of water, a lamentably insignificant amount when it is realized that it would require more than hundred tons of water to furnish even one inch of irrigation water on the surface of just one acre.

When wheat was failing, Sir John was concentrating on cattle and dividing the big Powder River herd into ten smaller herds for placement on the farms. But after another year, this arrangement was changed and the herds were consolidated at Swift Current Creek where the famous order to indulge in dairying was carried out. The English directors agreed — on Sir John's recommendation, no doubt — that dairying would increase ranch revenue and Sir John ordered a creamery to be built at Swift Current.[4] Sir John offered a silver trophy for the ranch foreman whose efforts led to the biggest delivery of cream. It sounded very well in London but nobody considered the feelings of the old range cows whose longhorn forebears came over the trails from Texas; it would have been clear that they resented with maniacal hostility any human intrusion upon their private lives. Milking, understandably, produced some lively scenes and milk yields were low. Neither cows nor cowboys could find any enthusiasm for the enterprise and it did not last long.

The sheep-raising operations were somewhat better. Ten thousand head — a favorite figure with Sir John — were driven from Idaho and Montana to Maple Creek by William Riddle and James Ross in 1889. At the latter point, the flock was divided and the smaller bands were loaded on freight cars and shipped

A harvest scene on a big farm near Young, Saskatchewan.

Threshing scene on the J. G. Miller farm near Craik, Saskatchewan about 1910. (Photo courtesy Mrs. C. Hay)

to the respective ranches. But after a year, the flocks were brought together at three points, Swift Current, Kincorth, and Gull Lake. When John Oman entered the company's service as an experienced shepherd in 1892, the sheep numbered 30,000.

According to an editor's summary in 1889, Sir John's company "has eleven farms of 10,000 acres each along the C.P.R. in the Northwest. On these it has 7,800 ordinary cattle, 100 Polled Angus and Galloway bulls, 600 brood mares and 12 stallions. Sheep and swine are on the way. On the farms are eleven stables capable of sheltering 500 horses, sheds for 6,000 head of cattle, shelter for 33,000 sheep and pens for 3,000 pigs. There are 200 laborers now on the farms. This season's crop amounts to 5,000 acres of wheat, oats and barley. It is intended to have 300 [milk] cows on each farm. Flax occupied 300 acres last year and was of excellent quality. The company expects to bring out a large number of immigrants next season with which to settle tracts of land between their farms. The capital of the company is £430,0000. . . ."[5]

General misfortune struck in 1893 with what became known as the "Great Sheep Depression," when wethers sold at Winnipeg at 2½ cents a pound and sheep exported from the "76" Ranch to England netted no more. Nothing proved profitable and the Old Country directors were unhappy. Sir John withdrew, leaving the way open for his able and experienced ranch manager, D. H. Andrews, to go to England in 1895 to effect a complete reorganization of the company. Andrews continued as manager, with more responsibility than he carried previously. The business showed improvement, even prospered prior to Andrews' death in 1906 when Crane Lake Ranch and the "76" brand were sold to Gordon, Ironside and Fares.

Sir John, who bought and blundered his way to a brief spell of agricultural fame, disappeared from the Canadian scene about as suddenly as he had appeared, leaving the country slightly wiser and probably no richer. But whatever the degree of success or failure, Sir John and his kind brought a new dimension of interest to the agricultural record of the West.

Chapter 14

HALF A MILLION NEW FARMERS

More important by far than the few individuals with oversize farms that rose and fell were the thousands of immigrants who were coming to occupy small farms and make homes on them.

Immigration to Canada was increasing but not at a spectacular rate until after 1896 when Hon. Clifford Sifton became minister of the interior and initiated policies that were felt around the world. Immigration numbers soared to a record 400,870 in 1914, the year marking the onset of World War I. Not all were coming to take western homesteads, of course, but immigration was reflected clearly in land settlement. Homestead entries between 1873 and 1914 totaled 536,253, with 454,806 or almost eighty-five percent of them being filed in the fifteen years after 1900.

The new activity inspired some bureaucratic boasting but more significant than the statistics and more significant than anybody seemed to realize at the time was the character or ethnic composition of the masses which were coming to farm. The striking feature was diversity and it reached the point where nearly every country in Europe was represented by at least one farming community somewhere in the West. One quality the newcomers seemed to have in common was a feeling of kinship for the soil.

Soon after the coming of the Mennonites and Icelanders, the West received 15,000 Chinese but they did not come to farm. The purpose in bringing them was to obtain cheap labor in pushing the CPR through the rockbound mountains and their main purpose in coming was to earn a dollar a day. Most of them returned to the homeland when the task was completed although some became laundry and restaurant operators at country points and rendered useful service.

Of the immigrant groups that followed to the West, most were definitely farm-oriented, including several Anglo-Saxon aggregations like the Temperance Colonization Society and York Colony from Ontario, and Capt. William Pierce's merry Englishmen at Cannington Manor. Still later there was the English Barr Colony at Lloydminster.

The Toronto people who joined to form the York Colony in 1882, settled where Yorkton, Saskatchewan, took the name. At the same time, the Temperance Colony Association, likewise starting in and around Toronto, won support by appealing to people with strong views about the evils of liquor. Here was a society offering them farming opportunities where the demon, booze, would not be allowed to show its ugly head. Organization was in June and J. N. Lake, W. S. Hill, and George W. Grant traveled west to inspect the 2,000,000 acres beside the South Saskatchewan River which were offered to them. Wisely, the Ontario men were taking surveyors with them to help in locating the land. The reports were favorable and the 150 miles between the chosen location and the railroad at Moose Jaw, instead of being a barrier, was seen as a safe distance between the settlers and the tempting odor of whisky.

A Winnipeg editor offered both commendation and warning: "The idea of establishing a Temperance Colony into which no liquor will be permitted to enter is a good one and commends itself to everybody. A Company has . . . applied for 2,000,000 acres which it is more than likely to get. . . . [But] in what way will they succeed in keeping whiskey out? There is no use building a wall round a colony for you could never get it so high, so close and so thick that sooner or later there would not be a decided smell of whiskey on the inside."[1]

A few impatient colonists moved to their new land

Before the advent of the railway, oxen trains such as this one brought supplies and equipment for the settlers.

The Barr Colonists camping at Saskatoon, 1903, prior to the two-hundred-mile trail journey to the area now marked by Lloydminster.

in the autumn of 1882 but the main body came via Moose Jaw and the 150-mile wagon trail in 1883. A few chose to escape the long trail trip by continuing on the railroad to Medicine Hat and there making rafts on which to float downriver to Saskatoon.

The Saskatoon pioneers may not have been successful in effecting a lasting isolation against booze but they did succeed in building permanency into the farming foundation of the community.

Farm colonies at that period, regardless of the ethnic origin of the settlers, varied like ladies' milli-nery — no two alike. Certainly, the manner of farming pursued at Cannington Manor was different from anything practiced elsewhere in the country, before or since. Many of the English gentry who followed Captain Pierce to that district south of Moosomin were well-to-do and had no intention of submitting to unusual frontier hardship. They would not allow themselves to become so immersed with farm toil that they would not have time for music, a bit of cricket, riding to hounds, and tea and crumpets at four o'clock.

Cannington's nearest counterparts were the farm settlement operated by the French counts at Whitewood at about the same time, and the French army officers, retired, who farmed a little later at Trochu. The counts were indeed aristocrats who were fascinated by the frontier but were giving up none of their loyalty to France. They were handicapped by lack of experience but made a serious effort to farm progressively. Their initial activity was in Rebellion year, 1885, when, strangely enough, a French-speaking German, Dr. Rudolph Meyer, selected the area for the inland adventure, and chose some of the land. The Count and Countess of Roffignac followed and settled on a picturesque valley farm to be known as Rolandrie Ranch. Count Soumillhac was next and developed Richelieu Farm.

The counts grew wheat, coarse grain and cattle, like other settlers, but did not restrict themselves to these. They searched for new crops and tried to specialize in something. Some specialized in race horses, some in purebred sheep. Others experimented with sugar beets, chicory, and unusual cheese such as Gruyère. The experiments were encouraging to the point of marketing products and then there were difficulties.

The French aristocrats built fine homes and lived better than their neighbors until, with novelty ending, the counts and their countesses moved back to Paris, leaving little behind except some charming social history. There was practically no connection between the settlements at Whitewood and Trochu although they were similar. The latter, which began with Armand Trochu in 1903, differed in having more colonels and fewer counts, and seemed to lose its identity when many of its people returned to France at the outbreak of World War I.

To the far southwest of the prairie area came the Mormons in 1887, bringing their resources of experience in Utah farming and imagination. An advance party under the leadership of Charles Ora Card, son-in-law of Brigham Young, drove north as far as Calgary in the previous year. In the back of their wagon, the Utah men carried a walking plow and at any point offering attractions for future farmers, they would hitch the wagon team to the plow and turn over a few furrows to expose the secrets of the soil. At Lee's Creek, south of Fort Macleod, they found the combination of soil, mountain scenery, and water for which they had been hunting and twelve families came by covered wagons in the following spring, to build and exercise their advanced ideas about such practices as irrigation, sugar beet culture, cheese manufacture, and mixed farming.

These English-speaking settlers with obvious advantages in communication were in no danger of receiving less than a fair share of public attention. The others, so recently separated — perhaps forever — from homes, relations and most that was dear in their lives, were the ones needing reassurances. Happily, they qualified for exactly the same homestead considerations as the most vocal Canadians but they were not sure and as they were seen flocking westward through the "Gateway" which was Winnipeg, they were homesick, sad, and often discouraged. They longed to talk with someone who could tell them in their own tongue of what they faced in homestead country. But they came on bravely, more Mennonites and Icelanders, more French and French Canadians, Jews, Hungarians, Russians, Ukrainians, Doukhobors, Scandinavians, Germans, Dutch, Danes, and others.

Perhaps the Jews who came in the eighties did not come expressly to farm but they and more of their people who followed accepted farming and some families remained on land in Saskatchewan for more than fifty years. Fleeing persecution in Russia, Poland, and Austria, Jews arrived at Winnipeg in 1882, hoping to establish themselves in the city. Failing to find what they wanted, they accepted the proposal to form a farming settlement and then founded the first Jewish farming colony, about twenty-five miles southwest of Moosomin, calling it New Jerusalem. But the people lacked farm experience and the first crop failed.

New Jerusalem had to be rated a failure but while it was being abandoned, another settlement was being started at Wapella, northwest of Moosomin, this one to be described later as the "first successful Jewish farm settlement."

When, on June 22, 1975, a cairn was unveiled to commemorate the Wapella settlement, the inscription explained; "Between 1886 and 1907, fifty Jewish settlers and their families led by John Heppner and Abraham Klenman, fled their European homelands to escape persecution and took homesteads around this lake and on lands extending six miles north and four

Doukhobor women furnishing the power to pull a walking plow at Kamsack, 1899. (Photo courtesy of Sam Stoochnoff)

miles southeast. This became the first successful Jewish farm settlement in Canada and was the forerunner of some dozen Jewish farm communities established on the prairies. Barish Lake is named for the Solomon Barish family who farmed the homestead on this quarter from 1894 to 1958."[2]

The Hirsch Colony, twenty-five miles east of Estevan and not far from the United States border, was founded in 1892 with help from Baron de Hirsch; it was another which proved that Jewish people could be good farmers, despite an allegation that they lacked aptitude for it. More settlements followed at Qu'Appelle, Lipton, Hoffer, and Edenbridge.[3] With the passing of time, however, most of the Jewish settlers, attracted by opportunities in the professions and business, left the western farms. Perhaps they did have more instinct for business than for agriculture but they carried their share of pioneering in the homestead period and did it well.

As branch lines were built in Manitoba and into the Territories, colonies of European immigrants sprang up. By 1886, the Manitoba and North West Railway reached Langenburg and was soon to reach and pass Yorkton. At once about a hundred Icelanders formed a nearby colony, calling it Thingvalla, and Germans working on the railway used their savings to form another, Hohenlohe, in the same Langenburg area. Danes came almost at once to settle near Yorkton, and the Church Colonization Land Company, formed by the Church of England in London, started a farm colony at Churchbridge, between Bredenbury and Langenburg, in 1888.[4] It was to this

church-sponsored colony that a London bishop was supposed to have addressed a communication advising the settlers to buy oxen instead of horses because they would need milk as well as power.

The Hungarians, assisted by Count Paul Esterhazy, settled along Stony Creek, northwest of Neepawa, in 1885 and another group with the same backing went in the next year to the area of the North-West Territories to be marked by Esterhazy, Saskatchewan.

Of course, the Swedes were on the farm frontier. A community of these people established north of the Qu'Appelle Valley in 1885 and gave the place the good name of Stockholm. Before long the Swedish settlers were going to more remote parts of the Territories, notably Wetaskiwin. Similarly, Norwegians settled to farm at Outlook and then New Norway, Camrose, Grande Prairie, and other places which now bear familiar names.

It was an important day in agricultural history when the first Ukrainians reached the West. It was 1891 and the two extremely important branch rail lines extending from Regina to Prince Albert and from Calgary to Edmonton had been completed. The two inconspicuous explorers from Eastern Europe, Ivan Pylypow and Vasyl Eleniak, were impressed, especially by the park belt. They reported glowingly and big crowds of peasant people began flooding through Winnipeg in 1894. Most were from the provinces of Galicia and Bukovina which were parts of the old Austro-Hungarian Empire but exact ethnic origins were not always clear and describing them collectively as Galicians or Ruthenians was inaccurate, like using the term Nova Scotians to embrace all Canadian Maritimers. Fully 20,000 of them came to western

Peter Veregin's house was one of the most elegant of its kind. The house was located at Veregin.

A thatched roof home of a settler near Veregin, Saskatchewan, built about 1910.

Canada in 1907, most of them eager to get away from Winnipeg to find their homestead quarters somewhere in the park country stretching across Manitoba, Saskatchewan, and Alberta. They were the most numerous of all the non-English-speaking newcomers to the West and, because of their peasant ways and lack of education, may have been the last to be understood. But they brought a great store of self-reliance and such natural love for the soil that members were seen to grab handfuls of it and bury their faces in it.

At first these Ukrainian people gladly lived a self-imposed segregation in their farm communities, clinging to their own language, practicing their own customs, plastering home exteriors, thatching roofs, constructing outdoor bake-ovens, and perpetuating resourcefulness. But a generation in the country brought major changes, with educated children advancing far in Canadian life. Integration was achieved without loss of the Slavic love of soil.

Seven hundred Doukhobors coming in 1899 looked like the first positive response to Hon. Clifford Sifton's immigration campaign. They, too, were a peasant people, a stubborn race with strong religious views embracing pacifism and communal living. They wanted nothing more than farmland and freedom. Most of them went to form a big colony at Veregin, near Kamsack. In their concept of peace, they were vegetarian, refusing to hurt either wild or domestic animals and were known to hitch their human friends to plows rather than inflict hardships upon horses or oxen. But they were not always peaceful among

themselves and internal conflicts led to three sects or categories, the Independents, Orthodox, and Sons of Freedom. In time there was a general movement to British Columbia, but not before the people left their imprints upon agriculture, especially in the Kamsack and Blaine Lake areas.

These various Slavic races — Poles, Ukrainians, Doukhobors, Russians, and so on — were the ones in whom Sir Clifford Sifton found his great satisfaction. In looking back upon his years as minister of the interior and writing about the kind of settlers Canada needed, he was obviously thinking about those Eastern Europeans. "We want the peasants and agriculturists," he said. "The pioneers have to be of the toughest fibre that can be found." He admitted indifference about nationality and British birth but he did not hide his views about the characeristics he hoped to identify in immigrant settlers. His thoughts seemed to be on an incoming Ukrainian: "I think a stalwart peasant in a sheep-skin coat, born on the soil, whose forefathers have been farmers for ten generations, with a stout wife and a half-dozen children, is good quality."[5]

The European settlers were important and so were the likes of the Barr Colonists who came to occupy land around Lloydminster in 1903, but the biggest influx of settlers in the first decade of the present century was from the United States. Between 1900 and 1914, over half a million immigrants entered Canada from the south and accounted for the biggest percentage of homestead entries. Clearly the main attraction was land and the movement was only arrested by the stresses of World War 1 — and then revived by the substantial movement in 1918 of those peace-loving men and women who were completely wedded to farming, the Hutterites.

Chapter 15

NEW MACHINES FOR NEW FARMERS

Except for improved walking plows and the acquisition of a few reapers, the Icelandic settlers at Gimli and the Temperance Colony settlers at Saskatoon used farm tools of practically the same design as those employed by the Red River Colonists more than half a century earlier. They planted their first grain crops by hand, employing exactly the same time-honored methods with which every adult male since Biblical times was familiar. The planting pace was slow and graceful, with measured strides; the sack of seed was suspended from the shoulders, leaving one or both hands free for casting alternately to the right and left. The operation did not take long, but as every planter knew very well, carelessness or lack of skill would condemn him convincingly when the crop began to grow.

A few of the first farmers at Saskatoon brought reapers, hauling them over the 150-mile trail from Moose Jaw, but most of them cut their first crop by using a cradle or scythe, bound the sheaves by hand, and threshed by means of that most simple of all farm implements, the flail, which could be made from two broken broom-handles connected by a leather hinge. These people had heard about "self-binding reapers" but had not seen one. They had seen mechanical threshers but had to wait a few years before having one in their colony.

Likewise, their first hay was cut with a scythe in the hands of a man who had perfected the slow, rhythmical sweep demanded by that primitive device. It was then bunched with hand rakes equipped with wooden teeth and finally lifted onto carts and into stacks with the aid of nothing more advanced than the three-tine forks which became painfully tiring by the end of a long and hot day.

A cart or wagon was the first piece of mechanical equipment to be acquired by a homesteader. A cart could be expected to cost forty dollars, a wagon fifty-five. A walking plow was the next item on the shopping list and would cost twenty dollars. It alone was already an ancient farm tool, as old as agriculture

The way it was done by the first settlers at Red River. (Dept. of Agriculture, Ottawa.)

Multiple ox teams known as Bull Trains moved much of the freight in the years prior to the railway.

itself. Very well did it deserve to be regarded as the symbol of agriculture. In its beginning it may not have been much more than a forked stick that could be pulled through the soil but it held advantages over spades and hoes which never succeeded in endearing themselves to human creatures. Better plows meant better agriculture as the Romans knew very well. They brought wheels to form a plow carriage, next a colter and then an iron moldboard which would turn a furrow. The Selkirk settlers, glad to obtain plows of any type, used the all-wood kind at first and William Laidlaw who was in chage of the Hayfield Experimental Farm complained in 1818 that Red River had never had a plow ''fit to turn the plain properly.'' The weakness of the wooden plows in gumbo soil accounted for the lack of progress until Laidlaw obtained iron for better ones. Ironically, the new plows almost failed their first test when from the big crop of 1824, the wheat from plowed ground was said to have yielded 44 bushels per acre and wheat from land prepared with spades and hoes, 68 bushels per acre.

It was in 1837 — the year after the Selkirk holdings known as Assiniboia were bought back by the Hudson's Bay Company — that a New England smithy, John Deere by name, made a steel plow with a moldboard that would take a polished surface. It was

one of the most important advances in farm machinery to that date.

The improved walking plows began coming to Winnipeg in 1877 — the year of the signing of Blackfoot Treaty Number Seven — and were immediately popular. The typical plow had a steel beam, two long wooden handles, a rolling or disc colter and steel moldboard and share to cut a furrow of ten or twelve inches in width. Of several makes available, the favorite was Verity No. 14 which had been fashioned expressly for Red River Valley soils after a Verity company representative, James Pickard, had visited the area in 1870.

Within a few years, manufacturers began offering plows on wheels which would allow operators the chance to ride and direct both the team and the machine from a metal seat. This, known as a sulky, brought new comfort for plowmen but at a price in added complexity. It was told of a Saskatchewan man that after ordering such a plow and having it delivered in a ready-to-go state, he encountered unexpected trouble: the machine was delivered with moldboard down and in plowing position and the new owner failed to find the mechanical secret of raising the plowing parts. When the exasperated owner was obliged to confess failure, he hitched his team to the machine and headed for home, plowing a six-mile furrow from the loading platform, down the main street and ending in his farm yard.

The two-horse walking plows and three-horse

Oxen served the early homesteaders on the trail and in the fields.

sulky plows by 1890 were giving place to four-horse and five-horse units in the form of two-furrow gangs, allowing settlers like R. Wyld of Battleford to tell about his "newly imported gang plow with which he turns over six acres a day."[1]

Farmers found pride in good plowing and entertained secret ambitions to have the straightest and most uniform furrows and the best weed coverage in the district. Conversely, poor plowing became a topic of community gossip, much as though it were immoral, like stealing horses or making home-brew. The secret longing to be recognized as the best plowman led to annual plowing matches which in a few instances assumed national importance.

The sulky plow was an advance over the walking plow.

The first western plowing match may have been held at Stonewall, Manitoba, in 1883. In the next year, J. W. Sandison, who became the "Brandon Wheat King," was said to have won his first agricultural distinction by capturing first prize in the plowing match at Carberry.[2] After another year, as the last spike was about to be driven in the transcontinental railway at Craigellachie, Portage la Prairie was conducting its first of many matches and challenging plowmen who learned the art in Ontario, Nova Scotia, Scotland, and many other parts.[3] The Portage la Prairie contests drew national and international fame and could even count Lord Byng, governor general of Canada, among its guests when the event was held at the Rutledge farm in 1922.

For a few earlier years, the West's biggest and most keenly contested plowing matches were in the Blyth district, southeast of Brandon, where the first one was held on the farm of A. Elder in 1897 and thirty-nine plowmen were entered. In the event of 1899, held on the farms of G. S. Charleson and D. R. Noble, seventy plowing contestants took to the field.[4] Most of them had walking plows which were still regarded as the instruments with which operators could demonstrate their skills most effectively.

Plowing matches became increasingly popular and departments of agriculture were pleased to promote them. They reached their pinnacle of popularity about 1921 in which year they were conducted in thirty districts of Manitoba alone. The promoters reasoned philosophically that the contests encouraged better plowing habits throughout the plowing year. "This

practice of doing well in one line," it was suggested, "soon becomes a habit and he [the plowman] unconsciously does his other work well and neatly. The consequence is that scarcely a single man who enters into plowing matches can be said to have an untidy farm, while it can be taken as the rule that they are superior farmers in every way. . . ."[5]

But plowing matches declined in numbers as plows gradually lost their standing in western fields. The change resulted mainly from the necessity of holding stubble and other trash on the surface of cultivated fields as a protection against soil drifting, and partly from the major swing to mechanical power and the availability of new cultivators with broad sweeps.

The early farmers showed no hurry about changing their seeding techniques. The ancient hand method was good enough, even though it did not cover the seed. There were occasions when the farmer brought a flock of sheep to a planted field for the purpose of tramping the seed into the ground but this was not often practical. Using peg-tooth harrows which a handy man could make, the fields planted by broadcast had to be worked thoroughly to cover the grain seed before the birds got a lot of it. The "gatling gun" broadcaster didn't change the principle and the first major innovation came with the introduction of mechanical drills developed from an invention of England's Jethro Tull. These came to Manitoba about 1880, the first being of the "hoe type," without depth control and not much to offer in seed control. But they were soon displaced by shoe drills and disc drills which brought greatly improved planting efficiency.

Machinery sales were increasing since the first wheat was shipped to Toronto. Even in that year a Winnipeg newspaper could report that: "Some 30 carts loaded with implements, comprising mowers, threshers, harrows, ploughs, drags, hoes, shovels, etc., have already left Winnipeg for the distant settlements."[6] It did not mean that the settlers were ready to surrender their inventiveness and rely upon imported farm machines. Even when Portage la Prairie held the Provincial Exhibition in October, 1883, the prize list was obviously catering to local ingenuity and self-reliance. No fewer than forty-five classes were offered for articles and implements of home manufacture, meaning made on the farms or made in Manitoba and the Territories. The list included buckboards, bobsleighs, phaetons, buggies, pitchforks, sulky horse rakes, root cutters, ox harness, harrows, strawcutters, ox yokes, fanning mills, reapers, mowers, dairy utensils, and canoes.

There was no doubt; the plow left the clearest imprints upon the history of world agriculture, but on the western Canadian scene, the most spectacular machinery changes were in harvesting equipment. The

The ultimate in farm machinery, the Case 110 HP.

best of proof came from a prairie pioneer's casual comment that he threshed his first homestead wheat with a flail and lived to see crop on the same land being recovered by means of a high-priced, self-propelled combine. It seemed to argue that the Agricultural Revolution witnessed in prairie Canada was in no way less unusual or important than the more widely heralded Industrial Revolution in Britain.

The first reapers, tracing their lineage from the Cyrus McCormick invention in 1831, did not reach Red River until a short time before the birth of the province of Manitoba in 1870. For the person whose operations were limited by the small acreage he could hope to harvest with scythe or cradle, the horse-drawn reaper that cut and left the crop in tidy bunches for hand binding, looked like a giant step forward, but there was already speculation about a reaper that would perform what some believed the impossible, to twist wire around each sheaf or bind with twine and actually tie a knot.

Wire which could be secured by a twist was relatively simple to use in machine binding and preceded twine by some years. But there was criticism from cattlemen who were afraid of injury to animals eating the straw and more objection from men operating threshing machines. It wasn't until 1877 that an American workman, J. F. Appleby, made a knotter which was good enough to be adopted by William Deering who hastened to incorporate it on his reaper and place a successful self-binder on the market.

The first sale of Manitoba wheat for shipment to Toronto in 1876 proved to be an incentive and according to the *Daily Free Press,* Winnipeg, there were by harvest season 1878, about "twenty self-binding harvesters. They are naturally objects of considerable curiosity wherever introduced. The other day, the

The threshing outfit of George Parkenson at Roland, Manitoba in autumn, 1897.

Jim Wyatt's binder being drawn by a four horse team whose total age was 129 years.

my duty to inform the public through your esteemed paper of the facts as they are. Now, I have used my binder two years and I have let my cattle run to the straw pile as usual and without any damage to the cattle, whatever. If my cattle ate any of the wire, it did them no harm. I have not lost a hoof this year and my cattle never looked better. . . . My candid opinion is that the statements that are made about cattle dying from eating wire and millers refusing to grind the wheat bound with wire are all false and are only used by unprincipled agents to sell their inferior machines."[8]

A year later, while binding with wire was still the

These binders were universally accepted at the time this picture was taken in 1907 on the J. G. Miller farm, Aylesbury, Saskatchewan.

agent of the McCormick machine, Mr. R. T. Haslam, drove a representative of the Free Press to Mr. R. Tait's in St. James to see one in operation. . . . As is generally understood, the binding is done with fine soft wire. The sheaves were all nice and shapely and strong enough for all purposes."[7]

One of those wire-using self-binders included in the editor's count was owned by the distinguished pioneer, Kenneth MacKenzie at Burnside, who, after hearing many expressions of fear and criticism about the dangers of wire in the straw, wrote to the editor to share a user's views: "There have been so many false statements made about my self-binder that I think it is

Breaking on the Falloon Brothers Farm, Foxwarren, Manitoba, 1907. (Photo courtesy of Mrs. Lillian Falloon)

most up-to-date method of harvesting, another Winnipeg reporter drove out "to Polson's farm near St. John's College" to see a Marsh self-binder at work, cutting and binding between twelve and fifteen acres of grain per day. "The wire used was 20 gauge, 20 pounds per reel."[9]

By 1883, twine binders equipped with those amazing inventions, knotters, were appearing on the market and binders using wire began to vanish. By 1884, Maj. William Bell of the big Qu'Appelle Valley Farming Company spread at Indian Head sent forty-five twine binders to cut in a single field and then compounded his mistake by ordering the teamsters and their 180 horses to stop to await a late train carrying English visitors who signified a wish to see a big wheat field at harvest time.

Perhaps the travelers had been reading John Macoun's new book, *Manitoba and the Great North-West*, published in 1882, and caught some of the author's enthusiasm for the wheat fields. The book, depicting the country as one of unlimited opportunity and himself as the great optimist challenging the relative pessimism of Palliser and Hind, was much in the public eye at that moment.

Born in Ireland and raised in Ontario, Macoun saw the West for the first time when he came as the botanist and naturalist with the Sandford Fleming party searching for a suitable route for the transcontinental railway in 1872. He was captivated from the first sight of the plains. As for the wheat potential, he wrote: "There is actually no limit but the want of a market." His reason for such confidence: "The soil is the best in the world."[10] Macoun made mistakes but his supreme optimism may have been just what the changing West needed at that time. Certainly, he was good for machine sales.

Farther west in the Territories, the reapers and binders were coming a little later. Both Regina and Edmonton were reporting self-binders in 1885, Lethbridge in 1887 and Battleford in 1888. The newspaper report from Regina told that: "On Monday last at Bayswater Farm we witnessed the working of two Toronto Light Binders — seven-foot cut — manufactured by the Massey Manufacturing Co. Mr. McCusker, local agent for the Company, started the machines and personally supervised the work during the afternoon. The draft of the machines was exceedingly light and the cutting and binding very neat and clean. Special mention may be made of the sheaf carrier which does its work to perfection."[11]

After reporting the delivery of one self-binder in 1885 and twelve in 1886, the *Edmonton Bulletin* credited one of the machines' with previously unrecognized adaptability, telling that: "The self-binder in J. Walter's field on Wednesday cut up and bound two pigs which formed part of the crop at that time."[12]

The self-binder reported from Lethbridge in 1887 was delivered to one of the well-known characters from frontier history, Dave Akers, and delivery was at notorious old Fort Whoop-Up, formerly the recognized capital of the whisky trade that drew the North West Mounted Police to that part in 1874. Officers of the main body of Mounties trekking westward in that year, anticipated a battle when they advanced upon the whisky stronghold on October 9 but were surprised to find the place abandoned except for Dave Akers and two Indian lady companions. Instead of being hostile, Akers was congenial and the police marched on to build Fort Macleod on the Oldman River, leaving Dave to enjoy his whisky trading memories of Fort Spitzie and Fort Whoop-Up and indulge in some farming. Now, like a reformed and respectable citizen, he was testing a Milwaukee Junior twine binder and bragging that it was running steadily since delivery "and has not even broken the binder twine."[13]

Perhaps the new binders coming to the Canadian market were indeed superior, as Dave Akers suggested. In any case, some were winning international honors, such as the first-prize award and gold medal gained by the Toronto Light binder built by the Massey Manufacturing Company of Toronto, at the Paris Exposition in 1889. Fifteen machines from North American and European manufacturers were entered and the winners were decided in field trials near Paris. "This," said the editor of the *Edmonton Bulletin*, "is a triumph for Canadian skill and enterprise."[14]

When Wilfrid Laurier's government came to power in 1896, binders and other machines were no longer novelties on the prairies. They were coming into the farming country by trainloads and farmers, complaining loudly about the injustice of import duties, were borrowing money and paying $155 for binders, $95 for shoe drills, $55 for mowers and $75 for wagons. As American and eastern manufacturers recognized, the western market for machinery was a bonanza.

The midwest, comprising Manitoba and the Territories, which produced 2,785,597 bushels of wheat, oats, and barley in 1881, yielded 29,551,078 bushels in 1891, and 43,252,664 bushels in 1901. The same area, with only 10,091 occupied farms by official count in 1881, had 31,815 in 1891 and 55,593 in 1901.[15] It could be presumed that all western farms in that latter year needed and owned binders and most of the occupants surveying their crops were wondering how they would find the necessary stookers to follow the binders.

At various times through the years, inventors and manufacturers produced mechanical stookers as attachments for binders. They had special appeal when farm help was in short supply during war years but the mechanical wonders were not sufficiently satisfactory to ensure their survival in farm practice. It required strong and able men to make good stooks with eight or ten sheaves in each. When the West had a big crop, there was simply not enough available manpower in the country to do the stooking and the railroads, in co-operation with governments, instituted the famous Harvesters' Excursions which brought thousands of easterners to the West and helped to overcome a recurring annual harvest problem.

Approximately 18,000 easterners came west on the excursions in 1901. The fare was low: ten dollars from any point east of Sault Ste Marie for the outward journey and eighteen dollars for the return journey. There was no sex discrimination because women were eligible but not many chose to join the uncertain adventure.[16] In most years, excursions would leave the East at six or more announced dates in late August and early September. The fact that the policy was continued for many years proved that it was useful. The announcement in 1920 said: "30,000 extra farm hands will be needed in Manitoba, Saskatchewan and Alberta to harvest the crop. . . . Low fares and high wages are the attraction. . . . Wages, it is expected, will be from $4.00 to $6.00 a day."[17]

Not all those who joined the excursions were useful in the West. Some couldn't handle the heavy sheaves; some didn't want to try, and some proved overly sensitive physiologically to western farm drinking water with high alkali content. But most of the harvesters were conscientious and some caught a vision of farming opportunity that brought them back, to stay.

Chapter 16

THRESHERS AND STEAMERS

Plowing, planting, cutting, binding, and stooking were important farm operations but were, in a sense, but operational steps leading, hopefully, to the season's grand climax of threshing. Even in the years of the flail, the crop could not be counted a success until it was threshed. But machine threshing changed the character of the harvest scene completely and dramatically, bringing longer working hours, more workers, and heavier toil while, strangely enough, adding immeasurably to the spell of enchantment. It was a fitting finale in the recovery of the golden grain.

It wasn't necessary for every grower to have his own threshing machine but as crop acreage became too much for flailing, the circumstances demanded that there be at least one threshing machine in every community — and then some practical means of furnishing the necessary pulley-power. Actually, Red River, Portage la Prairie, Prince Albert, and Fort Edmonton districts had small threshing machines, modeled after the 1786 invention of Scotland's Andrew Meikle, before they had self-binders.

At first, these threshers were driven with power generated by horses hitched to the long radial arms of sweeps or horsepowers, and later with power transmitted from the same horses or oxen through the more compact but no less brutal treadmills. Power units of both forms were used at Red River for many years to furnish the drive for gristmills as well as threshing machines.

The first piece of machinery to confuse and challenge the Selkirk settlers was a windmill. Those who ordered its shipment from London to York Factory meant well because the settlers would need something better than horses and oxen for grinding grain and driving various mills, and nothing seemed more logical than harnessing the abundant wind of the

prairie country. Some people 150 years later were still arguing in support of a non-depleting, non-polluting source of power, like wind.

But because of its weight and awkwardness, the windmill sent from London remained unassembled at York Factory for several years and George Simpson did not hide his impatience when he wrote, in 1821, that the "iron mill" was likely to remain unused unless and until some person with mechanical skills was sent from England to put it together. Not very hopefully, he advised that the machine be returned to England and two years later repeated the recommendation because the mill was "eating itself up in rust."[1]

Company officials in London were reluctant about taking the retrograde step of bringing the mill back and arranged finally to have it forwarded to Red River, there to be made operational by an alleged expert, Mitchell by name, being sent the great distance from England expressly for the purpose. But the mill seemed to be a jinx and Simpson in 1824 showed further exasperation, doubting if Mitchell knew any more than the crofter settlers about windmills. Simpson put the man to work at the construction of a corn mill "to be wrought by oxen or horses," presumably one of the horsepower or sweep type.

Of the sweep which required the draft animals to pull constantly in a circle, and the treadmill with which the horses or oxen were obliged to climb continuously in order to use their weight to drive the gears or pulleys, the latter was considered the more efficient; in other words, two tons of horseflesh in motion on the treadmill would yield more thrust at the pulley than an equal weight of horses working at a sweep. But both demanded heavy work from the animals. Oxen were commonly excused from the

A pioneer steam threshing outfit before self-feeders and wind blowers were adopted in the separators, about 1890. (Manitoba Archives.)

A heavy steam engine breaking prairie sod with a twelve furrow plow.

An early threshing scene.

Threshing on Alex MacEwan's farm in 1899. Alex, father of Grant MacEwan, stands fourth from the left. The separator was the biggest made at that time and was equipped with the first feeder and blower seen in the area.

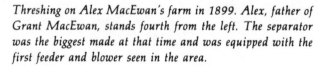

A threshing outfit pulling away to a new setting on the Myrick farm at Davidson, 1907.

sweeps because of a prevailing belief that traveling in a circle made them dizzy.

Fort Edmonton had a thresher driven by one of the long-armed horsepowers at least as early as 1866 when mention of it was made in the Fort Edmonton journal,[2] and it is supposed that Red River, with a somewhat more mature state of agriculture, had one at least that early. At whatever time the first one came to Edmonton, it would have been subject to the long delivery journey from St. Paul, Minnesota, by trail unless it came after the first trip of the riverboat *Anson Northrup*, which initiated the new service in 1859. In any case, the concluding thousand miles to destination would be by cart on that lifeline trail ending at Fort Edmonton.

Hon. David Laird who was the first resident lieutenant-governor in the North-West Territories demonstrated a practical bent when in 1878 — the year in which Battleford became the Territorial capital — he ordered a thresher and horsepower sweep to be brought to that place. The extent of its use is not known.

Steam engines were later in the prairie region although they were already making history in Britain, having been advanced by the inventiveness of James Watt whose successes contributed much to the Industrial Revolution, also by England's Richard Trevithick who showed how a steam engine could be used to move itself on rails, and George and Robert Stephenson — father and son — who in 1829 built the famous Rocket which startled the English residents with a speed of thirteen and one-half miles an hour.

In the Canadian Northwest there were stationary steam engines capable of driving threshers for some years before the first tractors appeared. They, like the first threshing machines, were hauled from St. Paul, mainly to replace the horsepowers in driving threshing machines. Manitoba's first was in 1874, judging from a

news item written on the day after the North West Mounted Police departed from Fort Dufferin to make the historic trek across the plains to build near the mountains: "The first steam thresher in the province is now in the warehouse," the Winnipeg newspaper reported. "It was imported by L. R. Bentley for Farquhar McLean, Portage la Prairie."[3] (The purchaser, although a well-known personality at the Portage, was not a member of the John McLean family.)

Again, the pioneer press left a valuable indication of the rate at which these mechanical wonders were being introduced in western settlements. A Moose Jaw editor could announce in 1881 that "the first steam thresher for the Moose Jaw district arrived on Monday. It was purchased by Battell Bros. . . ."[4] After four more years, it was reported by the Edmonton press that: "There are three steam threshers in the district this season — Bradshaw and Brunette, Lamoureau Bros., and finally, the Colonization Company's machine."[5] The same Edmonton editor recorded the threshing rates in effect at that time as one bushel of

A Case steamer breaking prairie sod.

"Off to the Elevator" — a four-horse team pulling one hundred bushels of wheat from the machine at Dundurn, 1908.

grain to the thresherman for every twelve bushels threshed, or seven and one-half cents a bushel. One of the steam outfits mentioned by the Edmonton editor, namely the one owned by Lamoureau Brothers, was said to have threshed 26,000 bushels of grain in that single season.

Still another report of a "first steam threshing outfit" appeared in the Lethbridge press in 1889 and referred to machines brought in for use in the progressive Mormon settlement at Lee's Creek at Cardston. The account gave indication of the current changes and improvements, stating that: "The first steam thresher for this district arrived here [Lethbridge] last night for Mr. C. O. Card of Lee's Creek. It is a New Model from Joseph Hall Manufacturing Co., Oshawa. . . . The machine is complete, having a 12-horsepower engine and the latest improvements including a stacker and grain bagger."[6]

Those stationary steam engines were seen as things of danger as well as wonder and the possibility of a boiler exploding was ever in the public mind, but for people with a compassionate feeling for over-

worked horses and oxen, they were like something sent by a benevolent Creator. They came on wagon wheels that looked too flimsy for the weight and were commonly moved by a two-horse team. When an engine had to be aligned to a threshing machine pulley, the awkwardness of the load was instantly clear, especially when the heavy thing was required to be moved backward with horses harnessed without the back-up breechings.

But the stationary steamer was only the forerunner of massive engines with the spectacular ability to move themselves and much more. The first in the North American region were made in the United States about 1855 and J. I. Case had some of them ready for the market in 1876. Over a hundred were sold in that year.

At once there were bigger threshers — very much bigger. The result gave evidence of both evolution and revolution. The farm worker using a scythe or cradle just a few decades earlier would have done well to cut and bind by hand the crop on an acre in a day. Then, with one of the earliest reapers hauled by a single horse, he could cut six or seven acres in the same time while a second man walked alongside to pull the cut grain from the platform as often as enough had accumulated for a sheaf to be tied later with its own straw. The same worker could achieve still more with the improved reaper fitted with a mechanical arm that

The world's first practical track-type tractor originated in 1904 when Benjamin Holt equipped his steam tractor with tracks instead of wheels.

would draw the cut grain off the platform without human intervention. The binder and the small threshing machine elevated him to a position of mastery and now, with the huge steam tractors and correspondingly big threshers, the man who so recently had been cutting with a cradle and threshing with a flail found himself part of a coordinated threshing crew clearing up to seventy-five or eighty acres in a day.

It was not to be overlooked that these steam engines which could propel themselves with their own steam were also able to perform various other services, including plowing, and the Regina newspaper, in the summer of 1883, made the claim that: "The first steam plow for this country arrived here on Monday. . . . The plow is built on the most improved principles and is supplied with 8 oscillating plows."[7]

The trend was unmistakably toward bigger machines and more improvements like self-feeders and baggers, also to higher costs.

One of the editors of 1889 told of the test of a band-cutter and self-feeder at Portage la Prairie, apparently as a May 24 attraction: "The band-cutter and self-feeder were attached to the . . . J. I. Case separator; a load of oats was placed on each side and as fast as two men could pitch the sheaves into it, it cut the bands and fed the grain into the [cylinder] — never a more severe test."[8] The writer was correct in his conclusion that the "band-cutter and self-feeder will certainly revolutionize the threshing trade," but not all the pioneer self-feeders worked as well as this one.

The threshing outfit bought by Alex MacEwan of Chater in 1898 was described as the biggest and most modern in western Manitoba, and cost him almost $4,000. In the opinion of one admiring spectator, it was the most spectacular "leap forward" to that date for Manitoba agriculture. The tractor was a Minneapolis of the return flue type with smoke funnel at the rear rather than at the forward end. Weighing about fifteen tons, it was enough to break nearly every bridge in the district, including the 18th Street Bridge across the Assiniboine at Brandon.

The 44-inch separator that accompanied came equipped with two of the most modern labor saving devices, self-feeder and wind-stacker. It was thus a combination of three machines, the basic threshing cylinder with teeth to beat out the grain, a winnowing machine to remove chaff and straw from the grain and, finally, the wind-stacker which left the mountain-like stacks of straw which were so commonly set afire as soon as the threshing outfit drew away. The stacker worked well but not the self-feeder, which gave trouble from the beginning and was finally removed to allow the owner to revert to hand feeding for the remainder of the first year.

When that MacEwan outfit moved about the country north of Brandon for custom threshing, the accompanying crew numbered thirty men. Eight teams hauled sheaves and two men remained constantly with each wagon. Two men worked as field pitchers, and after the self-feeder was removed, a total of eight men were kept busy at the feeder end of the machine, namely, the four occupants of the two bundle wagons that happened to be unloading, plus two men cutting bands and two more feeding the loose sheaves into the cylinder. Other workers who might classify as specialists included the highly paid engineer who held a certificate and collected $5.00 a day when ordinary teamsters received $2.50, the fireman who fed straw into the engine's firebox from five o'clock, A.M. until close to sunset, the waterman or tankman, the strawman or fuel teamster, the separator specialist who spent much of his time lacing belts and squirting lubricant into mysterious oil holes and, finally, the often distraught owner who, as general coordinator, tried to keep the men contented and the machine in motion.

The MacEwan outfit in the first autumn threshed for sixty days and served twenty-one Manitoba farmers. Threshing rates in that year were 5½ cents a bushel for stook threshing and 3 cents a bushel for stack threshing. The big machine was known to have threshed a thousand bushels of wheat in three hours on one occasion when members of the crew took strong exception to the dirty kitchen and unpalatable bachelor meals of the farmer they were serving. They gladly worked harder to escape the necessity of having to eat another meal at his place. The kitchen and the cooking must have been bad indeed.

Chapter 17

A DECADE OF DECISION, 1900-1910

The twentieth century began bravely. Gone were the fears and suspicions inherited from the fur trade that soil and climate were adverse for agriculture. Now, having passed the first practical tests imposed by the homestead years, farming was assuming a character of permanency and looking for appropriate direction and policies. What ensued was a decade of decision.

The census of 1901 showed Manitoba and the Territories with almost twice as much population as in 1891 and an additional 23,770 farms. Immigration was still rising like the morning sun and prospective homesteaders were being assured that free land was still abundant and shortage of capital did not need to be an obstacle in taking it. Single men coming to homestead, according to published advice, could get along with capital of $250 while married men should have a little more, say from $250 to $500.[1]

The Barr Colonists coming to the Lloydminster area in 1903 were the most conspicuous of the newcomers although the biggest influx at that period was from the south. Thousands were coming from the western parts of the United States, some of them, like Dr. Thomas Hays, Charles S. Noble, Henry Wise Wood, Christian Jensen, and Benjamin Plumer to distinguish themselves in leadership and service.

It went without saying that the face of the agricultural West was changing. The biggest change was in ranching which had hurriedly moved in to fill the void left by the departing buffalo herds. Now, having fully recovered from the killing winter of 1886-87, ranchers had accepted the necessity of living without open range. Gone were the general roundups. With barbed wire enclosing the ranges, cattle owners could exercise better control of herds — and better care in winter. Only with herd control could they hope

to achieve the improvement which could be expected from the use of superior sires. It did not mean that the rancher's worries were over. One of his latest concerns was the insidious parasitic disorder, mange, for which there appeared to be no relief except by a long and costly program of dipping.

Ranch land, of course, had a new generation of personalities. Those who drove their founding herds over the trails from Montana and Idaho were absent. Tom Lynch, the acknowledged "King of the Cattle Trails," died in 1891. The ranchers who were to become known as Canada's "Big Four Cattlemen" were now gaining prominence, George Lane and A. E. Cross in the foothills, Archie McLean on the plains, and Pat Burns in various areas. George Lane's "star" was rising rapidly, especially after 1902 when he, in partnership with Gordon, Ironside and Fares, bought the big Bar U spread with its 8,000 cattle and 500 horses, paying almost a quarter of a million dollars for it. That was fine until the misfortune of another tragic winter struck in 1906-7 and George Lane who had 24,000 cattle and calves in the autumn counted only 12,000 in the spring. It was enough to break lesser men but again George Lane was one of those who survived and prospered, ultimately becoming the sole owner of the Bar U Ranch with its good cattle and the biggest band of purebred Percheron horses on the continent or in the world.

But it was Pat Burns, the young Irish Canadian from Kirkfield, Ontario, who walked in advance of railroads from Winnipeg to file on a homestead at Minnedosa in 1878 and then after making his way to the foothills and fame with beef contracts, was now

Right: *The Big Four Cattlemen who backed the first Calgary Stampede in 1912. (Glenbow Institute.)*

emerging as the West's most influential force in both production and processing of meat animals. As the old century was greeting the new one, Burns was opening western Canada's most modern abattoir at Calgary and, at the same time, feeding about 10,000 cattle, mainly three-year-old and four-year-old steers. With unusual talent for finding markets, Burns was at this time taking his meat trade to distant parts of the prairies, remote mining communities in the British Columbia interior, and even the far-northern Klondike Goldfields.

Editors were pleased to pay tribute. One said: "Pat Burns, the Calgary Cattle King, is in town. A few years ago he was chasing his only steer across the plains. Today he controls the meat market of British Columbia."[2] Another said: "He is the Armour of this part of the world and is sometimes called the Cattle King of the British Northwest. Last year he shipped 3,500 carloads of beeves and he has now about 20,000 head in his yards. At the beginning of the Klondike gold

The Federal Government Tree Nursery at Indian Head was the source of millions of young trees used for prairie shelter-belts.

discovery, he got as much as a dollar a pound [for beef] on the hoof at Dawson."[3]

The marketing of prairie beef at faraway Dawson City was a feat for which Burns and his helpers were to be remembered, especially by appreciative men and women of the agricultural fraternity. Gold was discovered on Bonanza Creek late in 1896 and as soon as the news reached the outside, the rush began. An estimated 40,000 hopeful miners, and others whose purpose was to "mine the miners," went over the passes and negotiated the other dangers of the route in the next two or three years.

Burns may have been the first to sense market opportunity at Dawson and late in 1897 he sent William Purdue into the North with a small herd of mature oxen, animals selected to carry their own feed over winter trails. Purdue went through but before he was back to report his adventure, Burns was arranging with Billy Henry, Scottish immigrant at High River, to take a bigger herd to Dawson. One hundred and eighty heavy steers, four and five years of age, and twenty-two saddle horses were loaded at Cayley in June and Henry and eight other attendants were on their way. At Vancouver, the cattle were transferred from freight cars to 1,200-ton scows to be pulled north by a tugboat, the *Mystery*.

The ocean journey terminated at Skagway where the herd was unloaded for the long drive beginning with the Chilkat Pass and then onto the so-called Dalton Trail. Henry and his men drove for more than four months until they were near the mouth of the Pelly River where the mountains came almost to the river's edge to cut off further travel. The summer days had now passed and Henry, knowing the Lewes River might freeze over very soon, called a halt, to slaughter and make rafts. After almost 500 miles of overland travel from Skagway, Henry hoped to complete the journey by river. While half of Henry's crew was making rafts measuring 72 feet by 32 feet, the other half was slaughtering and piling the carcasses on the floating structures.

The river trip was estimated to be 150 miles and dangers and risks remained. There was still some fast water and as days and nights grew colder, there was the greater risk of the rafts being caught in river ice. But good luck traveled with the party and the cargo reached Dawson close to the end of October, just a few days before the ice ended all further navigation for the year and caught some rafts that were still upstream.

Having sold his beef, most of it to the North West Mounted Police at seventy-five cents a pound — and hides for dog feed at fifty cents a pound — Henry began the long walk of some 500 miles back to Skagway. He reached Calgary in February, to find Pat Burns assembling another herd for the profitable northern trade. This next trip for Henry was quite different; being a winter trip, he took sleighs on which to carry supplies, equipment, and feed for the cattle. It was a hard journey through the deep snows but with the big steers hauling the sleighs, Henry reached the destination, this time Atlin, with all his cattle charges. Of the animals, he said: "They were just common critters but they were as valuable as champions when we got them to Atlin."

A few other western Canadian cattlemen took herds over the forbidding northern trails from Skagway at the time of the gold rush madness, among them: Ed Fearon of Maple Creek; the Tuxfords and their brother-in-law, James Thomson, of Moose Jaw; Burchill and Howie of Brandon, and F. O. Sissons of Medicine Hat. Norman Lee of Hanceville, deep in the British Columbia interior, attempted a drive directly overland from his ranch but after driving for four months encountered misfortune and lost the beef and his months of work. But with either success or failure, the courage and fiber of the men who attempted such drives deserved the highest praise of those who attempt to capture the story of those years in western agriculture. Billy Henry, the last of the noble band, died at High River in 1972, age 105 years.

Calgary's annual Bull Sale which became a range-land classic, had its beginning at the same point in agricultural history, 1901. Presented under the auspices of the Territorial Pure Bred Cattle Breeders' Association, sixty-four cattle were offered by auction at the Frontier Stable. As an additional inducement to buy and use purebred bulls, the department of agriculture and the CPR were offering purchasers free delivery to any railroad station in the Northwest. It was still less than enough to induce extravagance on the part of buyers; the highest price of the sale was $250 and the average for purebred bulls was $85.17.

Planting trees was not like driving cattle over sub-Arctic trails but it was nevertheless an important feature of the decade. Moreover, nothing symbolized the new spirit of faith so well as the federal government's tree-planting policy which took form under Norman Ross who was working out of Indian Head at that time. William Saunders, who is remembered as the author of Canada's Experimental Farm system, was the first with a resolve to do something about the treelessness of the western prairies. First he would work to overcome the view that trees could never be grown successfully on prairie farms and then initiate a tree distribution from the experimental farms to private farms.

Ross, a Scot with an abiding love for trees and Shorthorn cattle, came to Indian Head in 1901 as the very man to carry out the Saunders ideas. In the next year, he was able to furnish seedling trees for 421 western farmers and then he made a request for a permanent tree nursery. The government responded with a quarter section of raw land south of Indian Head. The ground was broken and cultivated in the next year and became the principal source of the 400 million young trees distributed to change the face of the farming country in the next seventy-five years. Four hundred million trees planted three feet apart would have provided a single row long enough to encircle the earth eight times, or an eight-row belt to go all the way around the world once. In more practical terms it meant that every farmer had an opportunity to plant a shelterbelt or windbreak and many did, to enhance their own property and enrich the community.

That Decade of Decision did not see the first efforts in western farm organization but it did see some of the best and most lasting, notably in late 1901. Earlier attempts were made to bring western farmers together but not with much success. The American farm organization known as the Grange had a short existence in Manitoba, then the Manitoba and Northwest Farmers' Union which was started in 1883, the Farmers' Alliance promoted about 1891, the Patrons of Industry about the same time, and then the Grain Growers' Association of the Territories launched at Indian Head on December 18, 1901.

The Manitoba Grain Act passed by the government of Canada had a good purpose but was being abused. It was supposed to ensure a proper distribution of freight cars and uphold the farmer's right to load his grain directly from railroad platforms to cars and thus escape the alleged elevator monopoly. To guarantee fair treatment, car order books were supposed to be maintained. But in spite of the Manitoba Act, the car shortage of 1901 brought numerous complaints from farmers. Homesteader W. R. Motherwell and his neighbor, Peter Dayman, resolved to do something about it.

They were aware of a meeting being announced for Indian Head on December 18, 1901, at which Premier Rodmond Roblin of Manitoba and Premier Frederick Haultain of the Territories were scheduled to debate a Manitoba proposal to annex a portion of Territorial land. Motherwell knew that farmers from a large area would attend the afternoon meeting and believed many of them would be glad to remain for an evening meeting if they knew about it. He was right. The meeting was a big one and farmers were angry about the apparent disregard for the terms of the Manitoba Act. Before the meeting ended, the Territorial Grain Growers' Association was formed, with Motherwell as the provisional president.

Roderick McKenzie, Brandon, was director of the U.G.G. from 1909 to 1921. He was also the first secretary of the Manitoba Grain Growers Association.

The new organization, forerunner of the Provincial Grain Growers' Associations of Manitoba, Saskatchewan, and Alberta, received its first major challenge almost immediately and laid a charge against one of the CPR agents for failing to distribute freight cars according to the rules laid down in the Manitoba Grain Act. It would be a test case, to be held at Sintaluta and nobody expected the farmers to win. But they did win and the railway company was fined. The company appealed and lost the appeal, making it a convincing victory for the farm organization.

The grain growers' movement grew and in 1906, with A. E. Partridge as the moving spirit, the Grain Growers' Grain Company was formed to handle grain and took a seat on the Winnipeg Grain Exchange, much to the displeasure of other exchange memberships. The farm organization was evicted and then re-admitted. Meanwhile, the Growers' membership soared and led to an adventure in provincial government ownership of elevators in Manitoba, the promotion of the Co-operative Elevator Company in Saskatchewan, and the United Farmers of Alberta in the Foothills Province. As the years demonstrated, farm organization was another feature of the decade, especially when there was recognition of the various provincial livestock associations which were formed after Saskatchewan and Alberta became provinces in 1905. In the first-named province, for example, the Saskatchewan Stock Breeders' Association was organized with representatives from the breeders of cattle, horses, sheep, and pigs, in 1905, and four years later, the Saskatchewan cattle breeders, horse breeders, swine breeders and sheep breeders were set up as separate associations.

It was further evidence of maturity in the industry when decisions were being made at this time for the provision of specialized agricultural education. Ontario started an agricultural college in 1874, choosing a site at Guelph after rejecting one at Mimico because it was too close to a big and evil city like Toronto. Guelph, known for its "strong moral and religious tendencies," would offer a better atmosphere for young men from the farms. The first class, consisting of thirty-one students, was welcomed with free tuition, free board and room, free laundry, and a reward of fifty dollars for every student passing the examinations. One catch was a requirement of seven hours of practical work daily on the college farm. This did not mean a seven-hour day but rather, seven hours of hard work over and above the normal college day.

The first proposal to start an agricultural college in the West was in the eighties when Major Bell of the big Bell Farm at Indian Head advanced a plan. But the first agricultural course of consequence was offered by Wesley College in Winnipeg in 1902. It was for

W. J. Rutherford, first Dean of Agriculture at the University of Saskatchewan, became one of the best judges of heavy horses on the continent.

Hugh Sutherland, ex-M.P. from Winnipeg, was the leading promoter of the H. B. railway, started in 1910.

farmers and farmers' sons and the total anticipated cost was $100 for the winter session.

The Manitoba government in 1903 named a commission to inquire into the need for a provincial college and when the resulting report favored such an institution, the legislature voted $75,000 for the purchase of land. The chosen site was one of 117 acres of riverlots on the south side of the Assiniboine River. There, on what was known later as the Tuxedo Site, the Manitoba Agricultural College was built to follow the Ontario pattern of complete separation from the university, in 1906. W. J. Black was named as principal,[4] and the first course offered was to extend over two winter seasons and lead to Diplomas in Agriculture. Eighty-four pupils registered, each one making payment of $13.00, of which $5.00 were for tuition, $5.00 for contingencies and $3.00 for room and board for the first week. Before the end of the first two years, students were asking for extended courses leading to a university degree, Bachelor of Science in Agriculture. This was arranged and the first graduates received their BSA degrees from the University of Manitoba in 1911.

The distinction of being the first student to register at the college and thus the first to enroll in a university-recognized program of studies in agriculture in western Canada went to a young man from Carman, Thomas J. Harrison, later professor Harrison. And in the spring of 1911 when ten students qualified for degrees in agriculture, the first candidate over the platform and hence the first in western Canada was F. Walter Crawford, later comptroller of the University of Manitoba.

Of the ten members of that first graduating class, C. G. Partridge, J. C. Smith and H. M. Thompson lost their lives in the First World War. The others gained distinction in agricultural service, Ward Jones as superintendent of agriculture for the CPR; A. J. McMillan as a deputy minister of agriculture in Manitoba; J. C. Noble with the Dominion seed branch; J. C. Smith as livestock commissioner in Saskatchewan before going overseas; W. W. Thompson in the Canadian Co-operative Wool Growers, and M. J. Tinline as superintendent of the Brandon Experimental Farm.

Saskatchewan was the next province to provide for agricultural education and under the wise leadership of the first president of the University of Saskatchewan, Dr. Walter C. Murray, the province broke with tradition and brought the Agricultural College to occupy a place at the very heart of the university, beside the College of Arts and Science. Presided over by Dean W. J. Rutherford, the Saskatchewan college offered two courses, the degree course leading to the BSA and the associate course leading to the Diploma in Agriculture.

And following closely upon Saskatchewan, Alberta offered diploma courses at three schools of agriculture administered by the department of agriculture, at Olds, Vermilion, and Claresholm, beginning in 1913; two years later, the degree course integrated with the university, was started under the deanship of E. A. Howe.

If questions were asked about the leading agricultural triumphs in the decade in question, somebody among the pioneers would mention the Dominion

A gasoline engine, the newest caterpillar tractor, in 1908.

government's long-awaited promise to build a railway to the shores of Hudson Bay. Western farmers, handicapped by distance from world markets and the high cost of rail transportation, knew that a rail connection to a Hudson Bay port would make the distance from Saskatoon to Liverpool a thousand miles shorter than via Montreal. They knew that the northern water route had been used successfully by the Hudson's Bay Company for 200 years and even though the shipping season was relatively short, there was no reason why a railroad to the salt water would not lead to great economies. Almost every agricultural convention for years heard a resolution praying the government to build the railroad but the pleas seemed to fall upon deaf ears until western people talked about building the railroad themselves. But when a general election was called in 1908 and Prime Minister Wilfrid Laurier was campaigning for re-election of his Liberal government, he made the promise while speaking at Niagara Falls on September 18. "This railway is a necessity," he conceded. "The Government will build the railway."[5]

The sod-turning was in 1910 and progress was moderately good until World War I when all work was suspended. Nobody quarreled with the suspension but the long delay in resuming construction after the war brought loud complaint; the rails did not reach the Port of Churchill until 1929. The volume of shipping over the route was not as great as was expected but western farmers retained their confidence in the potential of the northern route and were sure the day

Gasoline tractors were challenging steam tractors in 1912. This one appeared at the Winnipeg tractor tests that year.

would come when the short cut to Liverpool would prove its great value to the western growers.

In at least one farm area there was no decision. In the matter of farm power, the conflicts were intensified rather than resolved. The horsemen lost none of their confidence; manufacturers were making steam tractors bigger and managing to sell them, and the noisy gasoline tractors were threatening as never before. Only the sweeps with their ever-winding motion and the treadmills like endless escalators were becoming obsolete. Further changes were coming but what would they be? The steam tractors, like the ancient dinosaurs, had to become bigger before they disappeared.

In the meantime there were strange developments in California where the mechanical monsters known as combined harvester-threshers or traveling threshers had caught the agricultural imagination. There, two inventive and industrial giants, Charles Holt and Daniel Best, seemed to be competing to build the biggest. When Best fielded a combine drawn by a steam tractor, replacing seventy-five mules, Holt came out with a combine said to have a fifty-foot cut. By 1904, the first combines were being fitted with auxiliary engines; by 1906 Holt was using a crawler-type tractor to haul the combine and by 1911, he was building the first self-propelled machine.

A combined harvester-thresher which may have been the first in western Canada was brought to Saskatchewan in either 1909 or 1910 to the order of C. P. J. Shand and Harry Edmonds of Spy Hill.[6&7] It was one of Holt manufacture cutting a twelve-foot swath, powered by a huge bull wheel and pulled by a 30-60 Hart-Parr gasoline tractor. Another combine appeared at Spy Hill about the same time and one at Aneroid — said to have been home made — in 1913, but more years would pass before such things would be widely accepted by prairie farmers. In the meantime, still bigger tractors and threshers were being introduced. Again, the California manufacturers, Holt and Best, led in the production of massive tractors. Holt's steam tractor No. 88, made in 1903, was equipped with drive wheels seven feet, six inches in diameter, each of them six feet wide and three on each side. With these six big drive wheels, the tractor had a total width of forty-five feet, eight inches. It is difficult to imagine why anybody would have wanted anything as big and cumbersome.

When it was no longer practical to make bigger threshing machines, George Lane, of Bar U Ranch fame, bought the biggest steam tractor available in England — one with upright cylinders — to be delivered at his grain farm at Champion. After furnishing it with two pulleys, he used it to drive two big threshers placed side by side. With this placement it was not possible for more than two of the ten stook

wagons to unload at the same time but Lane had four spike pitchers in addition to the two teamsters feeding into the twin machines, three pitching to each separator. The net advantages were doubtful although one saving was effected by having the separator man supervise two machines instead of one. Only Charles Noble adopted the idea and tried it for a few years.

Not far away, Ray Knight hit upon an equally novel plan, that of plowing with two big stationary steam engines fitted with cables. Perhaps the purpose was inspired by his interest in growing sugar beets and his wish for deep cultivation. The furrows were cut about twelve inches deep and the technique proved workable but not very practical.

Every steam tractor was heavy and demanding. A Case 110, a favorite for operations in big farm fields, hauled twelve plows in sod and weighed 38,000. Needless to say, it did not get along very well on soft ground. When plowing it required an engineer, a fireman, plowman, waterman, fuelman, and cook. Thus, even when burning straw or wood, its operational costs were high and it wasn't much wonder that neighbors were cynical, saying that "the surest way of going broke was for a farmer to buy a racehorse, a studhorse or a steam tractor."

Steam plowing outfits were for operators with big fields and ample turning space, like Charles Noble when he sent ten steamers to break land on his Cameron Ranch in 1918 and had them working around the clock, breaking 400 acres of new ground every twenty-four hours. It required about 100 men to run and service such a fleet of steamers.

The steamer of that day could turn over a lot of land in a day but it was at its best for threshing. Its power was steady, quiet and captivating for all except the farm wife who had the responsibility for feeding

Small gasoline tractor units were bidding for popularity by 1914. Shown here is a one cylinder, two plow tractor bought in that year.

The Rumely Oil Pull tractor was highly regarded at the time this picture was taken at the Winnipeg Tractor Tests of 1912.

the big crew of hungry men, whether the weather was fit for threshing or not.

Steam tractors might be in decline by the end of the decade but more makes were coming on the market while gasoline tractors, with internal combustion engines making a noise like thunder, were looking for buyers. Confused farmers wondered whom among the salesmen to believe. If there was an argument about the merits of two horses, the dispute could be resolved in the showring. Why not subject these new tractor things to a showring test? Directors of the Winnipeg Exhibition were the first to get the idea and in staging the Winnipeg Light Agricultural Motor Competition of 1908, they were not only offering a useful public service but were bringing to their city and show the distinction of presenting the first event of its kind in the world. Here was an opportunity for manufacturers to display their tractors if they were worth displaying, and a chance for prospective farm purchasers to see machines working side by side and on score-card tests.

Nine tractors were entered and seven appeared at the testing ground where they were required to haul loads and plow the tough gumbo sod. There were delays, breakdowns and embarrassment for the company representatives; and then the third day turned

wet and the heavy things floundered helplessly, necessitating a postponement, but finally, all the contestants were in the field and plowing was under test. Three tractors experienced further breakdowns. Two of them returned to the field; one did not. It was like a re-enactment of the biological law, "Survival of the Fittest," but the spectators loved it.

When scores were tallied, the gold medal was awarded to the Kinnard-Haines tractor, a 30-horsepower, 4-cylinder monster weighing 13,530 pounds, from Minneapolis, the biggest in the contest. It had pulled a 6-furrow plow, turned 3.2 acres in the time allotted and consumed 20 pints of gasoline per acre, leading to an aggregate score of 117.6 points. The silver medal went to a 9,920-pound entry from the International Harvester Company, with a score of 117 points. It meant that the heaviest tractor won the competition and the lightest one was second, which tended to confuse the farming people looking for some relationship between weight and efficiency. The third-prize winner was the Marshall Sons and Company entry from England, a 2-cylinder tractor weighing 10,680 pounds and the only one in the contest burning kerosene.

Prices, which had to be declared, showed the gold medal winner at $2,270, the silver medal winner at $1,800 and the English tractor at $2,700, all f.o.b. Winnipeg.

It wasn't a big show but it was the world's first and won praise from as far as the United States department of agriculture and Winnipegers were so gratified that they made plans for a bigger event in 1909, calling it the Farm Motor Competition of the World. And in that second year there were indeed more entries, steam as well as gasoline. The prize list announced three classes for gasoline tractors and one for steam. Of the twenty-two kinds of tractors entered, only five were steamers, and with no weight restrictions, the range was from 40,860 pounds for the heaviest steamer to 5,000 pounds for the lightest gasoline tractor, and strangely enough both carried the same maker's name, Avery.

Variation in type would have been evident on every hand. Gasoline tractors were present with 1-cylinder, 2-cylinder, 3-cylinder and 4-cylinder motors and traveling speeds ranged from 1½ miles per hour to 15 miles per hour. Likewise, prices ranged from $1,700 to exactly double, $3,400, for the 60-horsepower Marshall Sons English tractor.

For the gasoline and kerosene-burning tractors, the International Harvester Company qualified for the highest awards. The company's gold medal winner in the intermediate weight class was a 1-cylinder, 20-horsepower unit pulling 3 plows and plowing 1.09 acres in 75½ minutes on a consumption of 1½ gallons of gasoline per acre. And its price was $1,700 at Winnipeg.

Among the steamers for which there was still evidence of loyalty, the 120-horsepower Rumely was not the winner but caught much attention when plowing 4.23 acres in 75 minutes on fuel consumption of 580 pounds of coal. The top-scoring steamer was a Case rated at 110 horsepower and plowing 3.6 acres in 62 minutes on 442 pounds of coal.

Tractor competitions were adopted also at the Brandon exhibition but the founding glory belonged to Winnipeg where they were continued until 1914 when it was announced that the annual exhibitions were being discontinued. By that time, the big steamers were definitely in decline. More gasoline tractors were being sold and the new interest was in smaller units. The day of big tractors was passing but they had served two purposes, first in improving the effectiveness of farm workers and, second, in helping to convert thousands of immigrant farmers from inherited ideas of peasant farming. By exposure to bigger machines and obedient new power, no western farmer remained satisfied with a subsistence type of operation.

Chapter 18

NEW WHEATS FOR PRAIRIE GROWERS

Western agriculture advanced through the first decade of the new century like a conquering warrior. Wheat production soared from 63 million bushels in 1901 to exceed 100 millions in 1906 and 300 millions in 1911. The victories were not all on the wheat front, but the one that was to make the biggest and most lasting contributions to the future of agriculture and the country was the production of a new wheat, one destined to extend the wheat belt, improve farm security, and become a hallmark of quality around the world. The new wheat was Marquis and its creators were members of the Saunders family, Dr. William Saunders and his two sons, Charles E. and Arthur Percy.

Red Fife, tracing to seed that caught in a Scotsman's hat at Glasgow, was the dominant variety in the West since 1876. As everybody agreed, it had much in its favor and brought credit to itself and the prairies. It was a plump-berried, high-yielding, red spring wheat with unsurpassed milling and baking qualities, but it had one serious shortcoming: it was relatively late in maturing and was caught rather often by early fall frosts. Nearly every farmer knew the bitter experience of seeing an otherwise promising crop reduced to a miserable yield of shrunken grain from a single exposure to an early September frost.

Western farmers knew what they needed and prayed for a wheat with yield and milling qualities of Red Fife but that was a week or ten days earlier in maturing. Fortunately, the only Canadian in a position to do something about it heard the prayer. "Old William," as the elder Saunders was known, was a London druggist with an overriding interest in plants and animals. The Saunders family moved to a farm outside London, where he could practice his hobby of plant breeding. His earliest crosses were made with gooseberries in 1868 and he followed with apples and other fruits to obtain hardy varieties.

In 1886, Saunders became the first director of the Dominion Experimental Farm system and was soon aware of the western need for earlier wheats as well as fruits. He introduced new kinds from overseas and put them to tests and was impressed by a Russian wheat, Ladoga, which was ten days earlier than Red Fife and about equal in yield ability. What was not immediately evident was that Ladoga did not measure up to Canadian standards for milling and had to be discarded. Saunders then concluded that the best hope for success was in crossing Red Fife with selected early varieties. The first crosses were made at Ottawa in 1888. By this time, "Old William" had taught his sons, Charles and Percy, to conduct hybridizing and they were eager helpers.

Percy Saunders, in 1892, visited the three western experimental farms, Brandon, Indian Head, and Agassiz, and did some cross-pollination of wheats at each place. As a result of crosses between Red or White Fife and Ladoga, several named varieties were born, among them, Preston, Stanley, Huron, and Percy. But these new kinds were not entirely satisfactory and with growing demands upon the time of Dr. William Saunders, the crossing work languished for several years or until Dr. Charles Saunders was appointed Dominion cerealist in 1903. Assuming his work at the Central Experimental Farm, he lost no time in "dusting off" the accumulated samples of wheat hybrids and preparing them for a new series of rod-row plantings.

In the test rows of 1904, Saunders identified a plant with something special about it. It traced to a cross made by his brother Percy at Agassiz in 1892, between Red Fife and an early Asiatic wheat, Hard Red Calcutta. He watched it closely.

Dr. Charles Saunders, the originator of Marquis Wheat.

stalwart Angus MacKay of the Indian Head Experimental Farm. MacKay knew all about the heartbreaking disappointments that went with frozen crops and his judgment was known to be good.

But the way of the scientist is never easy and tragedy seemed to follow the Saunders wheat to Indian Head. Upon the receipt of the bag of seed, MacKay placed it in an open granary where he would study it later. But on his visit to the granary next day, the bag of seed was missing. Presumably a workman looking for feed for his hens or pigeons had lifted it. MacKay was horrified but did not call the Mounted Police. Instead, he penned a note and attached it to the granary door, announcing the disappearance of a few pounds of what might have proved valuable to the West and valuable to the world. He was inviting the person responsible to return the seed. The approach proved effective and next day, the bag of "chicken-feed" was back.

MacKay planted the new wheat with care in the spring of 1907 and saw it grow well. Sure enough, it was the only wheat on the experimental farm that escaped frost in that autumn. The results from 1908 and 1909 were no less encouraging and MacKay reported to Saunders that he was satisfied; this was the wheat for which the western growers were waiting and praying. Saunders chose to call the wheat Marquis and acted promptly to release it in five-pound samples to growers who requested it.

One of the small allotments went to a little Englishman, Seager Wheeler, who was farming at

It was easy to assess yield and grain appearance and maturity in the test wheats but, lacking proper facilities, it was difficult to determine milling qualities. With nothing better to serve his purpose, Saunders applied the chewing test, which consisted simply of chewing the wheats in question and studying the resulting gums. A good wheat gum was taken to mean gluten strength and the elasticity needed for a high-rising loaf of bread.[1] Some of the hybrid wheats under test seemed to inherit gluten weakness from the Hard Red Calcutta parent and were discarded. The one which caught Saunders' attention early, appeared to have derived the milling qualities of Red Fife and the early maturity of the Indian parent, which seemed ideal.

Saunders repeated the plantings in 1905 and 1906 and partially confirmed the happy combination of characteristics. But as he knew very well, the real test of the strain's merits would have to be made right on the soil of the West, for which a variety was being sought. By this time the seed had been increased to about forty pounds and for the 1907 planting, Saunders sent most of it, twenty-three pounds, to the

Seager Wheeler, Rosthern, Saskatchewan who forged the first link in a long chain of world wheat championships for the west when he won in 1911.

Samuel Larcombe of Birtle, Manitoba, an early western wheat king. (Photo by N. G. Ellis.)

Wheeler, showing Marquis wheat. Wheeler, back on the home farm, was one of the last to hear about it but he went to Calgary to receive the Sir Thomas Shaughnessy prize.

The cynics, some of whom are always present, said it was just another accident and such a success would not come again to Saskatchewan. "Lightning never strikes twice in the same place," they noted. But it did happen again. Wheeler entered and won the championship again in 1914, again in 1915, again in 1916, and for the fifth time in 1918. And when he could no longer compete, other midwestern Canadians took to exhibiting prairie grains in international competitions and won in most years. The record was enough to give western Canada a near-monopoly on world wheat championships. In sixty-five years of international competitions from the time of Wheeler's first success — first at Chicago and then at Toronto — wheat entries from western Canada won the supreme championship fifty-seven times (to December, 1979). And almost all the championship samples belonged to varieties which traced through at least one ancestral line to Marquis, to Red Fife, to a head that escaped

Dr. W. P. Thompson who, as head of the Biology Department at the University of Saskatchewan, proposed a wheat breeding program for the purpose of creating rust resistant varieties.

Rosthern. The little man, originally from the Isle of Wight, had been angry when the British Navy refused to accept him because of his short stature. Now, however, he was displaying skill as a plant improver and he welcomed the chance to conduct his own appraisal of Marquis wheat. The wheat did well for him and in 1911 he entered a sample at the Provincial Seed Fair in Regina and won the wheat championship. Neighbors coaxed him to send an entry of the same Marquis wheat to the World's Fair at New York but Wheeler laughed and said it would be of no use. The judges at the New York Land Show wouldn't look as his wheat, he was sure. But he yielded and forwarded an entry and then forgot about it.

As it happened, James J. Hill, American railway magnate, offered a one thousand dollar gold cup for the best sample of wheat at the World's Fair, "grown in the United States." Sir Thomas Shaughnessy, president of the CPR, chided him to open the contest to the world but Hill repeated: "Open to the United States." Shaughnessy replied: "Very well, my Company will offer a thousand dollars in gold for the best wheat at the show, grown anywhere in the world."

Sir Thomas Shaughnessy's hunch was a good one and late in 1911 it was announced that for the first time in history, the World Championship for Wheat had been won by a Saskatchewan man, Seager

An early combine working in a prairie wheat field.

A typical western harvest scene in 1938. The familiar row of grain elevators stands in the background.

David Fife's hungry ox, and to seed that became lodged in a scheming Scotsman's hat at the dockside in Glasgow. It was something to awaken the imagination.[2]

Just about every western farmer became a Marquis enthusiast. Purebred bulls, fancy hotels, rural schools, municipalities, and even babies were given the good Marquis name, and in 1915, it was Marquis wheat that carried the West to its record crop, a production of 360 million bushels — surpassing any previous year by more than a hundred million bushels. It was the year about which growers were to talk boastfully for decades, made the more remarkable because the spring was dry and not very promising. But the rains came when they were needed and for most growers the greatest problem was in getting the big crop cut, stooked and threshed under the wartime conditions that left them desperately short of help.

Marquis was great, as everybody agreed. But just as Red Fife had its shortcoming, so Marquis had one serious weakness and it did not come to light until 1916, the year after the bumper crop. The unsuspected

Harvesting wheat in the shadow of a huge government storage elevator.

truth was that the great Marquis, which seemed to have everything, could not stand against the slinking demon, stem rust, which was still unknown to most western farmers. What, at the midpoint of the growing season, looked like another big crop of Marquis wheat, became suddenly sick and seed development was arrested. Some farmers harvested light yields of low-grade grain; many others recovered big crops of straw and nothing more.

Farmers seeing crops destroyed by this rather mysterious disease felt completely helpless. The stem rust losses amounted to about $200,000,000 and growers wondered if the infection would remain to make rust a permanent crop destroyer and what they could do to control or eradicate the infection. What they did not understand at that point was that the life history of the rust fungus could not be completed in this area. As it was, the spores of infection would have to come floating in from the southern States and only if weather conditions were damp and muggy, could the organism grow where the spores settled. The life story was complicated and farmers were informed that there was no simple means of removing the danger.

It was Dr. W. P. Thompson of the biology department of University of Saskatchewan — later

president of the university — who proposed a genetic attack. While common bread wheats like Marquis were susceptible to rust, certain other kinds including some emmer wheats, possessed natural resistance. It would take some years to carry it out, Dr. Thompson warned, but his plan held the only hope, to make crosses between a quality wheat like Marquis and other kinds possessing inherited resistance to rust, bringing the best of both parent strains together in a new variety. Thompson's proposal, in effect, was to take the selected varieties apart, reshuffle the parts and build the best parts of both parents into a new variety. Those people for whom the science of genetics was still a mystery, couldn't hide their smiles of disbelief.

The National Research Council, the federal department of agriculture and the three midwestern universities agreed to participate in the program. The program was seen as being important enough to justify the construction of a special center to be known as the Dominion Rust Research Laboratory on the grounds of the University of Manitoba. The Rust Lab, as it was known, was opened in 1925.

Test plots on western experimental farms were dedicated to improving cereal grains and other crops.

A similar attack upon rust was announced by the United States authorities and in 1931 the Americans released the first of the new wheat varieties created to withstand stem rust; this was Thatcher, of which Marquis was a double grandparent. Being the first of the "custom made" rust resistant varieties, it was quickly adopted by Canadian growers and became extremely popular.

Meanwhile, the work was advancing at the various research centers in western Canada and two new varieties were licensed for distribution in 1935, Renown from the Dominion Rust Research Laboratory and Apex from the field husbandry department of the University of Saskatchewan. Four years later, the Dominion labratory had another rust-resistant variety called Regent and in 1946, still another, Redman, all of them with Marquis in their ancestry to contribute the quality for which western Canada's wheat was already famous around the world.

It might have been presumed that these new rust-resistant kinds retaining the treasured milling qualities would permanently end the rust menace for growers. But such was not the case because, while the new varieties were being evolved, Nature in her subtle manner was creating new strains of rust and a particularly virulent form known as race 15B was

identified. The latter was a strain against which even Thatcher and Redman and others like them were quite defenseless. The plant breeders were again alerted and as good fortune would have it, a new source of breeding material in the form of a rust-resistant wheat was discovered in a Manitoba field. Given the name McMurchy, it was used in new crosses and one of the results was Selkirk wheat which was able to resist all the rust strains including the 15B.

Then came Pembina, Manitou, Neepawa, Sinton, and still more. Each was a great success but it was still not the end because there was every likelihood that Nature would continue to generate new strains to challenge the plant scientists. Their task was to recognize new rust threats and be ready with a resistant wheat which retained that precious high quality of Marquis and yield of Thatcher, and all the other characteristics which Canadians had come to expect in wheat.

A similar story could be told about the production of Rescue and Chinook wheats which were bred primarily to furnish protection from wheat stem sawfly, the insect which laid eggs in the hollow stems of growing wheat. To confound the flies, the scientists delivered a wheat with solid stems and growers had instant relief.

And still the new kinds were members of the great Canadian wheat family, descendants of Marquis and Red Fife, with a bit of intermarrying to outside strains along the way.

The plant breeders, of course, had more than wheat to keep them busy. In furnishing new and better kinds of oats, barley, rye, flax, rapeseed, fruits, garden crops, and so on, their efforts were rewarding.

Chapter 19

DRY FARMING AND IRRIGATION

Seager Wheeler's world championship for wheat in 1911 made the Agricultural West appear like a young and beautiful debutante stepping into international society. But if spectators supposed the formalities were to be limited to one year, they were mistaken because the next year, 1912, held more and bigger surprises in capturing world attention.

It did something for agricultural self-esteem when it was announced that the 1912 meetings of the International Dry Farming Congress would be at Lethbridge where a Dominion experimental farm had been established four years earlier and where both dry farming and irrigation were receiving serious attention. Then, in the international competition of the Congress Seed Show classes, Henry Holmes from nearby Raymond repeated Seager Wheeler's success by winning the acknowledged wheat championship of the world. And while neighbors meeting at local livery stables were still talking about the Holmes wheat, J. D. McGregor of Brandon did the unheard-of thing and won the international championship for fat steers at the big Chicago show.

The Dry Farming Congress meetings, truly international in character, were said to be the most influential and important agricultural forums ever held in Canada. What was more important than getting the world viewpoint about the wise use of that great expanse of semi-arid treeless land? How much of it should be subjected to cultivation? Was the absence of trees on the prairie lands due to a lack of moisture or was low precipitation due to the absence of trees? Could dry farming and irrigation be conducted side by side in an area which remained dry, just as Palliser found it?

Drawing its members and supporters from farms, governments, agricultural colleges, and makers of farm supplies, the congress attracted delegates from many areas, even many countries including Russia, Germany, Australia, Holland, Persia, and China. The cosmopolitan feature in itself made the congress a novel convention in western Canada.

The Lethbridge committee was determined that this, the Seventh Annual International Congress, would surpass all previous ones. It did, even though there were some trifling disappointments, like the failure of the governor general and prime minister of Canada and the president of the United States to attend as expected. But the lieutenant-governors of both Alberta and Saskatchewan were present, also several provincial premiers. And the Lethbridge committee crowned itself with glory for its preparations — even took full credit for introducing a heavy October rain in a Dry Farming program, so noisy on the rooftops that sessions were interrupted.

The program of addresses by Canadian and United States authorities gave advice about farm machinery, cultivation, summerfallowing, farm power, windbreaks, markets, grassland management, and growing domestic grasses and legumes. But by editorial confession, "the greatest interest in the Congress centred about the winning of the Championship for the best bushel of wheat. There were some 300 entries in this section and competition was keen."[1]

With "some 300 entries" in the wheat class, it hardly needed to be added that the "competition was keen." What should have been told was that the winning wheat belonged to the Marquis variety, that it was from a field which came through a June drought to yield 33 bushels per acre, that the sample weighed 65¼ pounds per bushel and that Henry Holmes had been a serious student of dry farming since 1906.

The grain show had the essential character of a

world's fair and it is doubtful if class prizes were ever more handsome and more useful. The first prize in the class for the best bushel of hard wheat, open to the world, and won by Henry Holmes, was no less than a Type F Rumely Oil-Pull tractor, valued in 1912 at $2,500 and donated by the Rumely Company of Indiana.

For the best individual farm exhibit, A. Perrey of Cardston won a Fairbanks-Morse gasoline engine and pumping outfit, donated by the Canadian Fairbanks-Morse Company; a ten-foot Emerson disc-harrow was the first prize for the best farm exhibit of sheaf grains, this being offered by the Emerson-Brantingham Company of Illinois; a litter carrier, feed carrier and sanitary metal stalls and stanchions comprised the first prize for the best display of hay grown in eastern

Breaking the Canadian wheatlands with oxen about 1911.

Seeding on "Canadian Wheatlands" farms at Suffield, Alberta about 1914. Jas. Murray was the manager at that time. (Alberta Archives.)

Harvesting in the dryland area of Alberta. (Alberta Archives.)

Breaking dryland sod, about 1912.

Canada. There was an Oliver gang plow offered for the best bushel of oats grown in Canada and taken by J. Lanigan, Elfros, Saskatchewan, then a Van Brunt twenty-double-disc seed drill for the best sheaf of flax, "open to the world," offered by the John Deere Plow Company of Illinois and won by H. H. Jenkins of Pincher Creek. The best sheaf of hard wheat, open to the world, carried for first prize an imposing Stewart Sheaf loader valued at $500, donated by the Stewart Sheaf Loader Co., Winnipeg, and collected by R. H. Carter, Fort Qu'Appelle, Saskatchewan.

What prizes! And farmers were not the only ones who could qualify for them. The best essay entitled "Why it Pays Farmers to Build Good Roads" qualified for a road drag provided by a Spokane Company, and for the Alberta municipality making the best general showing, there was a Sawyer-Massey Road Grader offered by the Sawyer-Massey Company of Regina; the winner was at Cardston.

It should not have to be added that the Seventh Dry Farming Congress made a lasting impression upon the history of western agriculture.

While the International Dry Farming Congress was in session, work was going forward feverishly on a large irrigation project not far to the northeast, that of the Canadian Wheatlands Limited, a subsidiary of the

Cutting flax in Saskatchewan in 1915.

An aerial view of the PFRA Tree Nursery at Indian Head from which millions of seedlings have gone to furnish shelterbelts in prairie country. (D.R.E.E. Photo.)

Southern Alberta Land Company. The subsidiary, holding an option on 64,000 acres from the parent company, was engaged in breaking ground, two-thirds of which was to be made ready for irrigation, with water starting to flow by 1914. Twelve thousand acres were broken in 1911 and more in 1912 but the plan failed to mature and many of the ditches never carried water.

Lethbridge, by 1912, was nevertheless, at the heart of western irrigation development and shared Medicine Hat's interest in this scheme which had its beginning when the Southern Alberta Land Company was formed in 1909 with English capital and J. D. McGregor of Brandon as managing director. The land, formerly grazing land, was obtained from the department of the interior at a very small price on the condition that it would be irrigated. Some of the delegates to the Dry Farming Congress were driven out to see the development and get an impression of irrigation progress in Canada.

Congress speakers traced irrigation growth from its midwestern beginning beside Fish Creek, south of Calgary, in 1878. There, John Glenn, who shared with Sam Livingstone the distinction of being the first farmer in the Calgary region, took water from Fish Creek and conducted it a few hundred yards to irrigate twenty acres which are readily seen today on the east side of Number Two Highway at Midnapore.

Rancher John Quirk used water from Sheep Creek to irrigate some of his foothills land in the eighties, and the Mormon settlers following Charles Ora Card to build the Cardston community brought a knowledge of irrigation and soon put it to use. Calgary's William Pearce, who was one of the first to speak out on behalf of water conservation, was mainly responsible for inducing parliament to pass the North West Irrigation Act of 1894, intended to bring regulation and order to the developing irrigation.

Water resources and topography combined to bring distinct advantages to irrigators working in and near the foothills where most prairie irrigation water begins to flow. For the same reasons, Alberta forged far ahead of other provinces in irrigation acreage. Springbank farmers, nearby on Calgary's west side, organized in 1896 and took water from the Elbow River to irrigate 20,000 acres. It was the beginning of bigger things.

A Fort Macleod company secured a Dominion charter, then the Galt Railway Company, the High River and Sheep Creek Irrigation Company, and the Alberta Irrigation Company. When the Canadian Pacific Railway became active in irrigation, its operations were soon the biggest on the continent. Having obtained the odd-numbered sections for twenty-four miles on each side of the main line, the company was anxious to make its land both productive and salable and sought some consolidation that would allow irrigation. By an Act of Parliament in 1894, the CPR was allowed to take its allotment of land west of Medicine Hat in parcels that would make irrigation practical. A block of some three million acres to be watered from the Bow River was taken east of Calgary and development began in 1904. Then to raise the Bow River level and permit it to serve an eastern block, a large dam was constructed at Bassano from which ditches were carrying water in 1914.

Changes and setbacks were to come with the years but Alberta and Saskatchewan could look forward to achieving a goal of a million acres profiting from irrigation.

Chapter 20

MIXED FARMING AND DAIRYING

Wheat grown on western soil might be the best in the world and none but foolhardy persons would dispute it. Most newcomers, regardless of origin, were quickly converted to the philosophy of wheat farming with its seasonal operations, big fields, and summerfallow. The traditionalists, on the other hand, preached mixed farming the way it was practiced in Bruce County, just as though it had been decreed by the Law of Moses. Those who spoke for the departments of agriculture and the new colleges of agriculture took up the mixed farming cause and often gave the impression that the "cowless, sowless, lambless and henless farm" was a sin as much as a mistake.

Nobody disputed the conventional teaching openly but most farmers close to the practical problems peculiar to the prairies — like scarcity of water and uncertain feed supplies — were in no hurry to adopt the eastern and Old Country concept of diversification, involving much spreading of manure. They had their reasons: homestead regulations demanded a livable house on the quarter section, a certain acreage of cultivation, and residence for six months in each of three years, but they did not require breeding flocks or herds. What settlers seemed to understand better than the professional people was that prairie districts differed widely and some of them would grow grain better than they'd support the kind of mixed farming presumed by the Ontario formula. Moreover, didn't many of the homesteaders come west to get away from the endless chores of milking cows, slopping pigs, and hoeing turnips? Western farmers would diversify in their own good time and in their own good and practical way.

Nevertheless, dairying was the commonly accepted symbol of balanced farming and received substantial government aid. The Manitoba Dairy Act passed in Northwest Rebellion year, 1885, provided for the incorporation of cheese and butter-making plants and was seen as encouragement for mixed farming. At the same time, the sum of $2,500 was furnished for dairy instruction. It was the year, also, that witnessed an amazing new dairy aid, the mechanical cream separator. In making its public appearance in Manitoba, it was threatening to end that age-old task of "setting" fresh milk in tall "creamer cans" to remain overnight or until the cream had risen to the top and the skim milk could be drained off to effect separation.

When members of the Manitoba legislature, very much aware of their duty to encourage dairying, heard about a cream separator that was installed by Hon. Walter Clifford on his farm at Austin, a few miles west of Portage la Prairie, they declared an adjournment and drove from Winnipeg to see it for themselves.

Described as "one of the celebrated De Laval cream separators manufactured in Sweden," the mechanical wonder had been imported from England and "working satisfactorily for about a month under the management of an experienced buttermaker. At present he is making about 70 pounds per week from the milk furnished by 20 cows, over and above what is required for feeding; but the machine is capable of separating the cream from 50 gallons of milk per hour. It is driven by a small three-horsepower engine with 40 pounds of steam."[1]

Cheese factories were preceding creameries in the West and Manitoba, by this time, had two of the former; one was at Stonewall and the other at Rapid City, both having been started in 1882. Now, in 1885, the first creamery in the province and in the midwest, was opening at St. Francois Xavier, a short distance west of Winnipeg.

The Territorial pattern was the same, with the first

Canary Korndyke Alcarta, a Holstein cow, became the highest producer of butterfat in the world for four-year-old Holsteins in the 305 day division. She was owned by Ben Thomson of Boharm, Saskatchewan then purchased by the Government of Saskatchewan for $10,000.

two dairy plants being cheese factories, one started by Ebenezer Healy at Springbank in 1888 and the second, only a few miles away on the Elbow Park Ranch, in the next year. Then came the first Territorial Creamery, built by D. M. Ratcliffe at Big Hill Spring, also in the district west of and close to Calgary.[2]

Dairy plants increased in number rapidly but even by 1900, the factories had not overtaken the volume of butter being made on the farms of the West. In Manitoba, in that latter year, creameries produced 1,557,000 pounds of butter while the farm-made product amounted to 8,676,000 pounds. Every farm wife was a proud butter maker.

Throughout the nineties, leaders in both provincial and federal governments believed the West could and should be a great dairy country. Dairy projects could obtain government support when other farm enterprises could not. Traveling Dairy Schools were a government innovation of 1894, with staff supplied by the Central Experimental Farm at Ottawa. This school on railway wheels toured the country, spending a couple of days at each point and giving instructions about butter making, breeding and feeding of milk cattle, cream separators, Babcock testing, and so on.

Two years later, Manitoba started a provincial dairy school with the same motives.

There was continuing debate about which of the two main dairy products, butter or cheese, would dominate the western Canadian industry. J. H. Ellis tells that in 1895, Manitoba had fifty-two cheese factories producing 1,553,192 pounds of cheese, and only nineteen creameries with total production of 529,812 pounds of butter.[3]

At the Territorial Exhibition at Regina in that year, cheese was said to have won a major share of attention, partly, no doubt, because of the "big cheese" exhibited from the cheese factory at Innisfail.

The Saskatoon Calf Competition in 1929 brought nearly 1000 fat calves together. The calves were shown by boys and girls.

Weighing 1,300 pounds, it brought visitors back for repeat inspections. It was inspired by the huge cheese produced at Perth, Ontario, two years before for display at the World's Fair at Chicago. That masterpiece was made with the co-operation of twelve Ontario plants and J. A. Ruddick — later the dairy commissioner for Canada — was the chief cheese maker. It took 207,200 pounds of milk and the finished cheese weighed eleven tons, stood six feet high and measured twenty-eight feet in circumference.

Back in Manitoba, the provincial government, prodded by the Manitoba Dairy Association, was doing all in its power to maintain the growing interest. C. C. Macdonald was appointed superintendent of dairying and he set about to enlarge the scope and status of the government's dairy school. The ten-weeks' annual program enjoyed every favor and was allowed to occupy the new dairy building at the Tuxedo site of the Manitoba Agricultural College even before students were enrolled for the general course.

W. J. Carson was named both superintendent of dairying and professor of dairying.

Cow testing was introduced; higher standards of grading were adopted and more of the dairyman's production was going into the fluid milk trade. Dairying was changing but back of it all were the dairy breeds being brought to an ever higher state of efficiency and perfection.

Of the specialized dairy breeds, the Ayrshire was the first to arrive in the West. The Hudson's Bay Company in 1848 sent out a mixed lot of selected animals, including the Thoroughbred stallion, Melbourne, two Thoroughbred mares, two Ayrshire cows and an Ayrshire bull. The idea was worthy but the purebreds were ahead of their time and their identity was lost completely.

The Holstein or Holstein-Friesian from Holland was the next to appear and as time demonstrated, its role was a big one. Two Holstein cows and a Holstein bull named Selkirk, brought downriver to Winnipeg by pioneer Archibald Wright in 1881 were not only the first purebreds of their kind in the West but the first in Canada.

Cattle of this breed had big frames and great capacity for milk production and Western specimens like Canary Korndyke Alcartra and Alcartra Gerben were among those that gained world fame. The

Alcarta Gerben's production of butterfat made her the world champion producer in the 365 day division.

Four Clydesdale mares taking a load of seed to market at the University of Saskatchewan.

former, known locally as "Canary" was an Ontario-bred heifer brought west by Sam Sims of Manitoba and sold to B. H. Thomson of Moose Jaw, in whose herd she produced 26,396 pounds of milk and 1,080 pounds of butterfat in 305 days to establish a world record for butterfat in the four-year-old class, 305-day division. That the record was made on commonplace rations comprising sweet clover hay, sunflower silage, oat straw, crushed oats and bran, with a mineral supplement of salt and bonemeal, added to the significance of it all. When the record was announced in 1928, the government of Saskatchewan, to ensure that she would remain in Canada, bought Canary for $10,000 and placed her for keeping at the University of Saskatchewan.

A few years later, 1945, the Alberta-bred-and-owned Holstein, Alcartra Gerben, eating Alberta feed, made 1,409 pounds of butterfat in 365 days to become the world's butterfat champion for all breeds, bringing glory to the well-known Hays herd at Calgary. It was evidence not only of the cow's capacity but also of the western potential in dairying, which had once been in doubt.

The Holstein breed continued to rank first in numbers but the Jerseys, Ayrshires, and Guernseys

Dr. Gordon Taggart was superintendent of the Canadian Experimental Station at Swift Current, then minister of agriculture for Saskatchewan and eventually the deputy minister of agriculture for Canada.

Blonde Beau 7, the grand champion Yorkshire Boar of 1936, was bred at the University of Saskatchewan and exhibited by Alex McPhail of Brandon. Pig production was an important part of the mixed farming program in the west.

The Motherwell Farm at Abernethy in about 1914. Mother-well was a great advocate of mixed farming.

P. C. Colquhoun, a Maple Creek pioneer, advocated and practiced mixed farming. His own activities embraced dairy-ing, honey production and fruit growing.

gained prominence and made their contribution to the western record. The area that produced 2,302,144 pounds of creamery butter and 1,317,106 pounds of factory cheese in 1901, reached 28,490,412 pounds of creamery butter and 1,168,392 pounds of factory cheese in 1921, and 39,951,000 pounds of butter and 20,131,000 pounds of cheese in 1975. If it was a measure of mixed farming progress, it should have been convincing.

Mixed farming by any standards, however, presumed much more than milk cows. It called for the growing of forage crops, grain crops, soil-building legumes, cattle, horses, sheep, pigs, poultry, and even bees. It took time to build up the frontier herds and

flocks and the census of 1881 showed livestock numbers in Manitoba and the Territories as still low, just 27,609 horses, 731,153 cattle, 6,419 sheep, and 20,133 pigs. But ten years later, the corresponding populations showed horses to have increased by more than five times, cattle by more than six times, sheep by fifteen times and pigs by three times. By 1921 when the horse population had reached its peak of 2,506,577 in the area, cattle of all kinds had reached 4,235,293 head; sheep, increasing more slowly, were at 842,981, and pigs, which fluctuated like the price of wheat, were at 1,231,778.

As for the domestic bees, there was doubt when the first arrived. It wasn't easy to believe the story about the first ones being herded into Manitoba by bee drivers or herders. The *Edmonton Bulletin* of 1888 gave a good clue to the first in the country: "The two hives of bees brought in by express about a month ago by Messrs. J. Knowles and Thos. Henderson, are doing well so far. About half of the bees were dead when the hives arrived but notwithstanding this and the continuous rainy weather, both swarms have done well and are gathering honey rapidly. . . . They are of the Italian variety and came from Niagara Falls. This is the first attempt at the introduction of bees.[4]

By 1910, the Canadian statisticians could count 735 hives in Manitoba, 24 in Saskatchewan and 80 in Alberta. From that time honey production soared.

Eastern critics continued their aspersions about "one crop farming" in the West but the fact was that western producers were diversifying at a reasonable rate. If, for example, Alberta's total livestock population of 1971 were divided evenly between the province's 62,702 farmers at that time, each one would have between two and three cows to milk, fifty-four other cattle to look after, twenty-four pigs, eight sheep and a flock of hens. He would indeed be a mixed farmer, with a full complement of chores.

Chapter 21

BREEDING FOR BETTER BEEF BULLS

Many people questioned the midwest's suitability for specialized dairy cattle and dairying but beef cattle with a reputation for hardiness invited no doubts. "Kootenai" Brown declared that where buffalo chose to graze, beef cattle would do well and, except for the reverses of a few bad winters, time proved him right. Almost as soon as the prairie bison disappeared, range herds of beef cattle appeared and multiplied. Simultaneously, farm herds were started by thousands of homesteaders whose purpose was to sell steers and surplus heifers on the beef market. A big prairie

production of beef cattle was assured. The sale of cattle could and would rank next to that of wheat.

At first the need for numbers ignored quality. In the Red River settlement, any horse was better than no horse, and any cow that would freshen and furnish some milk was like a treasure, regardless of her conformation. Cattle improvement had to wait until animal numbers would allow settlers and ranchers to reject breeding stock with ill shape and inferior quality.

Kenneth MacKenzie and Walter Lynch brought the first purebred Shorthorn cattle to western Canada and met to challenge each other with their best in the Portage la Prairie showring. Then, to strengthen the area's claim to being the first Shorthorn stronghold, John Barron from Elora, Ontario, settled on the

Gainford Marquis (right) was regarded as the greatest breeding bull of the Shorthorn breed in his time. He is held by Charles Yule who later became the manager of the Calgary Exhibition and Stampede.

Carberry Plains in 1878 and four years later founded his Shorthorn herd with the purchase of a heifer, Lady Fairview. Thereafter, he was scouring Ontario for good breeding stock and had the fortune to secure the bull, Topsman, that proved to be both a showring and breeding success. This bull, in 1899, was champion at Winnipeg for Barron and champion at Toronto for his new owner, Capt. T. E. Robson of Ontario.

What followed was a succession of nationally famous western Shorthorn herds which revolved around one eminently great cattleman, James Yule, the Aberdonian who had worked for Amos Cruickshank of Sittyton before coming to Canada in 1880. In Ontario, he managed the herd of John Dryden and came west in 1897 to manage a herd being established by Hon. Thomas Greenway, premier of Manitoba, on his farm at Crystal City. After six years, "Jimmy" Yule went to operate the Sir William Van Horne farm and herd at Selkirk and as usual Shorthorn breeding prospered under his direction. But while at Selkirk, Yule suffered injury from an attack by a bull and never fully recovered. In 1911, he accepted an offer from H. L. Emmert, a Winnipeg businessman with a farm at Oak Bluff and an ambition to own the best

Shorthorns in Canada. It was an ambition which the Winnipeg man, after giving Yule a free hand to buy and sell as he chose, had reason to believe he had realized. If the caliber of herd sires was an indication, the Emmert herd when it had Browndale, Gainford Marquis, and Oakland Star at the same time, would have to rank as outstanding in Canada.

The American-bred Browndale, with the great Avondale as his sire and also grandsire on his dam's side, was Yule's selection soon after going to Oak Bluff. Gainford Marquis, about to become the greatest Canadian Shorthorn of his time, was bred in England and brought to Canada by James Watt of Ontario in 1911. The bull was undefeated in 1912 and after the Brandon exhibition of that year, he and the champion cow, Dale's Gift 2nd, were bought by Robert Caswell, one of the original Temperance Colony settlers at Saskatoon in 1883. The price for the bull was $7,500. Shown in Caswell's name, Gainford Marquis and Dale's Gift 2nd won the two Shorthorn grand championships at Toronto exhibition later in the same year.

Very soon thereafter, Gainford Marquis was sold at $5,000 to Hon. W. C. Sutherland who was building a superior herd of Shorthorns and stud of Clydesdales at Saskatoon. On the evening of the day of Mr. Sutherland's purchase, he was offered $500 more than he had paid for the bull but explained that as long as he was breeding Shorthorns, he would keep Gainford

Glencarnock Victor II, grand champion steer at the International Show in Chicago, for J. D. McGregor, Brandon in 1913.

Marquis. Early in the next year, however, while Jimmy Yule was still acting for Emmert, the entire Sutherland herd of fifty purebred Shorthorns was sold to the Manitoba buyer and Gainford Marquis changed hands again at $5,000. Finally, in 1915, following the death of Mr. Yule, James Watt, the original Canadian owner of Gainford Marquis, bought the entire Emmert herd, including Browndale and Gainford Marquis. Browndale was sold later to James Douglas of Caledonia, Ontario, where he became recognized as one of the greatest sires of the breed and Gainford Marquis remained in the Watt herd until his death at fifteen years of age. An indication of the latter's prepotency as a sire will be found in the record of his offspring

winning the get-of-sire class at the Toronto National Exhibition every year from 1914 to 1920.

Hon. Walter F. C. Gordon-Cumming may have been the first to breed the Scottish black and polled cattle, the Aberdeen Angus, in the West, having made an important importation to the Quorn Ranch in the foothills in 1889. In the next year, two herds were started in Manitoba, one by Robert Hall of Griswold,

Bullion IV, one of the most famous sires in the Polled Hereford breed. He was bred by Mossom Boyd on the Prince Albert farm.

Blackcap Revolution was one of the great show and breeding bulls of the Aberdeen Angus breed. He was brought to Canada by J. D. McGregor, Brandon, in 1921 and was later sold back to the United States for $15,000.

J. D. McGregor (left) brought fame to Glencarnock Farms of Brandon, Manitoba by popularizing the Aberdeen Angus breed and promoting mixed farming.

Frank Collicutt of Willow Springs Ranch, Crossfield, Alberta for some years owned the biggest herd of purebred Hereford cattle in the world.

near Brandon, and the other by Hon. Walter Clifford of Austin. The latter was not only among the first to breed and exhibit cattle of the breed in the West but he was the first president of the Canadian Aberdeen Angus Association.[1]

But the outstanding western breeder of the black and polled Scottish breed was James D. McGregor of Brandon whose successes led to his Glencarnock Farm being dubbed the "Ballindalloch of America."

"J.D.," with members of his family, arrived at Winnipeg in advance of the railway in 1877 and there his father bought and sold horses and cattle for a few years. After watching Hon. Walter Gordon-Cumming's importation of forty Aberdeen-Angus females and three bulls, "J.D." obtained a financial interest in the herd and ultimately bought it and brought it to Brandon.

McGregor who was successively a homesteader, cowboy, gold commissioner in the Yukon, national food controller in wartime and lieutenant-governor of Manitoba, was honored in 1928 by having his life-size portrait hung in the Gallery of the Saddle and Sirloin Club in Chicago, beside portraits of McCombie, Cruichshank, and other greats.

Upon his return from the Klondike in 1904, McGregor threw his full energy into the raising of cattle on his Glencarnock Farm. With James Bowman of Ontario, he imported the Scottish sire, Prince of Benton, and began showing cattle about 1906. But if McGregor's herd went virtually unnoticed in that year, it certainy seized the spotlight in 1912 when the Glencarnock cattle entered major competition at the Chicago International Fat Stock Show, a recognized breed stronghold. For Canadian cattlemen it was almost beyond belief that McGregor's Leroy 3rd of Meadowbrook would win the grand championship for bulls of the breed; that Violet 3rd of Congash would win the reserve grand championship for females; that Queen Rosie of Cullen would be the first prize two-year-old heifer; that a Glencarnock entry would win first prize for breeding herd and, most astonishing of all, that Glencarnock Victor would win the coveted and prestigious grand championship for fat steers.

It happened just one year after Seager Wheeler won the world championship for wheat and brought westerners a new sense of pride and confidence in their agriculture. Then, one year later, before many cattlemen had recovered from their initial surprise, McGregor went back to Chicago with another steer, Glencarnock Victor II, and repeated the supreme championship victory. It was the first time that any exhibitor had won the steer grand championship twice in successive years.

McGregor was the means of bringing some of the best sires of the breed to Canada. Evreux of Harviestoun was an early importation that influenced the breed in Canada as he influenced the Glencarnock herd. After 1921, the bull which was to be acknowledged as "King of American Sires," Blackcap Revolution, was bought by McGregor at the Escher and Ryan sale in the United States for $4,000. Some people criticized McGregor for extravagance but after two years of service at Glencarnock, the great bull was fitted for the international show at Chicago where he won the grand championship for Mr. McGregor and was sold there for $15,000.

While the owner of Glencarnock was making his Brandon herd one of the best on the continent, he was making agricultural contributions in other ways, like organizing the Brandon Winter Fair, leading in growing alfalfa, and advancing the cause of junior calf clubs and baby beef contests.

The Hereford breed, ultimately a leader in breed popularity, made a slow beginning. Senator M. H. Cochrane included imported Herefords among the bulls he sent west to his foothills ranch in 1882 and Joseph Sharman and Sons had a herd of purebreds at Toddburn, Manitoba, in 1884. But when the second annual cattle sale — forerunner of the Calgary Bull Sale — was held in 1902, the only Herefords entered were those offered by Mossom Boyd of Bobcaygeon, Ontario, and Prince Albert, NWT. Only in that year were the first purebred females brought to the Alberta area which was to become a Hereford stronghold. These pedigreed females were placed on the Baxter Reed Ranch east of Olds, and some of them went later to help found the Frank Collicutt ranch herd west of Crossfield.

Mossom Boyd, with a farm near Prince Albert, may or may not have been the first in the area now known as Saskatchewan with Herefords, but he was certainly the first with Polled Herefords. In addition to being a pioneer in hybridizing cattle and buffalo, he was one of the North American founders of the Polled Hereford strain. Bullion 4th, one of the leading Polled

The main herd of the Matador Cattle company, about to cross the North Saskatchewan River when the company was retiring from ranching on the Canadian side.

Hereford sires on the continent was a product of Mossom Boyd's Prince Albert herd. A double great-grandson of the breed-founding bull, Variation, he was calved in 1912 and made a public appearance at Canadian shows in 1913 when he won his classes at Regina, Saskatoon, and Winnipeg exhibitions and was grand champion at Brandon. After proving his worth as a breeder, Bullion 4th sold in Indiana for $9,500.

The Hereford spread quickly to become the dominant breed on the ranges and then experienced a genuine "boom" period during the years of World War I. J. I. Moffat of Carroll, Manitoba, bought a son of Perfection Fairfax from Warren T. McCray of Kentland, Indiana, in 1915, for $1,575. That started the escalating prices paid by Canadian breeders. A few days later, Simon Downie and Sons of Carstairs, bought the bull, Beau Perfection 11th, from the same breeder for $1,750.

Sale records were shattered in 1917. At the McCray sale in that year, seventy-five head of Herefords featuring the progeny from the great Perfection Fairfax brought an average price of $1,750 and the highest priced bull of the sale, Martin Fairfax,

Red Ransom, Grand Champion Shorthorn bull at the Portage la Prairie Exhibition in 1948, was owned by the Widdicombe Brothers of Foxwarren, Manitoba.

Visitors inspecting the breeding Shorthorn herd owned by Claude Gallinger of Tofield, Alberta.

by Perfection Fairfax, was bought by George Fuller for his Arm River Stock Farm at Girvin, Saskatchewan, for $17,000. It was the sale sensation of the year.

In the same season, Frank Collicutt of Crossfield attended the O. Harris and Sons sale in Missouri and bought the two-year-old bull, Gay Lad 40th, for $11,900. Collicutt by this time had over 600 purebred Herefords and a short time later, with 800, could claim to own the biggest herd of pedigreed Herefords in the world. In the year in which he bought Gay Lad 40th, the Glengarry Ranch at Claresholm bought Gay Lad 16th, paying $20,000 and this bull was purchased a short time thereafter by Collicutt.

If the new purchasers were to exhibit their bulls, the summer exhibition contests of 1917 would be the most exciting in prairie history and, sure enough, the "Battle of the Giants," took place at Calgary where Collicutt, Fuller, J. A. Chapman, L. O. Clifford from Ontario, and others made entry. Prof. W. L. Carlyle from Oklahoma was the judge and ringside interest was at fever pitch. It was expected that the principal competition would be between Fuller's three-year-old, Martin Fairfax, and Collicutt's two-year-old, Gay Lad 40th. But to the surprise of all spectators, the grand championship came to rest with Beau Perfection 48th, a handsome two-year-old which along with other

members of the herd of Curtis Cattle Company had arrived quietly from Kentucky to make his home at Langdon, east of Calgary. In the next year, 1918, when the ring "battle" was renewed at Calgary, Frank Collicutt's Gay Lad 16th was grand champion and Beau Perfection was next to him.

Hereford progress was spectacular, just as Shorthorn and Aberdeen-Angus progress was spectacular. Each of the British breeds — including the Galloway — had its supporters. There was ample room for three or four beef breeds and their supremacy was unchallenged until showring standards which encouraged small, compact cattle with excessive fat to lean, brought protest. Ranchers and other practical cattlemen rebelled at the declining weight for age and demanded bigger cattle from the British breeds or some new breeds. They got both; breeders of Herefords, Aberdeen-Angus, and Shorthorns began selecting for size, and at the same time, new European breeds began to appear. In less than ten years a dozen or more new breeds — all except one from European countries — made their appearance and captured a big share of support. Instead of having three or four breeds of beef cattle, western Canadians could count at least fifteen — whether they needed that many or not. Actually, they didn't need that many and some of them were likely to have a short history in western Canada.

Chapter 22

FOR MORE AND BETTER HORSES

Horsemen chose to believe that the twentieth century belonged to them. Oxen, with their natural ability to live off the land, had served the homesteaders well but failed to arouse loyalty or enthusiasm and had no chance of being kept in use after their owners could afford or obtain horses. Steam and gasoline tractors were threatening but most horsemen

Horse teams discing on the J.G. Miller farm near Aylesbury, Saskatchewan, 1906.

gave the impression of being amused more than worried. They were thankful for horses and proud to be horsemen.

By 1911, the three midwestern provinces had 1,194,927 horses, 892,914 of which were of working age, being three years or over. It meant enough horses in total to allow four and one-half work horses and one and one-half young horses for every one of the 204,214 farms in the three provinces at that time. Thus, the farmer with an average allotment would

have enough horses for a drill-team or binder-team, but with extremely little horse power in reserve in case of colic or other disorder in the stable. The few young horses showed the farmer's wish to grow replacements and increase his work stock. He knew that as soon as his cultivated acreage had increased, as it was bound to do, he would need an additional outfit of work horses for his fields.

But even six horses meant early morning and late evening chores and the owner quickly developed a horseman's habits and skills. He became handy at trimming overgrown hoofs, drenching sick animals, breaking colts, driving field outfits with four reins, and possibly rolling manes. He talked in terms of hame-straps, bone spavins, catch colts, and currycombs. Capturing the spirit of the time, he wanted better horses as well as more horses. Even farm boys could dream of driving to town with a wagon team of well-matched and high-lifed drafters hitched with clean harness and Scotch tops. The Cadillac car was unknown but farmers with spans of Clydesdales or Percherons fit for the showring were in a Cadillac category.

Horse improvement, long a foremost agricultural objective, began when the Hudson's Bay Company sent the Norfolk Trotter stallion, Fireaway, from England in 1831, and then the Thoroughbred stallion, Melbourne, in 1848. But it wasn't until the country was being served by railroads that the first improving stallions of Clydesdale, Percheron, and Belgian breeding became available. Most of the work of improvement rested with a generation of horse importers and dealers who were catering to the urgent needs of thousands of settlers. They imported large numbers of Clydesdale stallions from Scotland, Percherons and Belgians from the United States and Europe, a few Shires and Suffolk from England, and work stock of any available color or kind from Ontario or other convenient source.

The purebred stallions were generally of good quality. The work stock made a motley collection, much of it older than buyers suspected, some of it with hidden vices and unsoundnesses.

Because of the number of dealers and importers having headquarters or sales stables at Brandon, that city by 1910 was the self-styled Horse Capital of Canada. There the pioneer firms of Colquhoun and Beattie, Alexander Galbraith, Trotter and Trotter, J. B. Hogate, Vanstone and Rogers, Ben Finlayson and others of note conducted a thriving trade. Beecham Trotter estimated that his firm of Trotter and Trotter paid out more than three million dollars for horses shipped to and sold at Brandon.[1] Furthermore, the fact that 607 outside mares would be bred to five Colquhoun and Beattie stallions standing at the Baubier Stable on 8th Street in Brandon in a single

season gave an indication of the booming state of the horse business.[2]

Farther west, the best-known Clydesdale breeders and importers included W. H. "Scottie" Bryce of Arcola, Mutch Brothers of Lumsden, and R. H. Taber of Condie. Bryce, who settled in the eighties and displayed either singular judgment or luck in choosing his horses, imported the famous stallion, Perpetual Motion, sired by the four times Cawdor Cup winner, Hiawatha — paying $3,750 for him. In the next year, 1906, he imported another even greater sire, the one that Canadians came to know as Baron of Arcola. This son of Baron's Pride was registered in Scotland under the name of Keystone but Bryce wanted him to carry the name of his Saskatchewan town and paid five pounds to have the registration changed. At the Winnipeg Industrial Exhibition in 1907, Baron of Arcola placed second to Sir William Van Horne's show horse, Lord Ardwall, but at Brandon in the following week, the placing was reversed, with the general approval of most members of the Clydesdale fraternity. In the years ahead, Baron of Arcola and his offspring tended to dominate the western showrings.

Horsemen did not forget that Bryce tried to buy one of the greatest sires in Scottish horse history,

Scottie Bryce of Arcola, Saskatchewan, a leading breeder of Clydesdales in the early west.

Bonnie Buchlyvie. While traveling with James Kilpatrick in 1912, he visited the Seaham Harbour stud and inspected the famous stallion and proposed a purchase. Although unsuccessful in this bid, he instructed Kilpatrick to seize any opportunity to buy the horse at any price up to 4,000 pounds. Three years later the horse was included in the Seaham Harbour sale and James Kilpatrick bought him at 5,000 pounds, then cabled Bryce that he could have the horse at the price paid. The message arrived the day of Mr. Bryce's funeral but Pete Taylor, son-in-law of Mr. Bryce, was convinced that if the great Arcola horseman had been living, Bonnie Buchlyvie would have been brought to Saskatchewan

After 1910, it was the stallion The Bruce, imported by the Grahams of Ontario and bought by R. H. Taber of Condie, that became the idol of the Clydesdale showring. The horse made his public appearance at the Winnipeg exhibition in that year and won the first of many championships. Some people said he was small but The Bruce was unsurpassed in quality, which he transmitted impressively through Taber's Hillcrest mares.

Then, as gasoline tractors were gaining farm support, the University of Saskatchewan at Saskatoon became a center of interest for Clydesdale lovers. A new series of events began in 1919 when the government of Saskatchewan, at the request of the organized horsemen, agreed to buy an outstanding Clydesdale stallion in Scotland. When it was found impossible to buy a mature horse of the caliber demanded, the committee bought two yearling colts, Craigie Enchanter and Bonnie Fyvie, and saw them delivered safely at the university farm where they would come under the supervision of Dean W. J. Rutherford and Prof. A. M. Shaw. But the two young stallions failed to live up to

A line-up of Percheron stallions at the Edmonton Spring Show in 1919.

expectations; Craigie Enchanter died a few months after delivery and Bonnie Fyvie developed stringhalt and was destroyed in 1926.

In the meantime, the university farm became the home of some of the best Clydesdales on the continent. G. A. Cluett of New York wrote to Dean Rutherford on February 1, 1923, offering to sell his excellent string of horses at a fraction of their cost. Cluett had seen Rutherford judging Clydesdales at the international show in Chicago and admired him. The writer admitted that he did not wish to see his band of horses scattered; he was anxious to have Rutherford take all the mares and stallion and continue the breeding program started.

In the Cluett band at the time were the imported five-year-old stallion, Kinleith Footprint; the Cawdor Cup mare of 1916, Rosalind; Craigie Sylvia, who had been grand champion mare at one of the international shows at Chicago; Langwater Jessica, Eva Footprint, Greenmeadow Muriel, Fyvie Queen, and others with similar aristocracy. "If I could feel that the best of them would be kept for breeding purposes at your University," Mr. Cluett wrote, "I would be willing to sell the entire lot to you for $10,000, which as you will realize is only a fraction of their value." Actually, Cluett had paid that sum of money for Kinleith Footprint alone.

The university made the purchase and thirteen of the most royally bred Clydesdales on the continent were delivered at Saskatoon. Among them was Langwater Jessica's stallion foal, Greenmeadow Footstep, by Kinleith Footprint, which in 1925 won the grand championship at both the Canadian Royal Winter Fair and the Chicago International.

While the government of Saskatchewan was voting funds for the purchase of an outstanding Clydesdale stallion in Scotland, the government of Alberta was doing the same and obtained Craigie Masterpiece, paying 2,500 pounds for him.[3] The horse was pronounced by no less an authority than Alex Galbraith as the finest representative of the breed ever imported to Canada.

It was a time when, according to showyard winnings, the best Clydesdale stallions on the continent were concentrated in the western provinces. Most of the Clydesdale stallion championships at the Chicago Internatonal show in a ten-year period from 1920 were won by western exhibitors, mainly Saskatchewan exhibitors. Wee Donald, owned by C. A. Weaver, Lloydminster, gained that championship distinction in 1920, 1921 and 1924; First Principal, owned by the Manitoba department of agriculture, in 1922; Mainring, from the Ontario stud of W. B. Clelland, in 1923; Greenmeadow Footstep, from the University of Saskatchewan in 1925; Forest Favorite, owned by Haggerty and Black of Belle Plain, in 1926; Sansovina, for John Sinclair of Congress in 1927; Lochinvar, the property of John Falconer, Govan, in 1928, and Sonny Boy, for A. Johnstone of Yellowgrass in 1929. And to make the record of those years still more noteworthy, three of the grand champions on the list were imported from Scotland by one man, Ben Finlayson, who began importing in 1909 and continued until his death in 1933.

A few of the massive, hairy-legged English Shires and compact Suffolk Punch horses were being imported in those early years but they failed to become popular. The Percheron and Belgian horses, on the other hand, were introduced relatively late but made friends quickly and ultimately passed the Clydesdales in numbers of registrations.

The Brandon Agricultural Society, through its president, C. Whitehead, and vice-president, F. Clegg, bought two Percheron stallions from M. W. Dunham of Illinois in 1884 and may have been responsible for launching the breed upon its western course. The two stallions were grays and both stood for service at the Kelly Livery Stable at Brandon in that first year.[4]

Senator M. H. Cochrane, in 1885, sent three Percheron stallions from the Dunham source of supply to his ranch west of Calgary and soon thereafter, the

A team of imported Clydesdale stallions in harness at the University of Saskatchewan. Bonnie Fyvie is on the off side and Kinleith Footprint on the nigh.

Brandon horsemen, Alex Colquhoun and Isaac Beatty, included Percherons in their importations. Beattie was ready to declare the stallion Halifax as the greatest Percheron handled by his firm and could tell of winning the supreme championship over all breeds at the Winnipeg exhibition in 1909 with him. It was after that show that the stallion was sold to George Lane of Alberta, on whose ranch he proved to be as outstanding as a breeder as he had been in the showrings.

It was an event of first importance in western Canada's horse history when George Lane in 1898 bought 600 grade horses and 32 pedigreed Percherons from James Mauldin of Montana. The grade horses were driven overland by the existing trails to Lane's ranch, while the purebreds received preferential treatment and were shipped by rail.[5] The Bar U Percherons did well and George Lane saw to it that the best breeding stock available in France or elsewhere was secured for improvement. Importations were made directly from the home of the breed in each of the years 1907 to 1910 and when Louis Aveline from La Perche visited Canada in the latter year, he pronounced the Bar U band of purebred Percherons as being as good as any in France.

In 1918, Lane reversed the usual order of shipments by sending the first consignment of purebred Percherons eastward across the Atlantic. Twenty-six mares and the stallion, Newport by Halifax, were sent to England and a bigger group consisting of fifty-three head was shipped to England in the next year. Of the

Langwater Jessica, raising her own foal and an orphan from another famous mare, Craigie Sylvia, 1930.

Paragon Fan, a Belgian mare owned by Rob Thomas of Grandora, Saskatchewan, was a consistent grand champion for many years.

Starlight Koncarness, a famous show Percheron mare, was bred and shown by Hardy Salter of Calgary.

shipment made in 1919, a London report noted: "Thirty-four Percheron horses bred by George Lane of Calgary were sold at Easton, Suffolk, and realized 7,018 pounds. Lord Minto bought a mare for 650 guineas. . . ."⁶

The Belgian, the last of the three major draft breeds to bid for western Canadian attention, had the most rapid rise to prominence. Its introduction to many parts of the prairie country was due to the efforts of the firm of Eugene Pootmans and Sons of Antwerp, Belgium, which opened an office and stable in Regina in 1910 and then started a breeding farm west of the city.

But the most spectacular contribution to Belgian horse history in the West was made by George Rupp, who migrated from his state of Iowa to settle at Lampman, Saskatchewan, in 1907. Horses of the breed were still unknown in many parts of the West, a situation which Rupp was determined to change. He founded his pioneer stud of carefully selected breeding animals in 1914 and two years later had the biggest band of purebred Belgians in Canada. At this point he bought the American-bred stallion, Paramount Wolver, sired by the greatest of North American Belgian sires known to that time, Farceur. The latter, imported from Belgium by William Crownover of Iowa in 1912, won the grand championship at Chicago in 1913 and then went to the ownership of C. G. Good and Son, also of Iowa, at the record sale price of $47,500.

Paramount Wolver appeared on the western exhibition circuit in 1917 and 1918 and shared championships with Dr. Charles Head's Fox De Roosbeke and was sold to be returned to Iowa at a sale figure of $11,400.

Rupp then appeared with the Belgian sensation of his time, Paramount Flashwood, also sired by Farceur. He was seen at the Canadian shows in 1919 and gathered a string of championships. But the crowning show success was later in the year when Rupp took him to the international Belgian show at Waterloo, Iowa, where he, as the horse from Saskatchewan where the breed was still pioneering, surprised the Americans by winning the grand championship for stallions.

Flashwood possessed substance, style and quality. At two and one-half years of age he was reported as weighing 2,090 pounds and when showing in his three-year-old form at Waterloo, he weighed 2,300 pounds. But Paramount Flashwood came to an early death in 1922 and in writing to one of the farm journals, the saddened owner stated: "I feel the loss very keenly as Flashwood was not only a horse but a part of the family. The loss is partly offset by a $25,000 insurance policy."

George Rupp left his Saskatchewan farm and returned to Iowa in the year after he lost Paramount

A thirty-two mule and horse team driven from the home farm east of Vulcan to the Calgary Exhibition and Stampede by Slim Moorehouse in 1924. When seen in Calgary, the outfit stretched a full block in length.

Six-horse teams in the showring at the Summer Exhibition in Saskatoon.

The winning six-horse team at the Royal Winter Fair, Toronto, 1932. It was owned and driven by Allan Leslie of Watrous, Saskatchewan.

Flashwood but he earned the right to be remembered as the owner of Paramount Wolver, Paramount Flashwood, and Pioneer Masterpiece, three of the Belgian "Greats" on the continent.

Still another son of Farceur — this one known as Monseur — was brought to western Canada by C. D. Roberts and Sons and sold to Robert Thomas of Grandora, Saskatchewan, for whom he distinguished himself as both a show horse and breeder. Monseur won the get-of-sire class at the Royal Winter Fair in 1922 and again in 1924, while the "get" of his son, Paragon Major, won the same award in 1928, 1929, 1930, and 1931, thereby bringing the coveted award to Robert Thomas six times in the first eleven years of Royal Winter Fair competition.

But by the years of Paragon Major's breeding successes, the Belgian and all draft horse breeds had fallen on troubled times.

Chapter 23

THE WAR YEARS AND AFTER

War is disruptive and cruel at any time and the "shockwaves" from World War I were felt over a bigger area than were those in any previous conflict. More than 600,000 young Canadians answered the call of the services and over 60,000 of those who saw Front Line action did not return.

For many others there were essential duties at home, making munitions, maintaining order, meeting the need for increased volumes of food, and so on. It was enemy strategy from the outset to blockade British coasts with the idea of starving the United Kingdom people into submission. German submarines roamed far in the Atlantic, sinking ships loaded with essential supplies. Wheat and other food upon which allied soldiers and civilians were depending were favorite targets for the submarines and losses were alarmingly heavy. Farmers in Canada were urged to produce more — at least twenty percent more — because, as proclaimed again and again: "Food Will Win the War."

But for Canadian farmers, increased production was extremely difficult. Their will was to comply and

Well-known Canadian cowboys competing at the Winnipeg Stampede of 1913.

IKE HERMAN   A.J. BRYSON   CLEM GARDNER,
CANADIAN CHAMPION   STEER ROPERS   WINNIPEG STAMPEDE 1913.

Florence La Due, the world champion lady fancy roper at the Winnipeg Stampede of 1913. She later married Guy Weadick of Calgary Stampede fame.

Dan Riley, who came to the Canadian foothills in 1884 and became a successful rancher, eventually sat in the senate of Canada.

deliver the increased supplies but after parting with sons and hired men to the armed services, expanded production seemed nigh impossible. There was no simple way of producing more wheat and cheese and meat with less farm help.

Public servants who were expected to be unfailing sources of timely advice were hard pressed to find helpful words. In generating more output with less input, they did not have much to offer except the age-old generalities about reducing waste and raising work efficiency. Hence farmers were told again and again to select their seed with care and clean it thoroughly before planting, to keep weeds down, and maintain farm machinery in a good state of repair in order to minimize delays and loss of working hours. The livestock men were told to exercise more thought about breeding and feeding practices, all of which the farmers had heard before. It was like a mother telling the members of her family to be good children.

Still, it was an opportune time to declare the principles of good farm management and the public figure doing it with better effect than any other was W. R. Motherwell, Saskatchewan's minister of agriculture. He was the one politician who, by 1915, could win and hold any farm audience. Already in the country thirty-three years, he was the young man, just out of Ontario Agricultural College, who came in 1882 to homestead. Leaving the train at Brandon, the westerly limit of rail service, he drove a pair of oxen from that point to choose a quarter section near where Aber-

nethy was located later. His natural leadership was easily recognized and after the province of Saskatchewan was formed, with Walter Scott as the premier, W. R. Motherwell became the minister of agriculture and held the portfolio for the next fourteen years, later to become minister of agriculture for Canada.

This typical Motherwell message was published in more than one of the farm papers in the war years:

TEN DRY FARMING COMMANDMENTS

1. Thou shalt have no other occupation than farming.

2. Thou shalt fallow thy land every third year, being careful to plough it both early and deeply.

3. Thou shalt cultivate thy fallow and not allow weeds or any other thing that is green to grow thereon, or winds to blow through it, for in such way the moisture which thy fallow should conserve will be wasted and thy days will be nothing but labor and sorrow.

4. Thou shalt not despise the harrow, but shalt use it even whilst thou ploughest, and shalt place thy chief reliance upon it thereafter,

whether in early spring, late spring, midsummer or autumn.

5. Thou shalt sow good seed early and down into the moisture, lest peradventure it cometh not up betimes. He who soweth his seed in dry soil casteth away many chances of reaping.

6. Thou shalt not overload thy dry land farm with seed, even as the merciful man doth not overload his ox or his ass. Thin seeding best withstandeth the ravages of drought and hot winds.

7. Thou shalt keep on thy farm such kinds and numbers of horses, cattle, sheep, pigs and poultry as the water supply maketh possible, and thou canst grow pasture, fodder, roots and grain for. Thus shalt thou be protected against adversity, and thus shalt thou give thy children and children's children cause to call thee blessed, inasmuch as thou didst not too greatly dissipate in thy lifetime the fertility stored in thy soil through many thousands of years.

8. Thou shalt not live unto thyself alone, but shall join the Grain Growers' Association, the agricultural society in thy district or any like minded organization that is good. Through these thou shalt work unceasingly for the welfare of thy district and the upbuilding of Saskatchewan agriculture.

9. Thou shalt study thy dry land farm and its problems unceasingly and ponder on ways and means whereby its fruitfulness may be increased, keeping always in memory the fact that not alone by speeches and resolutions, but also by intelligent and timely hard work shall production be increased and the economic salvation of thy country be wrought.

10. Thou shalt not covet thy neighbor's big farm. Thou shalt not covet thy neighbor's Big Four, nor his mortgage, nor his worry, nor his hurry, nor anything that is thy neighbour's.

Remember these dry farming commandments to keep them wholly.[1]

The help situation became worse rather than better and brought complaints but by one way or another, resourceful farmers managed to surmount the obstacles and make the war years as spectacular as they were agriculturally productive. The higher prices for farm produce triggered a new wave of big farming,

bigger expenditures for purebred breeding stock, supersize barns and the first clear acceptance of farm mechanization, especially in the form of light gasoline and kerosene burning tractors of two-plow and three-plow order.

The junior club movement, which began when E. Ward Jones, working under Dr. W. J. Black, principal of the Manitoba Agricultural College, organized a Boys' and Girls' Farm Club at Roland in 1913, was expanded during the war years, giving rise to club fairs, farm boys' camps and baby beef classes like the one conducted at Brandon Winter Fair in 1914. In due course the junior clubs became 4H clubs and flourished.

The most noteworthy of the big wartime farms was that of Charles S. Noble whose successes and reverses had a storybook quality. A native of the state of Iowa, he homesteaded near Claresholm in 1903 and broke his first land with a walking plow and pair of oxen, just like most other new people in homestead country. Seven years later he was buying and breaking a 5,000-acre spread northwest of Lethbridge, near where the village of Nobleford would be built. Then after another few years when the wartime call for more food was being sounded, Noble was buying the Cameron Ranch and bringing his holdings to 33,000 acres.

In the summer of 1917, ten big steam tractors pulling breaking plows were working around the clock to bring about 400 acres per day into the cultivated total. Visitors in the last year of war saw sixty-one binders at work and saw Charles Noble as a millionaire farmer. But reverses in the postwar period brought him to financial ruin. Still he was not finished. He wasn't one to accept failure and started again with nothing but his hands and experience. He rented back some of the land he had lost, then bought back some of it until he had regained about 8,000 acres and his place of eminence in the agricultural community of western Canada.

Another monument to wartime agriculture was "Horseshoe" Smith's big barn, said to be the biggest in the world. That 1915 barn has long since disappeared, its lumber having gone into the construction of scores of homesteaders' homes and stables. Only its foundation remained, showing the barn's dimensions to be 128 feet in width and 400 feet in length.

W. T. "Horseshoe" Smith came from Kentucky by way of Montana and Manitoba and settled beside the South Saskatchewan River west of present-day Leader about 1901. No doubt the opportunity for irrigation was a consideration in choosing the location. Having acquired 10,000 acres of land, he was at one time bringing irrigation water to 2,000 acres and was probably the biggest individual irrigator in Canada. With as many as 10,000 sheep, 3,000 horses and mules

W. T. SMITH'S RANCH
LEADER, SASK.
SIZE OF BARN: 128 × 400 ft. HIGHT 60 ft.
MATERIAL USED FOR CONSTRUCTION 875,000 ft. LUMBER,
30,000 SACKS CANADA PORTLAND CEMENT, 60,000 ft. CORRUGATED
GALVANIZED IRON ROOFING, & 7 VENTILATORS,
RANCH CONTAINS 10,000 ACRES, 2000 ACRES UNDER
IRRIGATION & IS LARGEST ALFALFA & CORN FARM IN SASK.

The big W. T. Smith barn, west of Leader, Saskatchewan, was said to be the biggest barn in the world. It was 400 feet long and 128 feet wide.

and 2,000 pigs, he needed the security of dependable feed supplies.[2]

One of his important sidelines was the sale of horses to settlers and this business may have prompted the big plan for a barn. The decision to build was made soon after the outbreak of the war and one of his first acts was to drive by democrat and team of mules to interview his banker at Maple Creek. Neighbors said he returned with $80,000 cash tied in a bran sack and then began to draw plans and order materials for a barn that would shelter 2,200 head of horses and other livestock. He wanted it to fulfill a dream and be the biggest — and it was.

Construction took thirty-two carloads of first-grade B.C. fir and a carload of nails. The dealers in nails refused at first to take his order seriously and he had to make a special trip to Winnipeg to get satisfaction. A hundred men were sawing boards and pounding nails through the spring and summer months of 1915, and when the building was completed, Smith ordered a barn dance in the loft and everybody within traveling distance was invited. Two orchestras — one at each end of the loft — furnished the dance music and the celebration lasted all night.

It was the year of the big crop on the prairies and Smith threshed almost a hundred thousand bushels, using two big steam-driven outfits to do it. But Smith, then seventy years of age, was ailing and his death three years later coincided roughly with the end of war. He had never married. There was nobody to follow him on the ranch. Creditors moved to protect their equity and the big barn was dismantled in 1920. Settlers in all directions needed lumber and bought the material, leaving only the extensive bunkhouses, a modest residence, and the indestructible foundations into the construction of which had gone 30,000 bags of Portland cement.

Smith's heart was that of a horseman and he, like many other horsemen, would have been slow to concede that tractors were on the march toward domination on farms. Even governments believed that more and better horses would make it unnecessary for farmers to invest in tractors for field work. The federal department of agriculture, early in 1915, was offering encouragement to horse breeding by announcing that farmers forming clubs for the hiring of approved draft stallions could quality for refunds of service fees amounting to twenty-five percent. Where they organized to breed the urgently wanted army remounts, the refund from the public treasury could be forty percent.[3]

But tractors with new shapes and sizes were appearing and nothing was interrupting their progress. The steamer, still a favorite for threshing, was losing its appeal for plowing. A generation of relatively small gasoline or kerosene-burning tractors — two-plow and three-plow sizes — was appearing and inviting attention.

Recognizing the growing interest, the Brandon exhibition of 1916 offered a Light Tractor Plowing Demonstration, the first of its kind in the West. The response confirmed that the tractor of the future would be small to fit the needs of the average farmer. Moreover, the small ones were likely to represent the best value in relation to investment because as a war measures arrangement the federal government was refunding the import duty on all incoming tractors for farm use which carried a cost not in excess of $1,400 in the country of origin.

A farm editor reported that 3,000 farmers were interested spectators on the third day of the tractor demonstration and offered an opinion: "The big tractors have had their fling and this is the day for the smaller power plant. Just how small or how large the popular tractor will be is still a debatable question. The smallest tractors at this demonstration drew two-bottom gangs while the larger ones pulled three, four and five bottoms."[4]

Nineteen tractors from thirteen different companies were entered in this noncompetitive plowing demonstration, among them the two-plow Peoria which was priced at $1,050 at Winnipeg; the three-plow Happy Farmer advertised for $850, Winnipeg; a two-plow Rumely complete with plows marked at $1,050 and a three-plow Rumely at $1,350, Winnipeg,

also complete with plows; and the Waterloo Boy costing a little more, $1,475 at Winnipeg.

The J.I. Case Company was still advertising steam tractors in seven sizes from 30 to 110 horsepower. Farmers were making complimentary remarks about them but were not buying. They were showing more interest in another J.I. Case product, the "Case 40" touring car which was on the market for $1,020, f.o.b. Racine, Wisconsin. The fact was that car manufacturers were bidding for attention in the same way as the tractor makers, and farmers were taking notice. They knew from reading the farm journals that they could, if sufficiently bold, buy an Overland car for $890 at Toronto, a Gray-Dort for $850 at Chatham, a Chevrolet for $650 at Oshawa, a Maxwell for $850 at Windsor, a Studebaker for $1,165 at Walkerville, a McLaughlin for $1,110 at Oshawa, or a Ford for $495 at Ford, Ontario — all prices being for touring car models.[5]

Before the end of the war, farmers were reading or hearing about at least a score of new gasoline tractors, many of them with curious shapes, reflecting the manufacturers' uncertainty about the farm needs and wishes. Among the new ones were the Bates Steel Mule, a 13-30 horsepower tractor with two wheels in front and a single caterpillar track behind, priced at $1,500, Winnipeg. The Rein-Drive tractor was one which would permit the farm user to feel at home riding where he had always ridden, on the field implement being pulled, and doing the driving, horse fashion, with two lines. The Cleveland tractor, with

The Titan tractor of 1914 won exceptional popularity as an alternative to the big and cumbersome steamers.

12-20 horsepower rating, had two caterpillar tracks and was priced at $2,050 at Calgary. Then there was the four-plow Gray with a single drum-like drive wheel the full width of the tractor. There was no lack of manufacturer imagination but among the tractors that proved popular and stood up well were ones of simple design like the 12-24 horsepower Waterloo Boy weighing 4,800 pounds, and the 10-20 Titan made by the International Harvester Company, both with two-cylinder motors.

Significantly, the biggest tractor influence of 1918 was one of the smallest tractors, the Fordson, a product of the Ford Motor Company in the United States. Some years earlier, Henry Ford expressed a hope of designing and producing a car, a truck, and a tractor which farmers could buy for a total of $1,000. It was not a hope that he was to realize but the intent was admirable. Now, in response to the widespread need for more farm power in allied countries, the Fordson was coming into production and the first 6,000 were being taken on contract by the British government. In February of that year, 1918, a news report from Ottawa told that the Canadian government was following the British example and ordering one thousand of the tractors to be resold to Canadian farmers at cost as part of the Canadian Greater Production Fleet.[6] The cost was not expected to exceed $800 delivered, and delivery would commence as soon as the British order had been filled and before any Fordsons were offered for sale through the usual trade channels.

The first of the new tractors began moving to Canadian farm points in May with the price fixed at $795 cash at place of delivery. Farm interest ran high and farmers who had never seen a Fordson were buying on faith. The first thousand sold quickly and buyers were generally pleased with this two-plow, four-cylinder invention designed along quite different lines. The Fordson was compact and fast and handy. It had no visible moving parts except its wheels and had a road speed of eight or ten miles per hour. It was soon evident that the Fordson was setting new standards in design and accounting for the retirement of many more farm horses in the postwar years.

Agriculture in that last year of the war appeared to be booming, even though 1918 was a dry year on the prairies. Grain and livestock prices were strong and some price records were being established. Hereford bulls seemed to be leading the price parade, with Martin Fairfax being brought to Saskatchewan at $17,000 and Gay Lad 16th to Alberta at $20,000. Still more sensational was the price of $106,000 paid for an eastern Holstein bull calf, Carnation King Sylvia, bred by A. C. Hardy of Brockville, Ontario, and bought by Carnation Farms, Seattle.

But nothing in western agriculture felt wartime

Herman Trelle (left) and J. C. Mitchell were both western Canadian winners of world championships for wheat.

measures more forcefully than wheat marketing. Wartime Britain was looking to Canada for wheat supplies and while German submarines were being used to try to starve the population into surrender, it was imperative that Canadian wheat be delivered. Prices and marketing were too important to be left to the speculative dealers or the Winnipeg Grain Exchange interests, and late in 1915 when the big crop of that year was being moved eastward, the government of Canada seized control of all wheat at the Head of the Lakes. The British government then placed its buying agency known as the Wheat Export Company, right at Winnipeg.

The Grain Exchange continued to function and prices continued to rise, reaching three dollars per bushel on May 11, 1917. As governments became more and more involved, there seemed no justification in maintaining the speculative market and the Winnipeg futures trading was suspended.

United States, facing the same problems, set up a giant state-run monopoly to fix prices and actually buy and sell. Canada did about the same by appointing the Board of Grain Supervisors on June 11, 1917. The board then established prices and directed distribution. In its first directive, to take effect on August 1, 1917, the board set the price of Number One Northern wheat at two dollars and forty cents per bushel, Fort William. The next step by government was taken in September, 1918, when the Board of Supervisors was given full control of grain marketing in both domestic and export areas.

The war ended a couple of months later but the marketing problems did not disappear and the board's responsibilities in the face of threatened famine in much of Europe remained for a time. But the grain speculators wanted to get back to their trade and there were pressures upon government to disband the board. Farmers, on the other hand, had but little faith in the Grain Exchange and opposed the return of the open market. It was known that the United States had set wheat prices for the 1919 crop and Canadian growers, through the Canadian Council of Agriculture, were asking the government of Canada for a National Wheat Pool or Wheat Board to retain control. The request was granted and Canada's first Wheat Board was constituted to handle the crop of that year. The Board announced an initial price of two dollars and fifteen cents per bushel and growers would be given participation certificates entitling them to further payment. That was fine while it lasted but it didn't last long.

Chapter 24

THE FARMERS IN ORGANIZATION AND POLITICS

For farmers dreaming of a time when they would have their own elected representatives in parliament and legislatures, 1921 looked like the year of fulfillment. A Farmers' Government in power in Alberta and a big block of Progressive members in the House of Commons brought reassurance and some quiet rejoicing. In the opinion of some of those in the agrarian movement, the acquisition of political power was a prime reason for farmer organization.

Complaints arising from unsatisfactory prices, tariffs, faulty distribution, and government policies were almost as ancient as agriculture and farmers recognized only two ways of dealing with them, one through organization to bring pressure to bear upon governments and the other by direct political action, meaning political participation. Certainly the two were not unrelated. Both presented difficulties.

Farmers were well aware of the need to band together in order that the industry might have a stronger voice. The farm scene was broad and it was not easy to obtain a united viewpoint. Moreover, it was easier to start farm organizations than to keep them alive and vigorous. Experience showed that it was easy enough to keep agricultural societies flourishing, but not politically oriented agrarian associations.

Reference was made in an earlier chapter (A Decade of Decision) to certain pioneer farm organizations such as the Grange which had been a powerful force in the United States and was introduced to western Canada through a local chapter formed at High Bluff in 1876. Likewise, the Farmers' Alliance and the Patrons of Industry were American-based farm movements which enjoyed brief popularity on the Canadian side. The latter, with a particularly strong political bias, seemed to be making headway

until its candidates were convincingly beaten in the general election of 1896.

Of the strictly "home-grown" farm movements, the first was the Manitoba and North West Farmers' Union organized in 1883. At its first meeting in Brandon, delegates drew up a Farm Bill of Rights and proceeded to agitate for government grading of grains, a railroad to Hudson Bay and reduction of tariffs — all good planks for a farm platform. But it was the Territorial Grain Growers' Association, founded at Indian Head in 1901 and with which the name of W. R. Motherwell will be forever linked, that gained distinction by escaping an early demise.

By 1906, this Grain Growers' Association was taking a giant step in both the farm and co-operative movements by forming the Grain Growers' Grain Company to market grains. With the militant A. E. Partridge from Sintaluta as the guiding force, this new company obtained a seat on the Winnipeg Grain Exchange where co-operatives were most unwelcome. The farmers' company was expelled from the exchange on a technicality but the Partridge determination triumphed and the Grain Growers' Grain Company was re-admitted.

In Alberta, the United Farmers of Alberta — or UFA — of which much was to be heard, was born when the existing Society of Equity joined with the Alberta Farmers' Association in 1909. It must have inherited unusual life and vigor.

These organizations were becoming interested in co-operative ownership of elevators, leading to the formation in 1911 of the Saskatchewan Co-operative Elevator Company and in 1913 of the Alberta Farmers' Co-operative Elevator Company. In the latter province in 1917, the Co-operative Elevator Company and the Grain Growers' Grain Company amalgamated to

Officers and directors of the joint board at the amalgamation of the Grain Growers Grain Company and the Alberta Farmers Co-operative Elevators, 1917.

The Canadian Council of Agriculture, Winnipeg, Manitoba, 1918.

Irene Parlby, who was named to a cabinet post in the 1921 United Farmers of Alberta government, was the first woman in Alberta to be called to such a post and the second in Canada and in the British Empire to be given a ministerial position. (Glenbow-Alberta Institute.)

Henry Wise Wood, long-time president of the United Farmers of Alberta and first chairman of the Alberta Wheat Pool from its inception of 1923 until 1937.

create the United Grain Growers Ltd., with T. A. Crerar being chosen to be the first president.

More farm organizations appeared, among them the Canadian Council of Agriculture which arose from an affiliation in 1909 and 1910 of what remained of the Dominion Grange as it was serving in Ontario with the Manitoba Grain Growers' Association, Saskatchewan Grain Growers' Association, and United Farmers of Alberta. Then there was the Farm Union of Canada (Saskatchewan) which began in Saskatchewan in 1921 and became strong and influential as well as controversial. Some years later, the Canadian Chamber of Agriculture was formed while the Royal Winter Fair of 1935 was in progress, a movement which would ultimately become the Federation of Agriculture. At times there seemed to be too many farm organizations, defeating the purpose of one strong and unified body speaking with a single voice. If it was fair criticism, the goal of unity was still to be reached.

In politics, the farmers had their best years immediately after 1919 when T. A. Crerar, who had been minister of agriculture in the Union government of Prime Minister Robert Borden, broke away in protest to a budget that gave what he believed was inadequate support to the principle of free trade. In his withdrawal, Crerar took nine other Borden supporters with him, thus giving rise to a group which under Crerar's leadership became known as the Progressives. The dissenters, mostly from the West and with strong

loyalties to agriculture, displayed vigor and enthusiasm and won immediate admiration from farming people across the country. In the following January, the Canadian Council of Agriculture called a meeting in Winnipeg at which its officers presided over the more formal launching of the National Progressive Party as preparation for a general election expected to be called very soon.

In that election of 1921, the Liberals took 117 seats and formed a minority government. The Progressives elected 65 members — more than half of them from the West — and seized the balance of power and enjoyed it.

These successes gained by the Progressives in the federal arena, coupled with the knowledge that the United Farmers of Ontario acting as a political party triumphed in the Ontario election of 1919, fired other provincial farm bodies to consider their own involvement. The most spectacular provincial success was in Alberta where Henry Wise Wood, president of the United Farmers, advised against involvement as a party. It was his view that instead of fielding their own candidates, the farmers should be well organized to use their political weight in influencing all existing parties.[1]

But the Alberta farmers chose direct political action and when the decision was made, Wood gave his full support to the nomination and election of his people. The election was on June 17, 1921, and

Albertans received their biggest political surprises. The Liberal party had been in power since the inception of the province in 1905 and seemed likely to get another mandate. But contrary to expectations, Wood's Farmers won in thirty-nine of the sixty-one constituencies and faced the necessity of forming the next government, for which they were totally unprepared. The newly elected Farmer members wanted their sagacious Henry Wise Wood to become their leader and premier but Wood chose to remain to direct his UFA organization and the choice for premier fell to Herbert Greenfield.

A year later, Farmer candidates won the provincial election in Manitoba and brought John Bracken from his position as president of the Manitoba Agricultural College to be premier.

By 1925, however, the federal Progressives were losing their earlier drive and effectiveness and in the federal election of that year the party's elected members were reduced from the previous 65 to 25. The Conservatives had the largest number of members returned — 116 to the Liberal's 101 — but the Progressives were induced to support Mackenzie King's Liberal minority to let it retain the government. Gradually, the Progressive lost their identity and some were attracted to other parties.

The agrarian party in Alberta, on the other hand, remained in power until 1935 when it was displaced by the new Social Credit party, and the Manitoba Farmers, or what became known as the Bracken government, had an even longer record of administration. The Manitoba group remained until its character was changed by coalition of the provincial parties in 1940 — with Bracken still the premier.

The Farmer governments in Alberta and Manitoba gave sound and enterprising administration, demonstrating clearly that the relatively quiet "sons of the soil" could do it. Their performance was in the same western spirit of reform that led to the birth at Calgary in 1932 of the Co-operative Commonwealth Federation or CCF party and a short time later of the Social Credit party which defeated the Farmers in the 1935 election.

Chapter 25

THE TRIUMPHANT BIRTH OF THE WHEAT POOLS

Out of the frustrations of the postwar years came the prairie wheat pools, the biggest self-help achievements in the history of agriculture.

War's end brought universal sighs of relief, naturally, but as wartime ills like farm help shortage eased, new ones appeared. Prices for farm products slumped as might have been expected, but nobody was ready. And to compound the farmer's plight, dry years came again. The low average of 10.2 bushels of wheat per acre across the West in 1918 and 9.3 bushels in 1919 indicated the extent of drought, and thoughts turned again to irrigation. Projects which had been suspended during the years of war received renewed attention and a few people were boldly discussing weather modification. Didn't California, some years earlier, have an experience with an alleged rainmaker, Prof. Thaddeus Lowe, whose price for a rainstorm was $8,000? The professor had observed that big army battles were frequently followed by rainstorms and his technique was to burn gunpowder on the ground and, at the same time, use balloons for setting explosions in the clouds.[1]

Farmers in the area of Medicine Hat heard about a more modern rainmaker and invited Charles Hatfield, said to have had success in coaxing rain from indifferent clouds, to discuss a contract. Hatfield came and a deal was made. What followed was reported this way: "Since Charles M. Hatfield, the rainmaker, commenced operations on May 1, in an area which extends for a radius of one hundred miles, nearly an inch [of rain] has fallen in all sections of this territory. His apparatus is set up in Chappice Lake, near this city [of Medicine Hat]. An organization known as the United Farmers' Association will pay Hatfield $1,000 an inch for a maximum rainfall of eight inches during the months of May, June and July. A guarantee fund

has been raised for the purpose. Precipitation gauges on which the demonstration will be judged, will be erected at Medicine Hat, Empress, Jenner, Vauxhall and Bow Island. Hatfield does not claim to be able with his chemicals to draw rain from a clear sky but maintains that he has acquired the science of tapping moisture-laden clouds."[2]

The arrangement was that Hatfield could collect on half of the rain falling in the three months and luck was with him because rain started falling a few days after he arrived. Farmers coming to town to buy raincoats expressed the hope that the miracle man would "shut it off" when they started haying. But other parts of the prairies were getting rain at the same time and Hatfield's claim to credit for any part of it was being questioned. He enjoyed the widespread public attention and he collected his fees but was not pressed to return in the next year.

In spite of Hatfield, most farmers regarded drought as a sort of penalty for sins and beyond the control of governments or themselves. Dryland farmers might have to suffer in silence. But low prices for grain were different and if governments did nothing to correct the injustices, the producers would have every right to attempt it themselves. The drop in wheat prices was too sharp to be accepted without a protest. The 1920 yields were better than in the two previous years but the prices were worse. Number One Northern wheat which had realized $2.24½ per bushel at Fort William in the last year of the Board of Grain Supervisors, 1918, was averaging $1.75 on the open market in 1920, then $1.29 in 1921, and falling below $1.00 in 1922.

The Board of Grain Supervisors with eleven members and full trading control, as constituted in June, 1917, was remembered favorably, almost affectionately. Not only had it paid $2.21 per bushel for the 1917 crop and $2.24½ per bushel in 1918 but it had also brought the closure of the trading in futures at Winnipeg and it gave wheat growers their first taste of stable prices.

It wasn't surprising that the termination of the Board of Grain Supervisors brought farmers clamoring for a Wheat Board with equivalent control over marketing. The growers got their board, even in the face of much government reluctance. The new board, with James Stewart from Maple Leaf Milling Company as chairman, F. W. Riddell who had been general manager of the Saskatchewan Co-operative Elevator Company, as vice-chairman and Henry Wise Wood as the third member, began at the middle of August, 1919, announcing that farmers would receive $2.15 per bushel, basis, as usual, Number One Northern, Fort William, also participation certificates, entitling the holders to possible later payments if there happened to be a surplus on the year's transactions. Some observers were sure there would be no further payments, and because the certificates were negotiable, some of them changed hands at prices as low as 10 cents per bushel. But along about midsummer, 1920, an interim payment of 30 cents per bushel was paid and still later, a final payment of 18 cents a bushel brought the total return on the 1919 wheat to $2.63 per bushel, Fort William basis, which might mean about $2.31 at distant Alberta points. Nothing more was needed to confirm the wheat grower's faith in the wheat board principle.

But the government had its own reasons for indifference toward the Wheat Board and ended its existence on July 31, 1920, allowing trading to return to the Winnipeg Grain Exchange.

Farmers wanted another Wheat Board and when it was being denied, their spirits rebelled. They recalled the pioneer years when railroads granted monopoly loading rights to anybody owning a local elevator and farmers had no choice but to accept elevator grades and weights and prices which often seemed suspiciously low. Reacting to those circumstances, the farmers, starting around Indian Head, organized the Territorial Grain Growers' Association and took a united stand which brought relief.

Now, as they were again in a position to be victimized by middlemen and were finding no comfort from a government that was refusing to provide a board, they were talking again about doing something for themselves. Many of their own people had misgivings about a big marketing enterprise operated by inexperienced farmers. "A farm-sponsored Pool won't work," they said.

Notwithstanding the pessimists, talk about a "grass roots" marketing organization became louder. Henry Wise Wood, speaking as president of the United Farmers of Alberta, urged an immediate study of a voluntary co-operative pool. He and his members were discovering the punching power of their own political muscle, having just seen their Farmers' party swept into power in the 1921 provincial election.

Farmers dreaming about organizing their own pool or pools needed the guidance of somebody with at least a modicum of experience with such things. Always when pooling was under discussion, there was mention of Aaron Sapiro, a California lawyer who had a record of success in organizing fruit and tobacco pools in his state. A visit from him would be helpful, but an obvious obstacle to people who had no funds for visiting speakers was the probable cost. But a conversation in the office of the managing editor of the *Calgary Herald*, Charles Hayden, brought the managing director, Col. J. H. Wood, into the discussion and a proposal that the *Herald* and the *Edmonton Journal* would jointly invite Sapiro and pay the cost. The invitation went by telegram and Sapiro agreed to come.

Two meetings were scheduled for Calgary on August 3, one a small gathering of farm leaders at which Henry Wise Wood occupied the chair, and the other a public meeting at the Victoria Park Pavilion in the evening, with Mayor George Watson in the role of chairman. Both meetings were fired by Sapiro enthusiasm and notwithstanding the lateness of the season, most of those present favored a short but vigorous drive for farmer contracts that would commit a minimum of fifty percent of the wheat acreage in the province.

Successive meetings were held at Edmonton, Camrose, and Lacombe and then Sapiro went on to Saskatchewan and Manitoba. An Alberta committee of seventeen members, with Wood as chairman, was appointed and given a provincial loan of $5,000 for organizational expenses. The campaign goal for the two weeks, August 20 to September 5, was a sign-up of delivery promises for a five-year period, covering a minimum of 2,842,798 acres of wheat. The contract provided that if the objective of a fifty percent acreage committal were not reached in the two-week period, signers would have until September 22 to withdraw.

The United Farmers of Alberta gave strong support and members worked hard, some of them, no doubt, neglecting their own harvests. The West had a big crop that year, exceeding 400,000,000 bushels of wheat for the first time. In view of the lateness of the season, nobody could be sure that the fifty percent goal would be reached and on September 5, it was clear that the goal had not been reached — not quite. The aggregate showed 26,719 signed contracts representing 2,616,721 acres of wheat, 226,077 acres short of the objective. The signers had their chance to withdraw but not many did — fewer than five percent —

A. J. McPhail, the first president of the Saskatchewan Wheat Pool.

The board of directors of the Canadian Co-operative Wheat Producers Ltd., 1924.

and most farmers were still enthusiastic. Acting on urging from the country, the committee decided to proceed with the formation of a marketing pool. With a Wheat Pool in 1923, Alberta was the first province to have one.

The upstart Alberta organization managed to market 34,000,000 bushels of wheat in that first year and the average price of $1.01, basis Fort William, left growers convinced that their big gamble was very much worth while.

Saskatchewan and Manitoba had the will and the enthusiasm but time proved too short and leaders in both provinces decided to concentrate their organizational effort upon 1924. The great and respected Henry Wise Wood, who might have been minister of agriculture in the Union government at Ottawa or the premier of Alberta in 1921, came to Saskatchewan to

The Lougheed building in Calgary where the Alberta Wheat Pool established its first office.

help with the campaign. It was fortunate that just as Alberta had Wood with some of the qualities of a Solomon, so Saskatchewan had Alexander James McPhail, the forty-year-old bachelor farmer from near Elfros, who had been secretary of the Saskatchewan Grain Growers' Association, and Manitoba had C. H. Burnell, with the same quality of dedication. They worked diligently and in Saskatchewan where the same fifty percent of wheat acreage was set as the minimum to be required for organization, McPhail, on July 16, 1924, wrote in his journal: "Wheat Pool over the top today."[3]

At that date the Saskatchewan committee had 46,509 signed contracts committing the required 6,433,778 acres of wheat.

With the organization of the three provincial pools completed, the leaders met in July and formed what was known commonly as the Central Selling Agency — more correctly the Co-operative Wheat Producers Limited, with McPhail as chairman, Wood as vice-chairman, and Burnell as secretary.

Manitoba was quickly concerned about elevators and found it necessary to lease elevator space at country points and terminals. This was not satisfactory and there was an instant demand for pool-owned elevators. The Manitoba members' contracts, in addition to providing for a pooling system, permitted deductions of two cents per bushel on deliveries for the purpose of acquiring elevators. A further deduction not exceeding one percent could be made for the creation of a reserve fund and the money from these, in the first contract period, was loaned to the subsidiary Manitoba Pool Elevators for the construction or purchase of elevators. Between 1924 and 1931, Manitoba Pool Elevators built or bought 152 country elevators. At each point where an elevator was obtained, a local Co-operative Elevator Association was formed to lease the elevator.

The prairie wheat farmers were in business in a bigger way than farmers had ever been before, and by the end of the first five-year period when new contracts were being obtained, they had handled and sold through their pools almost a billion bushels of wheat. The new contracts and the continuing farm loyalty confirmed the farm backing. That was good, but there were testing times ahead.

The Saskatchewan Wheat Pool building during the 1950s.

The West had another big crop in 1928 —, 545,000,000 bushels of wheat, making it the first time that production exceeded a half billion bushels. Canada was then in the position of being the world's leading exporter of wheat. The pools, with 150,000 members, were in a commanding position. The volume of wheat handled by the pools represented about half of Canada's total. Maybe it was dangerously big for men whose marketing experience at international levels was still limited.

For the wheat from that big crop, the initial pool payment was 85 cents per bushel and successive payments brought the total to $1.20. There was no complaint — except from competitors who had lingering trouble in accepting the giant co-operative. The principal controversy, internally, was about a proposal to secure legislation to establish a 100 percent compulsory pool. Aaron Sapiro — still a phantom in the pool movement — advocated it and Louis Brouillette, vice-president of the Saskatchewan pool, supported it. A. J. McPhail and Henry Wise Wood, on the other hand, were opposed to the compulsory feature, and unfortunately, ill feeling resulted. Events of the next year, however, almost destroyed the pools.

The year 1929 started bravely and pool leaders were optimistic. They were still confident when they fixed the initial payment for the new crop at $1.00 per

The Wheat Pool building in Winnipeg, 1928.

bushel, a figure which did not seem to be out of line when Winnipeg wheat was close to $1.50 per bushel. Even the bankers who furnished the year's credit agreed. But international forces were working obscurely. Perhaps they should have been recognized. A big wheat carry-over at home and abroad might have been identified as a threat. In any case, along in October, the economic "roof fell in," first at New York and then in distant parts. Wheat prices dropped and continued their descent until the pools were in danger of losing control of their grains. When the price of wheat reached $1.15 per bushel, which represented the initial payment plus a fifteen percent margin, the banks could have forced sales to protect their equity and were probably prevented from doing so only by the action of the three provincial governments which, on the pleadings of the pools, came forward to guarantee the bank loans, accepting elevators or other assets for partial security. Thus the pools were able to hold their wheat for the price recovery which everybody expected and which did not come. Instead of recovery, prices plunged lower and went below the amount of the initial payment made by the pools.

At year's end, much of the pool wheat had been sold below the initial price and the pools were left with big debts to the provinces, $3,300,000 in Manitoba, $12,500,000 in Saskatchewan, and $5,500,000 in Alberta. Provinces took over the elevator assets. In Manitoba, later, the Wheat Pool went into bankruptcy. Association leases were canceled and the local associations, by an agreement in 1931, were to buy the elevators for a total of $2,100,000 which amount the government agreed to take in full settlement of the debt. The payment which completely retired the debt to the province was made in 1949.

Pool enemies couldn't hide their satisfaction and were sure these reverses would end the pool menace forever. Even overseas grain merchants, who criticized the pooling policy of withholding grains when markets became dull, seemed happy.

But the pools were not alone in their financial woes. The depression was worldwide and it was going to be slow in correcting itself. Contrary to expectations, prices did not rebound and the pools had more trouble in financing for the 1930 crop. Again banks required guarantees which the provincial governments supplied. This time the pools resolved to make an initial payment of 70 cents a bushel. Surely that would be sufficiently cautious, even in a period of depression. But the price of wheat on the world market continued to fall and the pools were obliged to take the humiliating step of dropping the initial price from 70 cents to 50 cents. By November of 1930, the world price had reached about to the latter figure and

R. B. Bennett of Calgary, later Prime Minister Bennett of Canada, inspecting the loading of the first cargo at the Alberta Wheat Pool elevator in Vancouver.

McPhail expressed his gloom in his journel entry on November 14: "Everything is tottering."[4]

Pool members were worried. Some called again for a compulsory pool. Some were deserting. Pool executives had to submit to the will of their creditors. John I. McFarland from the Alberta Pacific Grain Company was brought in to become general manager and save what he could. Given full authority with the backing of the governments and the banks, he departed far from pool policy. He closed the London office of the Central Selling Agency and disturbed much co-operative pride by selling pool wheat on the Winnipeg market.

A summer meeting in 1931 brought a new pool

policy. In view of the recent failures, members were released from contracts, to sell their grain wherever they believed they could sell to advantage. They were urged, however, to continue to pool their wheat if they desired and to use pool elevators wherever possible. It marked a turning point, setting the pools on a new course, that of handlers more than sellers, especially after the Canadian Wheat Board became a permanent instrument in marketing. The pools became specialists in elevators and related services and did well.

In Manitoba, part of the debt was written off by the province while in Saskatchewan and Alberta, the debts were paid in full. The total debt payments including capital and interest made by the three pools was $31,731,302.78.[5]

When Manitoba Pool Elevators marked the fiftieth anniversary in 1974 and the troubles of the earlier period were largely forgotten, it could be reported that 22,000 farmer members owned 323 elevators at 211 points and handled about 63 percent of the province's grain deliveries. In Saskatchewan at the same time, the reports showed 1,528 elevators with capacity of 115 million bushels and handling "almost 68 percent of total deliveries." Alberta's anniversary account revealed 858 country elevators with capacity for 77 million bushels and a claim to handling 68 percent of total provincial deliveries.

Chapter 26

DEPRESSION, DROUGHT, AND DRIFTING SOILS

The Wheat Pools were not alone in feeling the brutal blows of the thirties. For agriculture everywhere — and for the rest of the community — they were the West's blackest years. Being forced to suffer a prolonged spell of depression or drought would have been bad enough but when the evil forces came together and remained together — like wolves hunting in packs — the results were devastating, leaving debts, eroded soils, depleted herds, broken dreams, and frustration in their wake.

If the beginning of the decade-long ordeal were to be pinpointed, it would have to fall upon Friday, October 18, 1929, on which date panic struck the New York stock market and sent its "shockwaves" over the entire western world. Trading on the preceding Wednesday was said to have shown "a nervous price tendency" but markets were always fluctuating and nobody seemed greatly alarmed until the next day when press headlines conveyed the more ominous news: "New York Market Breaks Sharply In Heavy Selling." But it was on Friday that the market "bulls" took to wild flight with the "bears" in pursuit. It became a day of confusion and fear, with the Manitoba press reporting the New York scene this way:

"Another billion dollars or more was lopped from the stock exchange values Friday when fears succeeded in dislodging support from Montgomery Ward, United States Steel and a long list of other blue chips. . . . Gloom prevailed in the bullish ranks as traders large and small saw fortunes wrested from them. Thousands upon thousands of dollars in profits melted away in the morning. . . . In the last hour, there was no attempt to stay the avalanche of sales and prices dropped like plummets into the abyss. In the after-

noon losses were figured in millions and at the close at least a billion dollars was lopped off values."[1]

Winnipeg wheat prices dropped about five cents a bushel which was like a disaster for speculators but most people were quite sure the decline was temporary. When the markets opened at the beginning of the next week, financial institutions brought their dollar resources with which to prop the trade and avert further collapse, but it didn't work.

Those people who made public utterances felt duty-bound to play the part of the optimist; the downward trend in prices for agricultural products would not last long, they were saying, and the reverse trend would offer opportunities for easy and rapid wealth. But instead of turning upward, prices continued lower and lower until wheat touched that almost unbelievable point of 38 cents a bushel for Number One Northern at Fort William, said to have been the lowest price in world markets in a hundred years.

As it was told by the *Manitoba Free Press*: "Shattering all previous low prices, wheat values slumped 3¾ to 4 cents Friday [Dec. 16, 1932] in the course of the worst break since last June. . . . December wheat dropped to 38 cents in store Fort William. On this basis it was worth only about 20 cents per bushel to the farmer at the elevator in Saskatchewan while to the farmer in the Peace River who pays a much higher freight rate, it was worth probably not more than 12 or 13 cents."[2]

Farmers found it difficult to accept what was happening, made worse by the fact that while the best milling wheat in the world was bringing less than $7 per ton in Saskatchewan, one of its byproducts, namely bran, was still being quoted at $13 a ton.

According to a later calculation, the Fort William prices on that December day, when No. 1 N. wheat touched 38 cents, would give wheat of equal grade an elevator price of 19½ cents a bushel at Calgary and Edmonton, and 12½ cents at Dawson Creek. The grower with No. 6 wheat could expect 11½ cents a bushel at Edmonton and 4½ cents at Dawson Creek. Feed wheat at Dawson Creek on the same day would have had a cash worth of 1½ cents a bushel. For 2 C.W.

oats, the elevator price would have been 7½ cents at Edmonton and 4 cents at Peace River points.[3]

A northern farmer whose story, for what it was worth, was told again and again, took a load of barley to the local elevator and discovered from the agent that deductions for handling and dockage totaled more than the cash price for the grain. The farmer was in debt to the elevator buyer to the extent of one dollar. The farmer, who did not have a dollar, said he was sorry he could not pay the debt but would bring the elevator man a dressed chicken or a few dozens of

This scene at Melita, Manitoba, shows the desolation resulting from drought and wind in the 1930's.

The same Melita, Manitoba area after rehabilitation.

eggs. The agent was agreeable and said: "Bring me the dressed chicken."

The farmer, appearing more upright than bright, arrived at the elevator a few days later with two dressed chickens and handed them to the agent. "But," said the elevator man, "one chicken would have satisfied your debt. Why did you bring two?"

"Yes, I remember," the farmer replied, "but today I am bringing you another load of barley."

The best butcher steers at the Winnipeg stockyards on that historic day of low wheat prices were quoted at $4.00 per hundred pounds, while bacon pigs were commanding $3.10 per hundred pounds liveweight, plus a premium of $1.00 per head on pigs meeting the Select grade standards. Fat lambs were bringing $3.75 per hundred. The Winnipeg produce trade quoted 20 cents a pound for creamery butter and 30 cents a dozen for fresh eggs. A Montreal market report gave the current price for the best bush or farm horses as $80 to $100.[4]

The lowest prices for livestock and livestock products came later. At the end of October, 1933, the Winnipeg stockyards' report named $2.50 to $3.00 per hundred as the price for good butcher steers. Feeder steers were trading between $1.50 and $2.00 per hundred, and good butcher cows, $1.40 to $1.60 per hundred.[5]

Leonard Nesbitt told of a farmer in the northeastern part of Alberta who hired a truck for the purpose of taking his six two-year-old steers to the stockyards in Edmonton. But the man had miscalculated and the returns from the steers were less than the rental for the truck and he had to borrow five dollars to buy gasoline for the trip home.[6]

On that famous day when wheat dropped to its lowest price in history, the three midwestern provincial premiers — John Bracken from Manitoba, J. T. M. Anderson from Saskatchewan, and J. E. Brownlee from Alberta — along with representatives of mortgage and other lending institutions, were meeting at the legislative building in Winnipeg to consider ways of dealing with the nasty debt situation without evicting occupants of farms and homes. When the conference ended, the premiers announced their intention of introducing to their respective legislatures in the coming February the legislative bills needed to prevent widespread seizures of homes and farms.[7]

Following closely upon the heels of the ruinous prices for farm products — as if part of a design — were those other wicked destroyers, drought, drifting soil, grasshoppers, and crop failure, reaching their climax in 1936 and 1937. By that time, even the Indian natives concluded that the Great Spirit was displaying his anger at the white man for greedy and rapacious ways and was using weather excesses to punish him for his sins. If extremes of heat in summer and cold in winter and weather-related plagues at all seasons were so intended, the palefaced transgressor should have heard the message.

The most obvious weather aberration was in the dearth of precipitation. Saskatoon, the Hub City, with an average annual precipitation record of 14.4 inches, reached that amount of moisture only once in the nine years beginning in 1929. While the decade was still young, the climatic variations led farmers to say again and again: "The weather has gone crazy."

Snowfall in the winter of 1930-31 was light and the dry and windy spring brought dust storms with

Cora Hind, a prominent member of the agricultural press (Agriculture Editor of the Winnipeg Free Press*), played an important role in the history of western agriculture by ensuring an informed rural public. (Glenbow-Alberta Institute)*

The Honorable James Gardiner, farmer and minister of agriculture for Canada (right) and L. B. Thompson, director of Prairie Farm Rehabilitation (left). Both men were leaders in the big rehabilitation during the 1930s.

unprecedented intensity. The weather of 1932 and 1933 suited the grasshoppers and they appeared in hungry hordes. A story was told about a farmer who saw his fields infested with hoppers and had no feed for his turkeys cooped up in the henyard. Thinking that his birds could live on the grasshoppers, he released the turkeys and gave them access to the fields, only to discover when the flock returned in the evening that the turkeys were stripped of all feathers; the ravenous hoppers which had been denuding all vegetation had turned on the turkeys.

January and February in 1936 at many western points were the coldest months on record and five months later, July was the hottest on record. It may have been the extreme heat more than the drought that brought the average yield in the three provinces to the lowest point since records had been kept. By the second week in July, crops were being "burnt up," and no wonder. The Winnipeg press reported that seventeen people died and twenty-one others were hospitalized from heat prostration during the second weekend of the month, when the temperature reached 108 degrees F. It was the worst temperature toll in the hottest weekend in Winnipeg history.[8] The heat brought thunderstorms without rain and crops deteriorated. As if that were not enough grief, the country was struck by the worst spell of soil drifting in memory, so severe that the CPR found it necessary to use its snowplows to clear the mounds of soil drift from tracks in some southern parts.

"The toughest year" for the West was the way 1936 was described by John Vallance, director of the new Prairie Farm Rehabilitation program, after touring the southern prairies with Hon. James Gardiner, federal minister of agriculture, and seeing the parched fields, the eroded soils, and the hungry cattle. His words coincided precisely with the July heat wave that brought temperatures as high as 110 degrees, registered at Brandon. An average wheat yield of 8.1 bushels per acre for the three provinces removed all doubt concerning 1936 being the West's "toughest year."[9] But as western farmers were soon to discover, the next year, 1937, was capable of being worse and was worse, especially within the Palliser Triangle where snowfall in the preceding winter was light and soil drifting continued off and on throughout the season.

The worst soil drifting of the decade occurred in early June. With a fifty-mile-per-hour wind on June 2, soil at Edmonton lifted sufficiently to make midday seem like night. Before the end of the day, Calgary, Lethbridge, and Medicine Hat were wrapped in the same ugly "black blizzard." Next day, the Saskatoon and Regina areas had it and airborne silt from the western grain fields was seen as a gray blanket over Winnipeg. As it moved, some of that silt was finding its way into both rural and urban homes to settle distressingly on dinnerware, window sills, bedspreads, and everywhere.

Drifting soil, of course, was the traveling companion of drought, and prairie residents, after 1931, became more or less accustomed to the rasping effect of sand on the move and the sight of drifting soil forming mounds on headlands, filling roadside ditches, burying fences and sometimes farm implements. When a machine company collector visited a Saskatchewan farmer for the purpose of collecting on a note or repossessing a seed-drill and inquired about where he would find the machine, the farmer, with a twinkle of mischief in his eye, pointed to a huge mound of fresh drift and said: "It's somewhere under that mountain of sand; if you want to see it, I'll lend you a shovel."

Nothing in the thirties was more depressing than the dust storms, and their effect upon the resources of the soil was one of the most costly disasters of those troubled years, 1937 in particular. Before the summer of that year was far advanced, most of the Palliser Triangle resembled a desert and it was evident that the year's growth of fodder would not meet the winter needs of even the shrunken population of livestock on farms. Livestock numbers would have to be further reduced and government action would be necessary. By freeze-up time, nearly half a million cattle were shipped out of the drought area.

According to E. W. Stapleford, 90,000 head of cattle were bought by the government agency and sold for what they would bring at the public stockyards, 70,000 were sent to the East for sale to owners of feedlots and more thousands were sent to graze on natural grasslands at Carberry.[10] Farmers understood that they could not qualify for relief feed for more than a minimum number of cattle and other livestock. The limit was placed at one work horse for every thirty-five acres of cultivated land, one to four milk cows depending upon the number of children in the family, one steer for meat, one brood sow and one other pig for every four members of a family.

A few resourceful farmers were able to retain above the fixed numbers of animals by gathering low quality vegetation which would not have been considered for feed in better times, like Russian thistles. These so-called thistles, which came from Russia by way of the Dakotas, possessed much of the drought tolerance of the native cacti and were the only occupants of the grain fields that seemed to be enjoying the conditions of 1937. On the 1,000-acre farm operated by the University of Saskatchewan at Saskatoon, the total feed harvested consisted of 200 tons of Russian thistles, making it seem like a proper year in which to conduct Russian thistle research. In consequence, the uninviting thistles were prepared and processed in almost every possible manner. They were cut green and placed in silos, cut when mature and stacked, blended with other and more palatable feeds like molasses, pulverized, and even cooked, but regardless of the method of preparation, they were still unappetizing and still objectionably laxative. That rather commonplace fodder of 1937 was still marginal, even as an emergency feed, and deserving of little better than the jocular description it received: "About as nourishing as wheat straw and as appetizing as barbed wire." But in spite of all that was said to belittle the feed, it was the means of bringing a few additional thousands of cattle and sheep through the winter.

Nobody wished to face another year like 1937 and more and more prairie people loaded their essential possessions on wagons and drove north, hoping to re-establish where rains would be more dependable and trees would not only break the force of eroding winds but furnish fuel for kitchen stoves. The province of Saskatchewan in September, 1935, created the Northern Settlers Re-establishment Branch to assist the large number of discouraged farmers who hoped to escape from drought and wind and find independence in the friendly park belt.

Some of those who fled north were disenchanted by the difficulty of bringing tree-covered land to cultivation but most of the refugees adjusted quickly and succeeded. One who went to Carragana, east of Tisdale, wrote cheerfully on January 25, 1938, saying: "I shall have 100 acres in crop this year and aim to break 50 more on the farm. . . . It was hard to leave our farm in the South after 30 years of our young lives being spent there, but the thought of more relief and no prospect of a crop decided us to try to earn our living and give our boy a chance to be a man. If we can only become self-supporting and eat our own bread again we shall be repaid for our efforts."[11]

It has been said many times that the troubled years of the thirties brought out the best in some people and the worst in others. The resourceful ones survived and some made history. The circumstances, in a few instances, produced violence, as on occasions when unemployed masses clashed with the police. It happened at Regina on July 1, 1935, and the conflict was marked, unhappily, by the throwing of rocks, gunshots, tear gas and the death of Detective Charles Miller of the Regina police force. Forty-two rioters and citizens were injured and damage was estimated at $50,000. It was seen as Regina's worst day since a cyclone struck the city exactly twenty-three years before.[12]

A few rural areas witnessed violence too, as at Arborg, Manitoba, on November 29, 1932, when 500 farmers, made angry by what they considered heavy taxation in the light of prevailing prices for grains and livestock, demonstrated. It was the announcement of a tax sale that finally triggered the demonstration. After parading on the street, the farmers rushed the municipal office, manhandled the reeve, tore the clothes from his back, scattered municipal records on the floor, and threatened a tar and feathering. They finally demanded and obtained the reeve's resignation. Three Mounted Policemen were helpless against the aroused farmers.[13]

But while some of the victims of the depression were angry, some found reasons to laugh at their troubles. People elsewhere had troubles also; it might be cold comfort but it was noted with a laugh that the price of harem wives, according to the Mideastern news, had dropped from $250 and $40 each and had thereby paralleled the falling price of wheat. And as Saskatchewan farmers were quick to observe, the order from German authorities to shorten shirt-tails as a measure to save cloth came long after prairie shirt-tails had been expropriated for patching overalls.

Moreover, at least a few agricultural inventions and institutions of lasting value sprang from the Depression Years.

Chapter 27
TRIUMPHS BORN IN ADVERSITY

If the sponsors of the World's Grain Show and Conference held at Regina in the summer of 1933 could have foreseen the weather woes of that time, would they have found the courage to proceed with the program — already postponed a year — or would they have tried to escape the added problems and embarrassment from bringing many of the world's leading agronomists to see the Canadian wheat fields bearing the grim marks of desolation? It was too much like having guests for dinner when the house was in complete disarray. The answer to the question will never be known but the responsible officials deserved praise for their refusal to surrender to the excessive heat, drought, drifting soil, and ruinous prices.

For the official opening, Hon. Robert Weir, Saskatchewan farmer at Weldon and minister of agriculture in Prime Minister R. B. Bennett's government, was the chairman while former Prime Minister Arthur Meighen, displaying the eloquence that was unsurpassed in his generation, delivered the opening address. It was then for the chairman to invite representatives from all participating countries to stand while the appropriate bars from their respective national anthems were played. Visitors promised that they would not forget either the grand beginning inside the exhibition building or the extreme heat outside. The temperature at the time was creeping up to 101 degrees Fahrenheit and nearby Moose Jaw reported 106 degrees on two days of that week.

Forty nations were represented and many internationally famous grain authorities were present, among them Sir John Russell who came to present a review of crop fertilizer experiments at Rothamstead over a period of 100 years.

In the grain show contests that followed, honors were widely distributed, with Canadian exhibitors doing well in spite of current weather troubles. Again, the supreme championship for wheat was seen as the most coveted award and with Prof. T. J. Harrison of Manitoba as the judge, the winner was Frelan Wilford of Stavely, a thirty-six-year-old farmer, born at Aurora, Ontario, and brought to the West as a child in 1902. Significantly, the first six prizes for hard red spring wheat were taken by Alberta entries. The runner-up for the championship was an exhibitor with a familiar name, Herman Trelle, of Wembley in the Peace River area, who won world wheat championships in Chicago in 1926, 1930, 1931 and 1932. At this show he was named the winner in the class for ten bushels of spring wheat.[1]

Visitors at the show heard with hope about an International Wheat Agreement and before the end of the year, the first agreement was signed with ten exporting countries and sixteen importing countries committed to its support. It was supposed to bring stability to the marketing of 562 million bushels, of which Canada's share would be 200 million. Argentina was to benefit to the extent of 110 million bushels, Australia, 105 millions; Danubian Basin countries, 54 millions; United States, 45 millions, and other countries, including Russia, 48 millions. The intent was good but the agreement was broken and it wasn't until 1949 that producers and buyers obtained one that really achieved its purpose.

For prairie people, the World's Grain Show was a pleasant interlude but the most difficult years were still to come. Human endurance would be tested, but within a year after the show, some rewards for perseverance were starting to appear, among them the first of the new rust-resistant wheat varieties. The first to be tried and adopted was the Minnesota variety, Thatcher, which had Canadian Marquis as a double grandparent. It was followed at once by Renown and Apex, the former from the Federal Rust Research Laboratory at Winnipeg, and the latter from the field husbandry department of the University of Saskatchewan. New kinds continued to make their appearance: Regent in 1939, Redman in 1946, Rescue, with resistance to wheat stem sawfly, in 1946, Selkirk, with resistance to the relatively new 15B strain of rust, in 1954, Canthatch, resembling Thatcher but with strain 15B resistance, in 1959, Manitou in 1965, Neepawa in 1969, and so on.

As is often the case, conditions must become seriously bad before the necessary steps are taken to make them better. So it was with the adoption of the Prairie Farm Rehabilitation Act — known generally as PFRA. But in the light of passing years, that PFRA

The Prairie Farm Rehabilitation Act, passed in 1935, made provision for water conservation in both large and small projects. The illustration shows a multi-purpose reservoir near Swift Current.

program may well be seen as the crowning achievement of the decade.

Perhaps it was Hon. R. B. Bennett's misfortune to have been prime minister of Canada between 1931 and 1935 when the best that governments could do seemed trifling to western farm fortunes. By 1934, most prairie farmers were on relief and, however guilty or blameless they might be, governments were being blamed. When farmers could no longer buy gasoline for their cars, they fitted the motor vehicles with poles and whippletrees and hitched their farm horses to provide the pulling power. Hitched this way, the vehicles became known as "Bennett Buggies."

The prairie record of production was going from bad to worse and editors and even members of the legislatures made proposals about turning Palliser's Triangle back to grazing for buffalo herds. So serious was the state of erosion and depletion that the land's return to its former productivity — even with normal rainfall — seemed doubtful unless far-reaching rehabilitation measures were adopted. Such a program

would require better land-use policies, new and improved cultural practices, and more attention to soil and water conservation.

The Canadian government's recognition of the need was demonstrated by the passage of the act in the spring of 1935. Funds were provided with which to take the first meaningful steps to aid the return of a vigorous agriculture.

The passing of the act did not make it rain and the prairie region was drier in each of the next two years than in 1935 but it gave the government a big role in the tasks of restoration and it helped "to make these people self-sustaining" which, according to the minister of agriculture, was a prime government aim from the onset.[2] It certainly helped to establish two points, first that much submarginal land brought into cultivation in error should now be returned to grass, and, second, that even the better prairie lands needed new and improved cultural methods and management.

The original act did not provide for community pastures but as submarginal lands were being retired from cultivation, the opportunity of assembling them for community pastures could not be overlooked. The act was amended accordingly and the idea of community grazing areas, as proposed by Robert Sinton at the National Livestock Association meeting in Ottawa in 1908 and later tested by the Saskatchewan government on the Matador Ranch, was adopted as one of the several principal purposes. It was immediately popular.

By the terms of the act, provincial governments were required to petition the federal government for the pasture program and select appropriate areas for pastures. Alberta had its Special Areas Act of 1927 and did not petition but Saskatchewan and Manitoba acted promptly and saw an ever-growing acreage of problem farm land being converted to its best use. Sixteen Community Pastures totaling 177,000 acres of margin-

al and submarginal land were formed, fenced, furnished with watering facilities, and made ready for cattle in the first year.

By regrassing where it was needed and bringing good management to the pastures, the carrying capacity was increased greatly. At the outset it was found to take an average of fifty-eight acres to feed a cow for the season but eighteen years later, through the combined effect of better management and better rainfall, the carrying capacity was trebled. One of the best aids in pasture improvement was found in the use of the imported crested wheatgrass, outstanding for its drought resistance.

By 1970, the Community Pastures had grown to over two million acres, serving 6,500 farmers and grazing 140,000 cattle. And as they were growing in both number and acres, so was assistance in water development. George Spence, who became director, called it a crime to allow needed water to leave the dry parts and with PFRA assistance one way or another, the West, thirty years after the passing of the act, had 90,000 additional small bodies of water trapped behind small dams or in dugouts, also irrigation projects ranging in size from very small ones to the big St. Mary-Milk River project which was fashioned to furnish irrigation water for half a million acres. And the still bigger construction effort, the South Saskatchewan River dam at Elbow, was planned to

The Honorable James G. Gardiner farmed at Lemburg, Saskatchewan and went from premier of his province to the post of minister of agriculture for Canada where he played a big role in rehabilitation.

Cattle drinking from a PFRA dugout in the prairie area.

generate hydroelectric power while at the same time furnishing water for irrigation and municipal use. This dam, standing 210 feet high and named to honor the federal minister of agriculture at the time, Hon. James G. Gardiner, was opened by the minister on July 21, 1967.

As a sort of companion to PFRA of 1935, there came the Prairie Farm Assistance Act, or PFAA in 1939. It was the view of Agriculture Minister Gardiner that the country was not yet ready for crop insurance — if, indeed, such a high-risk area as the western plains would ever support it — but that something offering better farm security was needed in order to keep people on the land. The PFAA scheme was to be a modified form of compulsory insurance covering all grain-growing parts of the West. Farmers would contribute one percent of returns from wheat, oats, barley and rye delivered at the elevators. Thereafter, farmers in townships declared to be part of a crop failure area qualified for assistant payments from the fund. The one percent deductions brought substantial totals but it was never expected that these would meet all payments — and the subsidies voted from the public treasury were heavy. Roughly half of the money paid to farmers came from the treasury and half from the farm collections.

PFAA was frequently criticized but it did help to keep farmers on the land and it served to point out the areas in which land use was still faulty. There was no PFAA program in 1942, a year of heavy crop, but otherwise, the province of Alberta alone, between the first year, 1939, and 1955, had 52 townships in which farmers qualified for the payments in 12 out of the 16 years, 28 other townships which received payments in 13 out of the 16 years, 12 townships qualifying in 14 out of the 16 years, and 2 townships that were recipients in every year except one.

Of course, the thirties were trying, but they were not to be regarded as lost years and not without their triumphs. Hadn't entries from midwestern exhibitors won the world wheat championship in nine years out of the ten in that decade? Hadn't the University of Saskatchewan Barred Rock hen known as Lady Victorine, enjoying the attention of Prof. R. K. Baker, laid 358 eggs in 365 days to make the best production record in the world? Didn't the "strip farming" technique developed by the Koole Brothers at Monarch to check soil drifting, gain favor dramatically in Saskatchewan? Wasn't it in the thirties that C. S. Noble perfected a new blade-type cultivator which materially changed cultural practices across the American as well as Canadian plains? Weren't they the years that stimulated the greatest interest in planting shelterbelts and saw the formation of the Conquest Shelterbelt Association which coincided exactly with passage of the PFRA in 1935? Didn't prairie people benefit as never before from lessons about conservation of soil and water and all resources? The thirties were not really "lost years."

Strip farming, first implemented in the Monarch district in southern Alberta, was an important check against soil drifting. This photo was taken in south west Saskatchewan, 1949.

Chapter 28

WAR AND FARM RECOVERY

By 1939 when the evil forces of drought and depression seemed to be retreating and World War II was just beginning, the three midwestern provinces had 295,000 farmers, most of them trusting in debt adjustment legislation to spare them from bankruptcy. In Saskatchewan alone, creditors under mortgage and sale agreements wrote off $27 million of debt and the provincial government canceled another $27 million in relief claims. Simultaneously, municipalities wrote off $46 million in taxes and relief claims and the Dominion government forgave $27 million of loan money. Farming people were still short of cash but thankful for relief from debts that could have been crushing burdens. "A magnificent achievement," an editor said of the debt adjustment progress.

What politicians called "Agricultural Reconstruction," most farmers saw as simply "beginning again." The economic climate appeared more hopeful and the farm scene generally brighter, except for the price of wheat. The crop of that year was the best in a full decade — 494 million bushels, which represented an average yield of 19.1 bushels per acre. Not since 1930 had the western yield been above 16 bushels to the acre. But prices which had risen to an average of $1.31 per bushel in 1937 had dropped back to only 76½ cents in 1939. It was the best price the Canadian Wheat Board could obtain on world markets paralyzed by war. Most of Canada's former customers were unable to buy and farmers were obliged to accept a five bushel per acre Wheat Board delivery quota. Sounding a long-standing impatience, the editor of the *Farm and Ranch Review* said: "The disastrous world wheat situation has for years been a standing reproach to our civilization."[1]

It was reassuring that productivity was returning and farmers were generally grateful for the new wheat

varieties from which they could choose. As the Searle Grain Company discovered from a 1940 survey, 41 percent of the wheat planted across the West in that year was Thatcher; 27 percent was Marquis, followed in order by Red Bobs, Renown, Apex, Regent, Reward, and Garnet.

Following the good crop of 1939, the effusive farmers planted heavily in 1940 — too heavily for an export market that would take only 230 million bushels that year — and the 514 million bushels of wheat harvest resulted in glut and more depression in prices. The Canadian carry-over of 480 million bushels at the end of the 1940-41 crop year brought the Wheat Acreage Reduction program with the federal government paying subsidies of four dollars per acre on wheatland turned to summerfallow and two dollars per acre on land transferred from wheat to coarse grains or forage crops. But in spite of the subsidized reduction, the western wheat crop of 1942, totaling 529 million bushels, was the biggest in the West's history.

It was a situation with which western farmers would have to live for the duration of the war but, as they soon discovered, they were not without alternatives. The agricultural demands in this war were strikingly different from those of World War I and while Canadian contacts with many of the traditional customers for wheat were temporarily severed, the same wartime circumstances isolated the United Kingdom from former sources of foods of animal origin, thereby forcing that country to look to Canada for bacon, beef, cheese, butter, honey, and dried milk and eggs. Thus, the British market presented Canadian farmers with a huge new opportunity as well as a patriotic duty.

Suddenly, the wheat country became pork

country. Canadian bacon cut to conform to Wiltshire sides had been moving to Britain in moderate amounts for some years and meeting the tough competition presented by the high-class Danish bacon, considered the world's best. Now, when the war was only a few months old, the British ministry of food contracted to take Canada's total output at prices based on $18.01 per hundred pounds for Grade A sides at eastern tidewater. In May, 1941, the price was reduced to $16.81 per hundred, and later in the same year, raised to $19.60 per hundred. The latter price was supposed to be the equivalent of about $15.00 per hundred pounds for pigs on foot at Winnipeg and farmers agreed that marketing their grains in this manner was the only way by which they could hope to get a return of $1.50 or $1.75 per bushel for their wheat and barley.

The production of pigs and bacon became at once an industry of Empire importance and a popular enterprise among farmers and others. Governments conducted promotional campaigns and pigs commanded unprecedented prestige. Even urban people took to raising pigs as sidelines. A Saskatchewan lawyer changed his office hours to end at three P.M. because he had to go to the country to feed his pigs. A church minister thought well enough of this fashionable enterprise to preach a series of sermons on Wiltshire sides and Yorkshire pigs. And a school

A Lacombe pig, representative of a new breed developed at the Canada Experimental Station in Lacombe, Alberta.

teacher's only complaint was the ever-present faint odor of pigs in her classroom.

As just about everybody came to know, the way a person could be expected to know the National Anthem or the Ten Commandments, a Wiltshire side was half of a selected carcass of pork, with head and feet removed, the back bones, breast bones, shoulder blade and aitch bone cut out, and the ham trimmed. The name was derived from the district in England which gained early fame for the high quality of its pork marketed in such sides. In the course of time, British merchants wanted nearly all their bacon supplies in this form, with weight close to 60 pounds per trimmed side.

By 1943, Britain was calling for 600 million pounds of bacon from Canada and agreeing to pay $22.50 per hundred for Grade A carcasses at the eastern seaboard. Canada's farmers were delivering accordingly and glad to have this profitable outlet for their grains. More than 60 million bushels of otherwise unsalable wheat was sold through pigs in each year between 1941 and 1946.

Nine million pigs were marketed in Canada in the single year, 1944, with almost two-thirds of them going from western farms. Such numbers made it possible for the Canadian shipments of bacon to exceed two billion pounds in the war period. It was a substantial contribution to the war effort and the shipments of cheese, milk powder, dried eggs, and other animal products were only a little less noteworthy. Nobody could view the annual contracts in

1944 and 1945 to deliver 7,500 long tons of dried or powdered eggs — equal to about 48 million dozens of shell eggs — with anything but admiration.[2] To meet the export needs in cheese, dried milk, butter, and honey, it required production increases on the farms of fifty percent or more.

Even the pigs, the hens, and the cows appeared to be co-operating, a point which was not overlooked when the Hays and Company cow, Alcartra Gerben, on March 24, 1945, completed her 365-day production of 1,405 pounds of butterfat from 27,745 pounds of milk to become a world champion. On that day, 500 guests gathered to pay tribute to the Calgary Holstein and all other working farm animals and drink a toast in Alcartra Gerben's own milk.

Of course it was to the farmer's advantage to sell his surplus grains through bacon or cheese or eggs but the increased production was not accomplished without strenuous effort and in some instances, hardship. By 1944 it could be said that Canadian agriculture had lost 400,000 young men and 100,000 young women to the armed services and war industry, making for an inevitable shortage of help on farms. Nor was it to be overlooked that mixed farming or livestock farming had a higher labor requirement than grain growing.

To ease the farm labor crisis, farmers were turning more than ever to mechanization. Rural electrification was extended and farmers, with more spending money than in previous years, were buying tractors — 96 percent of them with rubber tires. The 112,624 farm tractors on midwestern farms in the second year of the war represented about 70 percent of the Canadian total. Moreover, the trend was toward bigger field units and O. B. Lassiter, farming at Chin, thirty miles east of Lethbridge, would, in 1947, hitch eight tiller-combines behind a tractor to allow one worker to cultivate a swath 48-feet wide.[3]

War ended in 1945 and the trade in livestock food products did not slacken. European herds had been almost wiped out. Dairying in some areas had disappeared and cropland had been overrun and neglected. Europe faced the threat of famine and Canadian food products — including wheat — were needed urgently. The Canadian wheat carry-over of 343 million bushels on July 31, 1945, fell to 74 million bushels one year later. And Britain in the first postwar year, 1946, was still relying upon Canadian producers for 450 million pounds of bacon, 60 million pounds of beef, 1,750,000 cases of eggs in the shell, and 5,000 long tons of dried eggs.

But everybody knew that Canada's exclusive position in supplying British needs would not last much longer. Farm leaders hoped to hold the British market for at least moderate quantities of bacon and cheese. There was concern about the future of the wheat trade, and the continued pressure upon the federal government for guaranteed prices led to the signing of the loudly heralded and highly controversial British Wheat Agreement. As signed in 1946, it was seen as an invention — good or bad — of the minister of agriculture, Hon. James Gardiner.

By its terms, Britain was guaranteeing to take a total of 600 million bushels over a period of four years. Canada was undertaking to sell and Britain was undertaking to buy 160 million bushels in each of the first two years, 1946 and 1947, and 140 million bushels in each of the next two years. The British price in the first two years was set firmly at $1.55 per bushel. For the remaining two years, the price would be negotiated but was not to fall below $1.25 in the third year and not below $1.00 in the fourth. The deal seemed attractive at the time it was drawn because, as everybody realized, the future of the international trade in wheat was very uncertain. It was also evident — or should have been — that the agreement could turn out to be a source of disadvantage to growers. It was a big gamble and as time passed it appeared that British buyers were the bigger winners. When world prices advanced, the agreement became the object of much political criticism. Farmers who had welcomed the guaranteed sales and guaranteed price for at least a portion of their production became critical and angry when they realized that they might not have obtained the full world value for their grain.

In carrying out the terms of the agreement, farm wheat was still channeled through the Wheat Board. The initial payment was $1.35 per bushel, basis Number One Northern at the Lakehead, and deliveries over the four years were handled as in a pool, with final payments when the net returns were determined.

The expiry of that agreement marked the end of ten years during which Canadian agriculture had prospered on British government contracts, and western farmers, who had been close to bankruptcy, were enjoying higher incomes than ever before.

The war years left other legacies, some of them lasting. One was the chlorinated hydrocarbon insecticide, DDT, another the weedicide, 2,4-D. The latter, discovered in 1940, was produced commercially in 1944 and tried cautiously on about 100 acres in the West in 1945. It captured immediate interest and was being used on eight million western acres in 1949.

Rapeseed, which was introduced and grown on 4,000 acres as a wartime source of vegetable oil in 1943, was found to do well and its humble beginning led to western plantings of more than six million acres in 1978 and a crop rating that made it second only to wheat.

There were big changes in farm machinery. Perhaps the biggest were in the further displacement of horses by tractors, the growing popularity of

This potash mine near Esterhazy, Saskatchewan, is the property of International Mineral and Chemical Corporation.

harvester combines, and the rejection of the plow in favor of the newer types of cultivators capable of loosening the soil and still leaving stubble and weed trash on the surface as a safeguard against wind erosion. Although 3,000 horse-plows were sold in Canada in 1950, only 17 of them were bought for use in the midwest, where their kind had almost disappeared.[4]

As tractors continued their advance toward complete domination in western grain fields, more and more draft horses became unemployed. The province of Saskatchewan which had a million horses in 1921 could still count 800,000 in 1941, but most of them were obsolete. When eating grass and other feed and returning nothing in service, they were seen as agricultural liabilities, at least until near the end of the war when stockmen were reminded of impending famine in Europe and the possibility of furnishing canned or frozen Canadian horsemeat.

The proposal to convert surplus horses to salable meat was discussed in 1943. At a meeting at Val Marie

on March 1, 1944, attended by 300 farmers and ranchers, the idea drew unanimous approval and an authorization for action. Local meetings followed to make other horse owners familiar with the plan, and before the end of the month, an organization meeting was held at Swift Current. L. B. Thomson, superintendent of the Swift Current Experimental Farm, was named to be secretary and instructed to prepare a plan along which the horsemen could proceed. Thomson's recommendation was for a co-operative slaughtering plant and with a loan of $50,000 from the government of Saskatchewan, the horsemen were buying an old power house at Swift Current to be converted to an abattoir. By October, 1945, the horsemen were in the meat business, with an initial order for 10,000 tons of pickled horsemeat for Belgium. A second plant was bought at Edmonton and canning facilities were installed.

There was no lack of horses for processing and by the end of 1947 over 100,000 horses had been handled at the two plants and horse owners had received cash payments of three million dollars. There were some reverses in 1948 and exports fell away but, strangely enough, a domestic trade developed, especially among European-born Canadians who were not strangers to horsemeat. By 1952, the co-operative, having processed almost a quarter of a million surplus horses and obtained about nineteen million dollars for the products, had pretty well completed the task for which it was organized and terminated its existence. Notices were sent to the 37,000 shareholders to inform them of the meeting which would be the last.

Nobody could say that the war years were idealistically sterile. The Food and Agriculture Organization was international in character rather than local but it found some of its best support in western Canada and should be acknowledged. Its birth was at a special United Nations Conference at Hot Springs, Virginia, in May, 1943, and it was brought to a functional state at a second conference at Quebec in October, 1945. Its purposes were to raise standards of living and levels of nutrition wherever there was need while, at the same time, trying to improve the position of the producers.

Sir John Boyd Orr, Scottish nutritionist and farmer who became the first director general, gave assurance in his report for 1948-49 that FAO was helping to bring scientific knowledge to the people who could apply it in the quest for improved production, handling, processing and distribution of foods. The report pointed, by way of example, at the battles against disease in livestock, insects in crops and other preventable losses, also at the programs in support of seed improvement, soil conservation, irrigation, mechanizaton where practical, and greater general efficiency in the needy and backward countries.

Some of the richest prizes to fall to Canada in the immediate postwar years were in the form of natural resources, and farmers, being big consumers of both potash and petroleum, had a deep interest in the discovery of potash in western Saskatchewan in July, 1946, and oil at Leduc, in Alberta, in February of the next year. It came as a particularly pleasant surprise that Saskatchewan, long regarded as "one-crop country," possessed potash deposits extending from Unity to Esterhazy which represented about half of the world's known reserves. Potash was not one of the essential plant foods likely to be lacking in Saskatchewan soils but it was noteworthy, nevertheless, that the province, which was one of the leading suppliers of grain for export, would now be one of the foremost suppliers of a fertilizer ingredient needed to grow wheat and other crops in many parts of the world.

Moreover, western farmers were coming to realize that they could not rely indefinitely upon the natural stores of fertility to support their cropping. It was one of the clearest lessons from the war and postwar years that the time had come to be more diligent in feeding the western soil.

Chapter 29

GLOOM AND DISASTER

Tragedies and near-tragedies furnished the head-line agricultural news in the first years after the midpoint of the century. What looked like a series of troubles began with the devastating Red River flood of 1950, bringing misery to thousands of both rural and urban people in the broad and fertile valley. Before the year was out, a wet harvest season resulted in the delivery of 100 million bushels of tough or damp grain at country elevators. Even at that, the grain driers were not nearly as busy as in the next year when wet grain became a major national problem. But it was the news in 1952 of an outbreak of one of the most insidious plagues in the livestock world, foot-and-mouth disease, that brought the most intense gloom and led farmers and others to wonder when, if ever, they would see the last of it.

"If this is a pattern of things to come," some were asking, "what's next?"

It was not the first time that the Red River had risen from its tortuous channel and gone on a destroying rampage but it brought the highest level of floodwater in eighty-nine years and by far the most costly damage ever. At its maximum the water covered 640 square miles of valley land on the Canadian side of the boundary and inundated various towns, villages, and a substantial part of the city of Winnipeg. At the town of Morris where no fewer than 41 homes floated away or collapsed, the flood assumed a lakelike appearance with width of 20 miles. Within the bounds of Greater Winnipeg, 10,000 homes were flooded to one degree or another and 5,500 of them had water above the main floor. Some 75,000 residents quit the city until the flood had subsided.

From applications received for assistance in re-pairing flood damage, it appeared that 1,640 farms were injuriously affected. Damage totaled many mil-lions of dollars but, significantly, only one human life was lost.

Again rural ingenuity became evident and it served in the rescuing and saving of many farm animals and some property. At St. Adolphe, twenty-six cattle owned by six farmers were given refuge on an immobilized river ferry, until the animals could be evacuated by a barge. The same barge rescued cattle which had been elevated to a farmer's hayloft, and on a farm not far away, a granary served as an island of escape for six milk cows and two horses; even at that the owner found it necessary to raise the granary to prevent it from floating away with its cargo of live-stock.

At the University of Manitoba which was squarely in the path of the flood, dairy cattle and pigs were stabled for several weeks of the flood crisis in railroad boxcars spotted on nearby tracks by a co-operative railway company. The university sheep were placed in the hayloft above the horse stable and feed for all the marooned animals was delivered daily by rowboat. One of the attendants remarked at the end of the flood that he found new sympathy for the feeding problems which Noah of old must have faced.

The Manitoba people discovered the cruelty that water is capable of inflicting. And before the end of the year, farmers in all three provinces were ex-periencing the woes of too much rain at harvest time and too much water in the grain they were trying to thresh. Every bushel of out-of-condition grain re-quired special attention if it was to be saved from spoiling. Mechanical driers were installed at terminal elevators and ingenious farmers made some of their own. But as time was to reveal most brutally, the damp grain problems of the next year were big enough to make those of 1950 seem small.

Accompanying the West's biggest crop of wheat — 529 million bushels — the hopelessly wet autumn brought what Rt. Hon. C. D. Howe called "unprecedented problems" for producers and all handling agencies. Speaking in the House of Commons on March 7, 1952, he reported that 186 million bushels of tough and damp wheat, oats and barley from the 1951 crop had been accepted at country elevators and he believed there were still "36 million bushels of threshed damp wheat on farms in the prairie provinces," and "about 150 million bushels of wheat and 135 million bushels of oats and barley still to be threshed" — meaning that that much was buried under prairie snow.[1]

It added up to 222 million bushels of tough and damp grain in storage somewhere and 285 million bushels under the snow. And as everybody realized, drying was like a race against time because grain with high content of moisture would be inviting spoiling as soon as weather turned warm in the spring. Facilities for the movement of grains were choked and markets

A view of the University of Manitoba campus during the disastrous Red River Flood of 1950. Damage to rural, as well as urban structures, was great.

suffered. The crucial drying equipment was totally inadequate. According to the *Country Guide:* "The unfavorable harvest weather of 1951 may turn out to be one of the major crop disasters on record."[2]

If damp grain was the most serious tragedy in 1951, at least one farm organization, the United Grain Growers, sensed the appearance of another; namely, inflation, then raising its ugly head as never before. Farm costs were rising and more people and more organizations should have been taking warning. "Continued inflation in Canada may seriously reduce purchasing power of western agriculture," a United Grain Growers' report noted. The peak of purchasing power had been reached in 1948 and was, by 1951, in decline.[3] And then delegates to the forty-fifth annual convention received a resolution counseling with prophetic understanding: "Farm organizations of Canada should give inflation immediate study as constituting the most serious danger to agriculture."[4]

A wet harvest season and the imprisonment of millions of bushels of unthreshed grain below the snow were bad enough, but for farming people of the time, the biggest scare of all came with the news headlines on February 25, 1952: "Foot-And-Mouth Disease Identified In Saskatchewan."

The diagnosis of foot and mouth disease on a farm east of Regina brought gloom to the entire agricultural community.

Western people knew something of the terrible price that other countries had paid in the fight against the hated destroyer, only to find, in many cases, that it had become so firmly entrenched that hope for eradication had to be abandoned. The United States had experienced outbreaks on a few occasions and succeeded by costly slaughter and disinfection to terminate the highly contagious thing. Canada had never known an outbreak but was able to benefit from the experience of the United States and other countries. One of the big Canadian worries was that if the infection were to reach the wildlife, such as deer and moose, eradication might never be accomplished.

The Canadian Health of Animals Division of the department of agriculture was at once confronted with its biggest test. The technique to be followed would be similar to that employed in the United States and United Kingdom, namely, a vigorous slaughter pro-

gram with deep burial and lavish disinfection. The story began in a farming community a short distance east of Regina where a farmer hired a young immigrant to help in doing stable chores. A couple of weeks later — November 26, 1951, to be exact — some cattle on the farm were sick. The owner was told that the disorder was probably indigestion and he should try drenching his cattle. But the sick animals did not respond to the treatment and more became sick. By this time, the trouble was believed to be from a virus infection but representatives of the Health of Animals Division became suspicious and sent samples for further tests to department laboratories in the East.

On February 24, 1952, the loathsome foot-and-mouth disease was identified and the bad news broke on the following day. Farming and ranching people

Cattle which had been exposed to foot and mouth disease are being brought together for destruction and deep burial in a pit.

across the country were stunned and wondered if this might be a "knockout blow" from which the livestock industry of Canada would never recover.

The news was followed by emergency measures, swift and sure. The United States ordered an embargo on all Canadian livestock and animal products. British Columbia, followed by Quebec and Manitoba, announced embargoes and trade ground to a halt. A contingent of veterinarians and Mounted Police was moved into the Regina area and quarantines of the strictest kinds were imposed. On the very day after the disease was confirmed, PFRA bulldozers began digging trenches in the frozen ground near McLean, east of Regina, to become graves for mass burial of animals found to be sick or under suspicion due to exposure. The quarantine zone extended for forty miles in all directions and affected eleven municipalities. Packing plants stopped buying livestock and even feed grains came under the quarantine order.

By February 29, the distasteful work of slaughter by shooting was started, with Mounted Police conducting the operation. Sick cattle and other animals under suspicion were herded into the new pits where they were shot and then buried with lime and ten feet of soil over the bodies. The first slaughter consisted of 238 cattle and 68 sheep. By March 17, the animals killed included 1,069 cattle, 129 pigs, 97 sheep, 1 goat, 2 horses, and 1,610 poultry. In addition, 13,192 eggs were buried. The horses were animals used in tests and the goat was the mascot of the Saskatchewan Roughriders Football Club.

In the meantime, a search was started for the German immigrant boy who had been hired to perform chores on the farm east of Regina. When located, he was subjected to tests but no trace of infection was found. The certain source of the infection was never established.

The impact of the outbreak was felt across the country. Winter Fairs were canceled or postponed. The Calgary Bull Sale was set back to a later date. Stockmen believed they were going broke when they could not sell their animals. And every sick critter across the nation was suspect. Rumors of new outbreaks came from widely scattered points, including Ontario. Each rumor was investigated but no outbreaks were confirmed except a few which were identified in Saskatchewan, none farther from the original outbreak than Weyburn.

With the passing of weeks and then months, confidence was returning and on May 20, Canada's agricultural minister. Hon. James G. Gardiner, said publicly that in his personal opinion, the disease was finally and completely buried deep in the earth. Some people believed that the Weyburn outbreaks made the minister's statement dangerously optimistic, but as time was to show, Mr. Gardiner was right. The measures taken, which may have seemed ruthless to some observers, were shown to be sound, and on August 19, just a little less than six months after the outbreak was identified for what it was, Canada was officially declared free from foot-and-mouth disease. It seemed too good to be true but a year passed and then twenty-five years passed with no recurrence. It was one of the great triumphs in the history of agriculture.

Chapter 30

A NEW DAY FOR AGRICULTURE

Canadian and American farming had come a long way. With giant strides, progressive farmers moved forward to enlist the aid of chemistry, genetics, mechanics, and electronics to transform their operations. A better understanding of vitamins, minerals, fertilizers and pesticides was sufficient to bring complete change to farm returns as well as practices. By 1960 it had reached the point where the average farm worker was producing enough food for himself and twenty-two other people, doubling the output per worker of twenty years earlier.

And the most productive years were still ahead. Using wheat as the indicator, the 1960s and 1970s surpassed the 1950s by an average of more than 100 million bushels per year in the prairie region and, at times, the market couldn't take the volume. Science and mechanization could explain much of it.

Whether described as revision or revolution, the changes marked a new day for Canada and for agriculture. The evidences of a new order were everywhere to be seen. Nationally, as the St. Lawrence Seaway was being completed to open officially on July 26, 1959, and allow ocean-going ships to load grain relatively close to the prairies, the South Saskatchewan River dam was being started to furnish power and irrigation water near the very heart of the wheat country, and the Trans-Canada Highway was nearing completion, to be opened officially on September 3, 1962.

The changes in farm fields and farm stables were less dramatic but scarcely less important, certainly no less important to the twelve percent of Canadians who were still living on farms in 1961. Gone was the tedious routine of feeding and cleaning and harnessing horses at early morning hours and in its place were the demands of oiling and repairing and bigger bills to be paid. Gone were the tasks of pitching hay with three-tine forks on the hottest days of the year and stooking with blistered hands and aching backs. Gone, or almost gone, were the quarter-section farms operated as subsistence units without specialization and without even the slightest concern about income taxes.

In embracing the new technology, 1960 might have been seen as the pivotal year. Chemistry was brought to the aid of farmers as never before. The sale of the new pesticides in the West increased by 24 percent in that year, to reach $33 million; it was an increase of 70 percent in four years. And no less significant was the sale of commercial fertilizers which rose from 61,837 tons in 1956 to 209,624 tons in 1962, an increase of more than 300 percent in six years.

These spurts in the use of technological aids and in productivity were not restricted to Canada and were not without attendant problems. All the wheat-exporting countries were reporting mounting stocks of unsold grain. Canada's carry-over at July 31, 1961, reached the disturbing total of 608 million bushels and farmers were conceding that selling wheat might be more difficult than growing it. But as demonstrated many times, wheat fortunes could change unexpectedly, like foothills weather, and at the beginning of 1961 when market forecasts were gloomy, China appeared as a completely new customer. That Far East country, hitherto unknown in the wheat trade, placed a January order for 28 million bushels of wheat and 12 million bushels of barley, and before the end of the year, brought total purchases to 94 million bushels of Canadian wheat and 37 million bushels of barley, to qualify as Canada's leading customer. Other surprise purchases during the year were made on behalf of Russia, Czechoslovakia, and Poland, and the big carry-over of 608 million bushels fell away to 326 million bushels in 1962.

Wheat, of course, was not the only farm product to gain prominence in the new order. United States writers and leaders pronounced hybrid corn as the

Romnelet sheep were a breed created specifically to meet the needs of the sheep industry in the range areas.

Pacific, a Simmental bull, sold at Lacombe in 1971 for $175,000. (Photo courtesy of the Canadian Simmental Association, Calgary.)

outstanding agricultural achievement of the period. Its potential in raising food production was believed to be so great that it might furnish an extra forty pounds of pork for every person in the United States.[1]

While American workers were proclaiming their hybrid corn as "the agricultural achievement of the Century," Canadians might have been speculating about the leading agricultural achievements and events on their side of the boundary in the same period of time. Finding answers could be a first-class exercise, deserving recognition in the concluding chapter of any treatise on agricultural history.

Anyone attempting to choose and rate the outstanding events and accomplishments in the present century could expect arguments but certain nominations would seem to be almost beyond challenge, such as the development of Marquis wheat and the rust-resistant varieties that followed. The benefits were enormous and nationwide. Then there were the soil surveys started in 1921, the formation of the prairie wheat pools in 1923 and 1924, and the bitter experience of drought and depression in the thirties. All were historic landmarks.

Choosing the most notable successes and failures in western agriculture in the second half of this century, or the years of the "new order," would present bigger problems. One person would point to the plant breeder's continuing successes in furnishing new crop varieties, "tailor-made" for changing needs, with more to come — perhaps an acceptable variety of

the wheat-rye hybrid known as triticale under study at University of Manitoba, or an early maturing soybean suitable for western farms.

Another adjudicator would name the brilliant accomplishment by Canada's public workers in stamping out the dreaded foot-and-mouth disease in Saskatchewan in 1952, or the success of the animal geneticists at the Lacombe Research Station in developing a new breed of pigs, the Lacombe, with light shoulders and heavy hams and created with 55 percent of Landrace ancestry, 23 percent Berkshire, and 22 percent Chester White.

Could the cattlemen's sudden interest in many new breeds imported from European and other countries after 1966 merit a place in the history of agricultural highlights? Until this new rage, none but British breeds — Shorthorn, Hereford, Aberdeen Angus, and a few Galloways — enjoyed the beef producer's attention. But the cattle of these breeds were allowed to become compact in form, overly refined and small, and practical cattle growers, demanding more scale and weight, were inviting the introduction of heavier kinds from Europe. A few

Cadet Roussel, an imported Charolais Bull, sold by auction for $81,000 in 1974.

Brown Swiss had been imported many years earlier but failed to establish themselves at that time. Cattle of the Charolais breed were imported directly from France in 1966 and were immediately popular. They added something to cattle history when a one-quarter interest in the imported bull, Cadet Roussel, was sold at Calgary in July, 1974, for $81,000. The seller was the Rudiger Charolais Ranch, Calgary, and the buyer, Van Enterprises, Ltd., Burnaby, British Columbia.

The Simmental breed from its native Switzerland, was next on the western scene, in 1967, and soon attracted attention. Four years after the breed's arrival, a bull, Pacific, was sold by the Lacombe Research Station in the first auction of Simmental bulls in Canada, at Lacombe, for $175,000. The purchaser was the American Breeder Service (Canada) Ltd., Bragg Creek, Alberta.

Next came the Limousin cattle from France in 1968, then the Maine-Anjou, also from France, in 1969, the Tarentaise from Switzerland in 1971, Blonde D'Aquitaine from France in 1971, Chianina from Italy in 1971, Gelbvieh from Germany in 1972, Murray Greys from Australia in 1972, Penzgauer from Austria in 1972, Marchigiana from Italy in 1973 and Romagnola from Italy in 1973. All had their friends and backers but the multiplicity was confusing and it should have been evident that all would not and

probably should not survive. Which ones would win a permanent place in Canadian agriculture remained to be seen.

Somebody searching for the achievement of the period will mention the rising popularity of artificial insemination in cattle husbandry. Its use increased by forty percent in one year to account for the impregnation of fourteen percent of all Canadian cattle in 1959.

The story of the half century could turn out to be about the continuing evolutionary changes to more costly and more sophisticated harvesting machines and farm tractors ranging to 400 horsepower and cost exceeding $75,000.

Indeed, one of the most worthy achievement stories might be about the introduction and acceptance of government-sponsored crop insurance, which had its first test in Manitoba in 1960. Although it was a federal-provincial scheme, the earliest demands for it came from the West and its record and status should be noted. A Royal Commission appointed by the

government of Manitoba, reported in 1955 that full crop insurance was beyond the ordinary economic resources of the province but that did not end the discussion and the federal government in 1959 passed the Crop Insurance Act which would permit the provinces to make all-risk crop insurance available to farmers and provide help in financing it. The federal government would pay fifty percent of administrative costs and twenty percent of premiums in any one year. There would be no compulsion and the scheme would not be operative unless at least twenty-five percent of the farmers in an area wanted it. Manitoba was the first province to enter into a formal agreement to provide the insurance. Saskatchewan was next and then Prince Edward Island. Alberta entered in 1965. Farm numbers were low at first but increased steadily until 98,000 Canadian farmers paid about $115 million in premiums to obtain one billion dollars of insurance protection in 1976. Crop insurance was relatively late in coming but quickly took the appearance of a permanent fixture.

There were still scores of agricultural enterprises worthy of historical recognition but it was quite possible that the most significant part of the record of

A massive, high-powered modern tractor illustrates the evolution of farm power in a few decades.

the years would be the changing ways of farm living in a single lifetime. By 1976 when the West could have and should have celebrated the 100th anniversary of the first outward-bound shipment of wheat, there were still many farmers with vivid recollections of farming with horses and spending much of their lives with them. The horse farmer started his day at an early hour with chores and finished it at a late hour with chores and if he had pigs to feed and cows to milk, an escape from chores for more than a few hours was impossible.

He hitched four horses abreast to a seed-drill and binder, and five or six in tandem formation to a two-furrow gang plow and had lots of time for meditation as he made the one-mile rounds of the fields at the rate of two per hour or twenty per day. He might become tired of the unchanging rear-end view of his horses but the long hours with his thoughts explained the development of individuality and imagination unmatched in other walks of life. It found expression in earthy farm stories woven into the lore of the time and the picturesque speech which, although not always grammatically correct, was distinctive and refreshing.

That farmer was part of an independent rural community with a one-room school dignified with white paint, a country church with a long shabby stable for parishioners' horses and, perhaps, a nearby

railway village presenting at least one elevator and a general store that stocked and sold everything when the operator was able to locate the wanted goods. Radio and television were still unknown and rural electrification seemed too remote to be considered seriously. The only organized services other than the public school was a beef-ring or, perhaps, a telephone installation with ten or a dozen farm neighbors on a party line.

Up to 1921 when thirty-five percent of the population of Canada made their homes on the land, farmers had more political strength than they realized, but in that particular year, the Alberta Farmers' party surprised everybody by winning thirty-nine of the sixty-one constituency seats in a general provincial election. It was both possible and democratically proper in a province where sixty-two percent of the people were still farm residents.[2] But by 1976, when the Canadian farm population had fallen to less than five percent of the total and Alberta's farm residents represented about ten percent of the province's people, it was easy to see how such political success could never be repeated.

Many of the changes in farm living were related to the drop in the number of farms and the increase in size. There was consolidation of farms and some abandonment of building sites. The once-proud farmstead structures left standing as derelicts told the story. Only big farms were efficient and profitable, it was told too often. One way or another, farming was looking more like an industrial operation with big investments and more complicated accounting. Farm-

The Fordson tractor of 1918 brought the light, versatile tractor to public attention.

ers were being caught up in the whirl of a fast-moving business society and the family farm character of earlier years was being shattered.

Statistics for 1976 showed Manitoba's 29,963 census farms averaged 628 acres per farm, while Saskatchewan's 69,578 farms averaged 939 acres, and Alberta's 57,310 averaged 864 acres.[3] For the entire midwest, with more than three-quarters of the arable soil of Canada and fifty-two percent of the farms, the average size of 156,851 census farms was 852 acres. It was an increase of about eighty percent over the average farm size of twenty-five years earlier.

And in support of the business image, the midwest in 1976, according to federal government statistics, had 9,884 farms from each of which sales had totaled $75,000 or more.

What had been fairly described as a land of "half-section farmers" in 1926, had become a land of "five-quarter" and "six-quarter" operators. And notwithstanding the added responsibility, most operators had more leisure time than their fathers had when farming quarters and halves.

The new agriculture was an almost completely mechanized industry which the active members of its generation seemed pleased to accept. The midwest of 1976, with 320,979 farm tractors, 298,701 farm trucks, 142,465 farm automobiles, and 126,989 grain combines, had what worked out to slightly more than two tractors, slightly less than two trucks and more than three-quarters of a combine per farm. It helped to explain the mounting and sometimes crippling investment.

But the increase in the size of farming units — impressive though it was — became completely overshadowed by the rising trading prices for land and equipment. Farm real estate was soon among the commodity leaders in the inflationary spiral. Investors wanted land for the security it offered and developers hoped for fast profits by converting farm land to residential subdivisions. Sellers offered no objection to the inflated prices and nobody could blame the owners who hoped to retire on the proceeds from a sale for taking all they could get. The high overhead did not seem to be such an obstacle for young people taking over family farms where there was the benefit of parental compassion, but for those forced to borrow for the full purchase of land and power machinery, the capital debt and interest could be frightening.

The extremely high price of both land and machinery without corresponding increases in returns from farm produce created a situation that should have been seen as a serious national problem. When the prices asked for an improved one-section farm and the appropriate power machinery totaled over a quarter of a million dollars and annual interest charges could be as high as $25,000, the outlook would be

Sugar beet production became part of the new diversification. Shown in the picture is a pile of beets awaiting processing at Taber, Alberta.

most discouraging to young people who were needed in agriculture.

It gave point to the remark that "young fellows who couldn't afford to go to university in other years, took to farming; now those who can't afford to farm, go to university."

Something more than the ordinary loan or mortgage was needed. What had functioned under the Canada Farm Loan Board and later as the Farm Credit Corporation was intended, with federal government backing, to advance funds for farm purchases and expansion. It served well enough and in the fiscal year of 1975-76, it approved 9,945 loans for a total of $641 million.[4] That would represent an average of about $64,000 per loan. Such a loaning service helped many people to start or expand in farming but it wouldn't be able to do much in lightening the new and more massive burdens of debt.

Saskatchewan's politically controversial Land Bank program offered hope by permitting the bank to buy a farmer's land and rent it back to the farmer or his son or some other person. After five years, the renter could continue renting or he could buy the land. There was merit in being able to rent before buying.

Some observers saw hope for young farmers in the co-operative farm idea, exemplified by the Matador Co-operative Farm established on the once-famous Matador Ranch, north of Swift Current. There, in 1946, seventeen veterans who chose farming as a career and elected the co-operative way began on totally unimproved land and pioneered. By 1950 they had broken up 8,250 acres and were finding success.

While writers made much of "average western farmers," there were really no such creatures. Individuality was not dead and by 1976 there were more farm specialists in more lines of agricultural endeavor than ever before. Diversification, which had been trumpeted loudly in pioneer years without much immediate response, was finally becoming more evident but not according to the Ontario formula. The mixed farm presented as a model in 1920, with milk cows, steers, pigs, sheep, poultry, bees, and both cereal and forage crops, was increasingly difficult to find. Diversification and specialization came together in the new agriculture but not on every farm. The diversified nature of the total production should have impressed those easterners whose perennial criticism was that westerners were "one-crop farmers." Perhaps the critics had a point; perhaps wheat did dominate the crop scene to an ill-advised degree but with the passing years the big western "food basket" was becoming ever richer with the range of its products.

Livestock and livestock products gave evidence. If all the farm animals counted in the midwest at the first of June in 1976 had been divided equally among the West's 156,851 census farmers, each one would have 58 cattle, 13 pigs, 2 sheep, 114 hens and chickens, 12 turkeys, and 3 geese and ducks. That individual created for statistical convenience could very properly insist that he was a mixed farmer with enough chores to keep him as busy as farm cats in a stackyard.

In growing field crops, the diversification was no less evident. Wheat, oats, barley, and tame hay were still leading crops, of course, but there were more than a million and a half acres of rapeseed, over three-quarters of a million acres of flax, over half a million of rye, and smaller amounts of buckwheat — mainly in Manitoba — field peas, sugarbeets — restricted to Alberta and Manitoba — potatoes, mustardseed, sunflowers, soybeans, vegetables and fruits, and one acre of tobacco in Manitoba. It was proof of a broader diversification than most Canadians had recognized.

Agriculture was still changing and would probably change much more. Some of the trends could be reversed. Some people living on the land were already convinced that farms were becoming too big. A bigger farm is not necessarily a better farm. Somebody will suggest also that too much has been said about farm efficiency and not enough about making the farm the best of all places to raise a family and live in harmony with the great Community of Nature. The economics of farming is important but it is not everything and it would be sad if the opportunities for rich farm living were ignored.

History tells that agriculture has always had its "ups and downs." Agriculture can be expected to have more "ups and downs," but if the race is to endure, agriculture must endure. Let it be the concluding word that Canada's agricultural land is the nation's most precious treasure and being its caretaker — protecting it against depletion and erosion and those forces which nibble at it constantly for urban expansion and recreation and rights of way — must be the most noble of all callings.

NOTES

Chapter 1   The "Ugly Duckling"

1. Sir George Simpson, Evidence before the Select Committee of the House of Commons in London, "Looking into the Affairs of the Hudson's Bay Company," *Parliamentary Papers*, 1857, Feb. 26.

2. John Palliser, *Palliser Report*, presented to the Houses of Parliament, May 19, 1863.

3. Bishop Alexandre Taché, quoted by John Macoun in *Manitoba and the Great North-West* (Guelph: World Publishing Co., 1882), p. 454.

Chapter 2   The Bold Selkirk Experiment

1. Hudson's Bay Company Minute Book, Meeting of Feb. 6, 1811, H. B. Co. Archives, Winnipeg.

2. "A Highlander," letter to editor, *Inverness Journal*, June 21, 1811.

3. Miles Macdonell to Lord Selkirk, July 17, 1813, Selkirk Papers.

4. John Spencer, Proclamation issued on instructions of Miles Macdonell, Jan. 8, 1814, Selkirk Papers.

5. Grant MacEwan, *Cornerstone Colony* (Saskatoon: Western Producer Prairie Books, 1977), p. 71.

Chapter 3   An Experimental Farm and the First Pigs

1. William Laidlaw to Lord Selkirk, July 22, 1818, Selkirk Papers.

2. Ibid.

3. Nicholas Garry to George Simpson, Feb. 23, 1831. Used with permission of the Governor and Committee of the H. B. Co.

4. Robert Campbell, journal, *From Highlands to Fort Garry, 1830-71* (1890), Glenbow-Alberta Institute Archives.

5. George Simpson to the Governor, Deputy Governor and Committee of the H. B. Co., Aug. 10, 1832. Used with permission of the Governor and Committee of the H. B. Co.

Chapter 4   The Struggle to Get Cattle

1. Elliott Cowes ed., Alexander Henry's journal of March 29, 1808.

2. John Pritchard to Andrew Colvile, Aug. 29, 1820, Selkirk Papers.

3. Lord Selkirk to John McDonald, Midmills, Scotland, May 19, 1819, Selkirk Papers.

4. Thomas Clark to Robert Dickson, April, 1814, Selkirk Papers.

5. Joseph Rolette to Lord Selkirk, Jan. 12, 1817, Selkirk Papers.

6. Lord Selkirk to Newport Kent, April 20, 1818, Selkirk Papers.

7. Lord Selkirk to Michael Dousman, Sept. 21, 1819, Selkirk Papers.

8. Adam Stewart to Lord Selkirk, Jan. 30, 1820, Selkirk Papers.

9. Andrew Bulger to Andrew Colville, Sept. 1, 1822, Selkirk Papers.

10. Ibid., September 8.

11. Andrew Colvile to Colony Governor Robert Parker Pelly, June 4, 1824, Selkirk Papers.

Chapter 5 *The Sheep Drive from Kentucky*

1. Robert Campbell, journal, *From Highlands to Fort Garry, 1830-71* (1890), Glenbow-Alberta Institute Archives.

2. Ibid.

3. Ibid.

4. Ibid.

Chapter 6 *Palliser, the Agricultural Explorer*

1. Sir George Simpson, Evidence before the Select Committee of the House of Commons in London, *Parliamentary Papers, 1857.*

2. Alexander Isbister, Evidence before the Select Committee of the House of Commons in London, *Parliamentary Papers, 1857.*

3. John Palliser, *Solitary Rambles and Adventures of a Hunter in the Prairies* (London: John Murray, 1853).

4. Henry Labouchere, letter of instructions to Palliser, Mar. 31, 1857. Copy included in *Palliser Report* to Colonial Office, 1862.

5. Census at Red River, May, 1856 (appendix of Report of Select Committee on H. B. Co.).

6. Dr. James Hector, account of visit at Fort Edmonton at the end of 1857, *Palliser Report* presented to Colonial Office, April 4, 1862.

7. John Palliser, General Report of Explorations, presented to Colonial Office, April 4, 1862.

8. Grant MacEwan, *Harvest of Bread* (Saskatoon: Western Producer Prairie Books, 1969).

9. Henry Youle Hind, *The Canadian Red River Exploring Expedition of 1857 and Saskatchewan Exploring Expedition of 1858*, 2 vols (London and Toronto: Longman, Green, Longman and Roberts, 1860).

Chapter 7 *Hope and Hoppers in the Sixties*

1. *Nor'Wester*, Dec. 28, 1859.

2. Ibid., Aug. 28, 1860.

3. Ibid., Dec. 28, 1859.

4. Ibid., July 22, 1863.

5. Ibid., July 11, 1860.

6. J. H. Metcalfe, *The Tread of the Pioneers* (Portage la Prairie Old Timers Assoc., 1932).

7. Robert B. Hill, *Manitoba, History of its Early Settlement, Development and Resources* (Toronto: William Briggs, 1890).

8. Exodus 10:15.

9. *Nor'Wester*, Aug. 7, 1868.

10. Ibid., Dec. 17, 1868.

Chapter 8 *A Land Survey, then a Homestead Policy*

1. Hon. William McDougall to Lt. Col. J. S. Dennis, July 10, 1869, Sessional Papers (No. 12) Govt. of Canada, 1870.

2. J. S. Dennis, memorandum prepared at Fort Garry, Oct. 11, 1869, Sessional Papers (No. 12) Govt. of Canada, 1870.

3. Return in the House of Commons, Feb. 2, 1881, printed in the Annual Report of the Dept. of the Interior, 1880-81.

4. Dominion Lands Act, Statutes of Canada, 35 Vic., Ch. 23, 1872.

5. Grant MacEwan, *The Sodbusters* (Toronto: Thomas Nelson and Sons, 1947).

Chapter 9 *Came the Mennonites, then the Icelanders*

1. *Manitoban*, July 21, 1873.

2. John Lowe, secretary for Dept. of Agriculture, letter to Messrs. David Klassen, Jacob Peters, Heinrich Wiebe, and Cornelius Toews, July 26, 1873. Copies survive with many western Mennonites and Hutterites, with same message in report of Dept. of Agriculture for 1873, Sessional Papers, 1874.

3. *Winnipeg Daily Free Press*, Nov. 13, 1874.

4. Ibid., May 4, 1876.

5. Col. Patrick Robertson-Ross, report to prime minister, 1872, Sessional Papers, Govt. of Canada, 1873.

6. Canadian Citizenship Branch, *The Canadian Family Tree* (Ottawa: Queen's Printer, 1967).

7. *Winnipeg Daily Free Press*, Oct. 12, 1875.

8. Margaret McWilliams, *Manitoba Milestones* (Toronto: J. M. Dent and Sons, 1928), p. 158.

Chapter 10 Making Wheat and Cattle History in 1876

1. Grant MacEwan, *Harvest of Bread* (Saskatoon: Western Producer Prairie Books, 1969).

2. *Winnipeg Daily Free Press*, May 1, 1876: "Today Winnipeg supplants Fort Garry as the name of the Post Office here."

3. *Nor-West Farmer*, Dec. 20, 1902.

4. *Winnipeg Daily Free Press*, Oct. 13, 1876.

5. *Manitoba Free Press*, Oct. 23, 1876.

6. *British Colonist*, Victoria, Feb. 5, 1878.

Chapter 11 Cattle where Buffalo Roamed

1. L. V. Kelly, *The Range Men* (Toronto: William Briggs, 1913), p. 178.

2. Annual Report, Dept. of the Interior, 1890, Sessional Papers (No. 17), 1891.

Chapter 12 Farm Fairs on the Frontier

1. Ezekiel 27: 12.

2. Cornelius Walford, *Fairs Past and Present* (1883), p. 40.

3. Grant MacEwan, *Agriculture on Parade* (Toronto: Thomas Nelson and Sons, 1950).

4. *Manitoba Free Press*, Nov. 9, 1872.

5. Ibid., Dec. 7, 1872.

6. *Saskatchewan Herald*, Battleford, Nov. 17, 1879.

Chapter 13 The Big Farms on the Frontier

1. *Brandon Sun*, Jan. 7, 1892.

2. *Edmonton Bulletin*, Oct. 6, 1888.

3. *Calgary Tribune*, July 17, 1887.

4. *Lethbridge News*, Sept. 18, 1889.

5. *Edmonton Bulletin*, May 18, 1889.

Chapter 14 Half a Million New Farmers

1. *Winnipeg Sun*, Dec. 15, 1881.

2. *Western Producer*, July 3, 1975.

3. Abraham J. Arnold, *The Contribution of the Jews to the Opening and Development of the West* (Historical and Scientific Society of Manitoba, Series III, No. 25, 1968-69).

4. *Morning Call*, Winnipeg, April 26, 1887.

5. Sir Clifford Sifton, "The Immigrants Canada Wants," *Maclean's Magazine*, April 1, 1922.

Chapter 15 New Machines for New Farmers

1. *Saskatchewan Herald*, Oct. 15, 1890.

2. Elton Historical Committee, *Homesteaders and Homemakers, History of Elton Municipality* (1973), p. 176.

3. J. H. Ellis, *The Ministry of Agriculture in Manitoba* (Manitoba Dept. of Agriculture, 1971).

4. *Winnipeg Telegram*, June 18, 1910.

5. Ibid.

6. *Winnipeg Daily Free Press*, June 3, 1876.

7. Ibid., Aug. 18, 1878.

8. Ibid., July 27, 1878.

9. *Weekly Times*, Winnipeg, Aug. 22, 1879.

10. John Macoun, *Manitoba and the Great North-West* (Guelph: World Publishing Co., 1882), p. 214.

11. *Regina Leader*, Aug. 27, 1885.

12. *Edmonton Bulletin*, Sept. 3, 1887.

13. *Lethbridge News*, Aug. 10, 1887.

14. *Edmonton Bulletin*, Oct. 26, 1889.

15. Canada Year Book, 1905.

16. Ellis, *Ministry of Agriculture*.

17. *Edmonton Bulletin*, July 15, 1920.

Chapter 16 Threshers and Steamers

1. George Simpson to Andrew Colvile, June 24, 1823, Selkirk Papers.

2. Hudson's Bay Co., Fort Edmonton Journal, Dec. 10, 1866.

3. *Winnipeg Daily Free Press*, July 9, 1874.

4. *Moose Jaw News*, Aug. 1, 1881.

5. *Edmonton Bulletin*, Sept. 26, 1885.

6. *Lethbridge News*, Sept. 4, 1889.

7. *Regina Leader*, May 17, 1883.

8. *Saskatchewan Herald*, June 19, 1889.

Chapter 17   A Decade of Decision, 1900-1910

1. *Edmonton Bulletin*, Mar. 21, 1904.

2. *Calgary Weekly Herald*, Aug. 15, 1901.

3. *Lethbridge Herald*, Mar. 29, 1906.

4. J. H. Ellis, *The Ministry of Agriculture in Manitoba* (Manitoba Dept. of Agriculture, 1971), p. 149.

5. Grant MacEwan, *The Battle for the Bay* (Saskatoon: Western Producer Prairie Books, 1975), p. 259.

6. *Farm and Ranch Review*, Sept., 1955.

7. *Farmer's Advocate*, July 23, 1911.

Chapter 18   New Wheats for Prairie Growers

1. A. H. Reginald Buller, *Essays on Wheat* (Toronto: Macmillans of Canada, 1919), p. 155.

2. Grant MacEwan, *Harvest of Bread* (Saskatoon: Western Producer Prairie Books, 1969), p. 85.

Chapter 19   Dry Farming and Irrigation

1. *Farm and Ranch Review*, Nov. 5, 1912.

Chapter 20   Mixed Farming and Dairying

1. *Winnipeg Weekly Tribune* — Review, "Portage la Prairie," June 19, 1885.

2. D. H. McCallum, *Historical Notes on Alberta Dairying* (Alberta Dairymen's Assoc., 1969).

3. J. H. Ellis, *The Ministry of Agriculture in Manitoba* (Manitoba Dept. of Agriculture, 1971), p. 129.

4. *Edmonton Bulletin*, July 14, 1888.

Chapter 21   Breeding for Better Beef Bulls

1. F. W. Crawford, *Aberdeen-Angus Cattle in Canada* (Canadian Aberdeen-Angus Assoc., 1944), p. 34.

Chapter 22   For More and Better Horses

1. Beecham Trotter, *A Horseman in the West* (Toronto: Macmillans of Canada, 1925), p. 243.

2. Isaac Beattie, as related privately. Mr. Beattie could not recall the exact year but believed it was soon after the beginning of the century.

3. *Edmonton Bulletin*, April 19, 1920.

4. *Brandon Blade*, Mar. 20, 1884.

5. *Lethbridge News*, June 15, 1898.

6. *Edmonton Bulletin*, Dec. 6, 1919.

Chapter 23   The War Years and After

1. *Nor-West Farmer*, April 5, 1915; also *Grain Growers' Guide*, July 31, 1918.

2. *Leader News*, April 20, 1967.

3. *Nor-West Farmer*, Feb. 20, 1915.

4. *Ibid.*, Aug. 5, 1916.

5. *Ibid.*, issues of 1916 and 1917.

6. *Grain Growers' Guide*, Feb. 20, 1918.

Chapter 24   The Farmers in Organization and Politics

1. William Kirby Rolph, *Henry Wise Wood of Alberta* (Toronto: University of Toronto Press, 1950), p. 85.

Chapter 25   The Triumphant Birth of the Wheat Pools

1. *Macleod Gazette*, Oct. 13, 1899.

2. *Edmonton Bulletin*, May 11, 1921.

3. A. J. McPhail, *The Diary of Alexander James McPhail* (Toronto: University of Toronto Press, 1940), p. 56.

4. *Ibid.*, p. 277.

5. Leonard Nesbitt, *Tides in the West* (Saskatoon: Modern Press), p. 272.

Chapter 26   Depression, Drought, and Drifting Soil

1. *Manitoba Free Press*, Oct. 19, 1929.

2. *Ibid.*, Dec. 17, 1932.

3. *Alberta Wheat Pool Budget*, Feb. 10, 1961.

4. *Manitoba Free Press*, Dec. 17, 1932.

5. *Ibid.*, Oct. 30, 1933.

6. Leonard Nesbitt, *Tides in the West* (Saskatoon: Modern Press).

7. *Manitoba Free Press*, Dec. 16, 1933.

8. *Winnipeg Free Press*, July 13, 1936.

9. *Ibid.*, July 11, 1936.

10. E. W. Stapleford, *Rural Relief in the Prairie Provinces* (Ottawa: Federal Dept. of Agriculture, 1939).

11. Ibid., p. 129.

12. *Winnipeg Free Press*, July 2, 1935.

13. Ibid., Dec. 1, 1932.

Chapter 27   Triumphs Born in Adversity

1. *Manitoba Free Press*, July 26, 1933.

2. Hon. Robert Weir, speaking in the House of Commons, April 10, 1935.

Chapter 28   War and Farm Recovery

1. *Farm and Ranch Review*, Sept., 1940.

2. *Western Farm Leader*, April 21, 1944.

3. *Farm and Ranch Review*, July, 1947.

4. *Country Guide*, Mar., 1951.

Chapter 29   Gloom and Disaster

1. Rt. Hon. C. D. Howe, debates of the House of Commons, Mar. 7, 1952.

2. *Country Guide*, Dec., 1951.

3. Ibid.

4. Ibid.

Chapter 30   A New Day for Agriculture

1. *Farm and Ranch Review*, Sept., 1960.

2. Facts and Figures, Govt. of Alberta, 1954.

3. Statistics Canada reports, 1975.

4. Canada Year Book, 1976-77.

INDEX